Earthwalking
Sky Dancers

Earthwalking
Sky Dancers

WOMEN'S PILGRIMAGES TO SACRED PLACES

EDITED BY **Leila Castle**

Frog, Ltd.
Berkeley, California

Earthwalking Sky Dancers
WOMEN'S PILGRIMAGES TO SACRED PLACES

Published by Frog, Ltd.

Frog, Ltd. books are distributed by
North Atlantic Books
P.O. Box 12327
Berkeley, California 94712

Distributed to the book trade by Publishers Group West

This is issue #56 in the *Io* series.

Cover photo by Kariel Daniels:
World Wheel; Site 9. Shoto Terdrom, Tibet, 1992.
"Rainbow Bodhisattva" Vijali
Title page photo by Cindy A. Pavlinac: Delphi

Cover and book design by Paula Morrison
Typeset by Catherine Campaigne

Printed in the United States of America

Library of Congress Cataloging-in-Publication Data
Earthwalking sky dancers : women's pilgrimages to sacred places/
edited by Leila Castle.
    p. cm.
    Includes bibliographical references.
    ISBN 1-883319-33-1
    1. Spirituality.   2. Women—Religious life.   3. Sacred space.
4. Pilgrims and pilgrimages.   I. Castle, Leila.
BL625.7.E36   1996
291.3'5'082—dc20
                                  96-4353
                                  CIP

1   2   3   4   5   6   7   8   9   /   00   99   98   97   96

ACKNOWLEDGMENTS

I WOULD LIKE TO THANK the following people who have given their encouragement, support, and assistance in so many valuable ways during the writing and editing of this book: Martin Gregory and Cindy Pavlinac, my computer angels; without their help and techno-wizardry this book would never have been written! My editors and the staff at Frog Ltd., Lindy Hough, Mary Buckley, Victoria Baker, and Anastasia McGee. John Steele, for his support and confidence in this project in innumerable ways. Dorothy Bielen, for her longstanding generosity and support. Susannah Woods, for reading and assistance in editing manuscripts. Michael Whelan for editing suggestions. Steven Goodman for reading and editing assistance with *Flesh of the Dakinis*. Special thanks to Tsultrim Allione for editing suggestions and contributing the title *Earthwalking Sky Dancers*, and to Namkhai Norbu Rinpoche, who together with Tsultrim, showed me the mirror. The women of my circles and tribal loved ones—especially Eileen McKearney, Hallie Austen, Froggy, and Little Bear—who have nurtured my heart and soul while I gave birth to this book. Gaea and Raven, for the gift of being a mother. All the women who have contributed to this collection, for adding a jewel to this necklace.

CONTENTS

FOREWORD

TWENTY-FIVE YEARS AGO, I had an experience I will never forget. I was in Austria, in a village on top of a hill. I had stopped at the village for dinner on the way to Vienna where I was born, and on impulse I had decided to drive up the hill to look at the sunset before dusk. The church was small and baroque, white, with a carved wooden portico. What intrigued me was the sign on it: *Frauenkirche*.

A Women's Church!

At that time I was still on the threshold of the journey of exploration that eventually led to *The Chalice and The Blade, Sacred Pleasure*, and other works reclaiming our lost Goddess heritage. But I already knew that if there was a church on a high place called a Women's Church, it must be on a very ancient site: a site dating back to a time when women were priestesses and the powers that govern the universe were not yet imaged only in male form.

The wooden door yielded to my hand. In the semi-darkness I saw another door, and I pushed it open. The interior of the church was lit only by a few altar candles, but I could hear the voices of women chanting. As my eyes got used to the darkness, I saw a circle of five old women dressed in black.

Mutter Gottes (Mother of God,) they were chanting, *Dein heiliger Leib* (*Your holy womb.*)

A chill traveled down my spine. For a moment I was transported back in time, almost as if a spell had been cast and I was in a different world, a world where I belonged.

The sound of a door opening followed by footsteps startled me. I saw that a priest had entered and was walking toward the circle of women. The women chanted one last invocation to the Mother. Then they crossed themselves, stood up, and bowed to the priest. The church was now his domain. They bowed to him again as they walked past him, and I was yanked back to reality.

Had I dreamed it all? Had I heard what I thought I heard? Did the women now slowly filing out of the little church know what ancient traditions lay behind their rite?

I stared at them as they turned, one by one, at the door to again cross themselves, curtsy to the priest, and depart. No, I thought. Perhaps in the deepest recesses of their unconscious minds they knew. But it was unlikely that they had any conscious inkling of what once was and was lost.

Today women all over the world are *consciously* reclaiming our lost Goddess heritage, for themselves and for us all. This book tells the stories of eighteen such women, from diverse religious and ethnic traditions. They are remarkable women and remarkable stories.

They are stories that illuminate my research over the last twenty years when, like a detective, I sorted through false testimony and half truths for clues to our real cultural heritage. Out of this research came the understanding that much that is happening in our time, including the women's spirituality movement, is not new or radical. It has ancient roots in a more peaceful and egalitarian time when what I call a partnership rather than dominator model determined relationships. Equally important, my work made it possible to see that the women's spirituality movement is integral to the contemporary struggle to create a more partnership-oriented world.

Books like *Earthwalking Sky Dancers* empower us in this struggle. They inspire us, as we read of the courage of women, not to slay dragons or kill human adversaries, but to explore new spiritual paths that often require extreme physical daring and endurance. They give us pleasure, as we vicariously follow the adventures of these women. They offer us a new mystical literature, written by women about the female aspect of the divine: mystical experiences and visions at sacred places that date back to the early Goddess religion.

Above all, they open for us new possibilities, not only for ourselves, but for our world.

Riane Eisler, author of
The Chalice and The Blade: Our History, Our Future
Pacific Grove, California
1996

SERPENT TALES

My bed stands beside two windows facing a lichen-covered old apple orchard. In late summer and autumn, when the apples ripen, the garden is filled with deer feasting on fallen fruit.

The night this book was conceived, I lay in the darkness asking the Great Mother for guidance and inspiration. Falling into a dreamy half-sleep, I was awakened by a raspy sound outside the window at the head of my bed. Peering out into the pale moonlit orchard, I was startled and enchanted to see a magnificent antlered stag facing me, inches away through the glass. The sound I had heard was his antlers hitting the wall as he grazed on the sweet fallen fruit. He stayed for hours. I didn't get much sleep. However, I did get the idea for this book—as if delivered by him, a messenger from a Dreamtime faery realm. I saw the entire book in an instant, turned on the light and wrote down as much as I could.

That was several years ago. He has remained a midnight companion and ally since. I delight in the sound of his antlers, and in his wild nature as the Horned God, consort of the Goddess in ancient Native European shamanic tradition.

I remember reading *Autobiography of a Yogi* by Paramahansa Yogananda. I was about twenty at the time. Feeling rather frustrated, I said to my boyfriend, "Why aren't there any books about a woman's spiritual journey?" He said, "That's for you to write."

Thankfully, there has been a wealth of women's writing on the sacred feminine since then—but not a collection of stories such as these that express a uniquely female view of our experience of the sacred feminine in relationship to sacred sites around the world. Until fairly recently, most well-known published

work in the field of geomancy has been written by men and rather than focusing on direct experience it has been more theoretical, scientific, and historical
(with the exception of *The Great Cosmic Mother: Rediscovering the Religion of the
Earth* by Barbara Mor and Monica Sjöö, and two lesser-known British women,
Katharine Maltwood and Mary Caine, who lovingly researched and wrote about
the Glastonbury Zodiac, or Star Temple, in Somerset, England).

After experiencing a geomantic initiation in Mexico in 1975, I devoured
everything I could find written on sacred places. John Michell's *The Earth Spirit*
and *The View Over Atlantis*, and the late Anthony Roberts' *Atlantean Traditions
in Ancient Britain*, were early inspirations. I was fortunate to later meet and
become friends with them both, as well as many other British geomancers (including several of the authors in this collection), when I lived in England. Here now
is my book—serpent tales of women's wisdom, stories of our initiations into the
sacred feminine and sacred places, stories of dragon priestesses of the Earth.

It is said that pilgrimage is a journey to one's true nature, the external journey
being a reflection of the journey within. Winding through inner and outer landscapes, my life has been a serpentine path of pilgrimage to sacred places. Along
the way, I have met and traveled with other women and men who have also
been touched by this wanderlust spirit of place. As if enchanted, we fell in love
with Gaia, the beauty and spirit of the Earth. She has many stories to tell, though
few people know how to listen anymore. We listened. We are still listening.

My original vision of this book was of a circle of women, like a ring of stones,
with each story a jewel from a different site. These stories are precious jewels
from each woman's life, gifts to her from the teachings of Gaia and her sacred
places. They are her treasures for us, meant to be shared with you, an offering
to the Earth Spirit in us all.

Each woman speaks from her experience at sites in every continent on Earth.
Although most of the authors are of European ancestry, several are of Native-
or African-American blood. I feel this is significant because it is through our
European ancestors that Western "civilization" has led a destructive tide of con-
quest, conversion, and colonialism since the waves of the Kurgan invasions of
the peaceful, egalitarian, Neolithic Goddess cultures of Old Europe, on into

Christianization and the Burning Times, resulting in our current global situation—the aftermath of World War II—as the theories of the late archaeologist Dr. Marija Gimbutas have brilliantly illustrated in *The Language of the Goddess* (Harper & Row) and *The Civilization of the Goddess* (HarperCollins).

When on pilgrimage to the Hopi land in Arizona in 1986, I prayed to learn what I could do to help the world. My prayers were answered by the wind, like Gaia whispering in my ear: "Teach your own people the ways of balance." We have inherited a legacy of violence and disconnection of unimaginable proportions, teetering on the edge of irredeemable nuclear and ecological disaster on a planetary scale. And this is old news.

We grew up in this. I hid—terrified—under my little desk at school in the fifties when air raid sirens screamed apocalyptic mock warnings. I had repetitive dreams of disintegrating in a great nuclear blast. But the Earth never abandoned me, never stopped playing with, healing, or teaching me.

All of us are born of sacred women and sacred places. My first sacred place was my mother's womb. My mother was unmarried, virgin in the ancient sense of belonging to no man. My father, a flower farmer with land that once grew lotuses in the Hawaiian Islands, was her lover. I was conceived near a beautiful beach—Lanikai—which means "Heavenly Waters," then born of their French ancestry in Berkeley, California, in 1952, and adopted at birth.

As a child I lived in several houses that bordered the Berkeley Rose Garden. The Rose Garden was like my own temple for sixteen years, my place of sanctuary, play, adventure, healing, and enchantment. It was built like a Greek amphitheater, in crescent-shaped terraces with hundreds of varieties of roses. In late spring the fragrance of roses in full bloom was beyond intoxicating; it was a visitation from Aphrodite herself. Wilder wooded groves of majestic oak and bay laurel trees balanced the more civilized gardens. At night the sound of the creek sang me to sleep.

My adoptive mother was born in Shanghai, China, the youngest of nine children. Her parents lived there for fifteen years in the early 1900s. I heard horrifying tales of piles of dead baby girls dumped at the edge of the city, ruthlessly discarded in favor of male heirs, and of women's feet being broken and bound, crippled for life so that they could wear the tiny silk embroidered shoes like the one my mother had kept to show me. This must have made a big impression on me—I loved to go barefoot.

Despite this early major tip-off regarding the status of women in the world, in my innocence I believed China was a long way away, an exotic foreign land. Those things could never happen here. Not in sunny California. I suppose we all find out the hard way; I certainly did. More subtle methods in American culture disguise the devaluation of the feminine. One day in the kitchen, my mother said, "If women ruled the world there would be no more war." It's difficult to see that we are roped into a patriarchal corral when we are born into it. California must be one of the most liberated places in the world, but even here we don't escape unscathed. I've got plenty of scars from busting out of many a "fenced-in" situation.

In the late sixties and early seventies, during the years I completed high school and went on to college, I felt very isolated and wild. I spent days alone swimming and meditating on rivers, riding my horses, painting, and dancing, alternating with anti-war demonstrations, going to rock concerts in San Francisco and exploring my sexuality. My mother had given me a copy of M. Esther Harding's *Woman's Mysteries* when I was eighteen, but this was long before much material of this kind was available. I felt like the ancient women she described in her book, but there was no cultural context for my experience—this was California in the Governor Reagan era! It was very confusing.

This next series of events led me to Oaxaca, Mexico, in 1975, where I first experienced the power of sacred places. While traveling through the Southwest, I had a vision. In the space between waking and sleeping, I suddenly found myself in another realm. I saw a naked woman, holding a pitcher of blood in her right hand and cradling a bowl of milk beneath her heart. Instantly I somehow became her, walking toward a crowd of waiting people. I felt hesitant and self-conscious. A brilliant flash of light dispelled my resistance and fear as I understood, this is my work and it is sacred. I stepped up to the people, blessing them with the blood and milk—the red and white essences of the feminine.

The image of this woman with the blood and milk was so compelling to me that I began a large painting of her called Dharma Lady. Within months I was pregnant—despite an IUD. I knew the moment I had conceived ... sunning on a boulder along the Yuba River I had watched a beautiful, naked, young preg-

Barbara T. Myman, "Birth of Knowing"

nant woman slide gracefully from a rock into the water and swim downstream, followed by a snake zig-zagging through the current. I was ovulating and had made love that morning. The IUD was later removed, but after months of being seriously ill and hospitalized, and then finally recovering, I miscarried. My grief was inconsolable. I broke up with my boyfriend and ran away like a gypsy with friends to Mexico.

Walking down a dusty dirt road in the tiny mountain village of San Jose del Pacifico, a little Indian boy approached me saying, "Hongos? Hongos?" (mushrooms). I followed him into the forest as he led me to his home. There his mother, a radiant young Mazatec woman, stood in the doorway of her hut, resting a basket of fresh, glistening blue mushrooms on her rounded, pregnant belly. She invited me to stay and eat the sacred mushrooms.

That evening I sat on the edge of the mountain ridges overlooking the Pacific Ocean far below, listening to the mushroom spirit sing to me. I watched in amazement as clouds began to form a gigantic, perfectly shaped mushroom cloud in the western sunset sky. It was big—huge—and looked like a nuclear explosion. I understood from the mushroom spirit that we had a choice: We could follow either the path of warfare and nuclear destruction or its antidote, *los hongos,* who would help us to reconnect with the ancient wisdom of the Earth. The cloud dissolved into the darkening sky as swirling mists rose from the sea, and I was left entranced by the sweet singing of the night.

I stayed in Oaxaca for six months, returning to the mountains and the mushrooms many times. I also discovered El Tule, the aged banyan tree called the Tree of Life, and Monte Alban, the magnificent temple ruins of the Zapotec—the Cloud People—where I often went to meditate. The place became my teacher, revealing many of its secrets. Over the months I began to realize that I was living in the midst of an ancient magical tradition, rooted in the teachings of the mushrooms and the Tree of Life, and stored at Monte Alban, with its temples arranged synchronistically in the pattern of the Kabbalistic Tree of Life. This knowledge and tradition was old (Atlantean . . . stellar . . . ?), layered underneath and woven into wisdom teachings all around the world. I understood that sacred places were connected to each other in this way, as keepers of strands of this ancient wisdom, and that it was possible for us to receive teaching directly from them. This was part of the "antidote," part of the healing for our culture and time. I was only twenty two years old and knew so little, but I wanted to follow these strands and learn more.

I returned to California on the trail of any information I could find about sacred sites and magical traditions. One evening I went to hear a Druid priestess speak at a bookstore in San Francisco, and by chance met a man teaching a class there on the Tree of Life and angelic invocation. He had an extensive library on everything I wanted to study and did healing meditations for the Earth every new and full moon, usually on Mt. Tamalpais and sometimes on Mt. Shasta.

Using an invocational system weaving goddesses and gods of many world traditions and cultures according to their corresponding qualities, we worked with Egyptian, Tibetan, African, Native American, Hawaiian, European, and esoteric Christian and Judaic deities and angels to create a Gaian Tree of Life.

I came to know the goddesses as they moved through me and learned to focus energy through my heart, visualizing sending healing and blessing to people or places anywhere in the world that needed it. We spent the next eight years traveling together to sacred sites doing these meditations. I liked the Tree of Life as a meditational image and form, especially because of its balance of male and female energy. The original Tree of Life represented the body of the Goddess as a pillar connecting Earth and sky, or perhaps it symbolized the sacred mushroom itself.

Our first pilgrimage together was a return to Mexico, back to El Tule and Monte Alban as Comet West circled the sun in February '76. At the full moon we were camping in a hammock in Palenque, in the rainforest beside the ruins. Before dawn we were led by a young Indian boy to the mushroom fields, where I felt blessed to witness what may have been the most astonishingly beautiful natural display I will ever see.

The fields were a lush emerald green. All around cattle lay peacefully in dark silhouette, their graceful horns looking like the Egyptian goddesses Isis or Hathor. In the western sky, a brilliant milk-white Virgo full moon was setting, while in the east the dawn sky was brightening with streaming colors. Venus sparkled like a shining jewel, accompanied by a dazzling twin with a great plumed tail—comet West. We took a ritual bath in a pool just beneath the temple ruins before eating the mushrooms we gathered that dawn. Our day was spent in prayer, meditation and joyous delight from the teachings we received in the courtyards and gardens of the ruins. The mushrooms revealed a great sense of playfulness and humor as well as tremendous power that was humbling. I was enchanted by the "flowery dream."

From Palenque we traveled to the Yucatan to celebrate the spring equinox at Chichén Itzá and were treated to another unexpected display. As we sat in prayer and meditation on the top of the Jaguar pyramid, I noticed people gathering below at the bottom of the very steep stone stairway, as if in a ritual observance of some kind. Later I discovered that on the equinox, the day we were there, is when a huge serpentine shadow is formed by the play of sunlight on the temple stairway as it descends to a stone snake-head on the ground.

Our last stop was Teotihuacan, outside of Mexico City. I barely made it there, becoming very ill, apparently from tick bites. I climbed the Pyramid of the Sun in a daze, making prayers and offerings of flower petals and incense, then wandered along the avenues and temples to Quetzalcoatl and the moon. Mexico will always have a mixture of beauty and horror for me. In its most ancient layers a great peaceful wisdom remains unbroken although terribly ravaged through time. Layered over this wisdom are hundreds of years of torture, rape, and the violent politics by domination and pathology, both native and conquistador/Christian which permeates the land with a sinister undercurrent, and nearly destroyed the people and sacred traditions they once held.

By summertime I was pregnant with my son. We lived in San Francisco, but made frequent journeys to Mt. Tamalpais. On the fall equinox, while my son's father climbed Mt. Shasta, I lounged in a hammock in camp. As before, I became extremely ill for several months, but slowly recovered. Being pregnant was living in a blissful altered state. Giving birth was mysteriously awesome, powerful, ecstatic. Raven Orion Taliesin Avalon was born at home with my beautiful full-blooded Aztec midwife Maria tending us, a year after Comet West circled the sun. I loved the voluptuous ripeness of pregnancy and breast-feeding, the rich beauty of my great full belly and creamy swollen breasts. Raven was a magical child, with spun-gold hair and a deep, calm nature. His placenta was buried beneath a tall, majestic old tree we called Grandfather, on Mt. Tamalpais where we often went to meditate. I carried him everywhere with me, in a Oaxacan shawl and never let him cry himself to sleep.

My relationship with his father was rocky at best. In my heart, what I wanted was a true partnership, but we never realized that. In the midst of our "spiritual" work together, we were far from domestic bliss, and eventually this hypocrisy doomed our relationship. Despite this, we continued our pilgrimages, which led us next to Hawaii. As we traveled to different sites in different cultures, I began to see how each place communicated, how it told me its stories through my direct experience in connection to it. The sites seemed so hungry for relationship, for communication with someone who could listen. It was as if an invisible network or web between sacred places and people had been damaged, or lay dormant and tattered from neglect. The spirits and ancestors still spoke there, and they were saying "Wake up!—life is so precious—love each other and take good care of this jewel of a planet, because you are blowing it massively!" A very simple message that seemed to be beamed from the heart of the Earth.

Around this time I had a vision, as I was meditating, of a very black-skinned Aboriginal man standing in the sun-baked Australian desert. He was naked except for a loincloth, and leaned on a wooden staff. His skin was the color of ebony and indigo, and he seemed as old and strong as the land itself. He didn't speak, but in my mind, I understood very clearly: "You people aren't holding your lines there." It was like an admonishment and warning that the invisible threads of a planetary web of interconnection, what the Aborigine people call *songlines*—had been dropped by this culture. So I have tried to learn what it is to "hold a line."

By the autumn of 1979, we were preparing our pilgrimage to the Great Pyramid in Egypt to celebrate the fall equinox and to pray for peace in the Middle East. Raven was two and still breast-feeding a little, but I sensed his sister very near, and was planning to open to her when we returned from this journey. She insisted on coming with us. I ovulated unexpectedly on the way to Glastonbury, England, and as I sat in meditation on the dragon ley that runs through the Abbey ruins that Pisces full moon, I felt her spirit enter my body as a dove-like shimmering light, through the top of my head into my womb-cradle. Welcome to Avalon, Isle of Apples.

We stayed briefly in Glastonbury for the full moon, visiting the Tor, Chalice Well, and the Abbey before going on to Egypt. Cairo overwhelmed me. I had not experienced this magnitude of poverty before; it was even beyond the miles of slums surrounding Mexico City. Sensitive and pregnant, and in a Moslem culture, I felt constantly harassed and like prey as a woman, despite my attempts to dress modestly. Only out in the desert near the Sphinx was I really able to sink deep into the energy there that runs through layers of time, dissolving the congestion of the outer crust of current culture, and there the spirits still reside. I spent a long while in the Queen's Chamber of the Great Pyramid, feeling a profound peace, in contrast to the King's Chamber which felt heavy and oppressive to me. This seemed to mirror the state of my relationship, which hit an even deeper low at this stress-point.

Delphi, Greece was a welcome relief after Egypt, although I left wanting to return one day in different circumstances—like sailing up the Nile to meditate in temples not overrun by tourists. In Delphi I felt a very strong pull to a certain temple area that took a long while to find. I wandered through the ruins all day and asked the guards where it was, but they didn't speak English or seem to know the place I described to them. Finally at sunset I found it, a circular temple with standing columns overlooking the gorge below that I now know is beside the Castilian spring, the original oracular site. It felt like home there, and throughout my pregnancy in the months ahead, I would return night after night in dreams in which I would sleep on a bed within the open-air temple. When I woke, I returned from a most healing and divine sleep, as if I had truly slept there.

From Delphi we returned for the Aries full moon to England and Glastonbury, where we visited Arthurian scholar Geoffrey Ashe at his home at the foot of the Tor, where Dion Fortune once lived. He led us up the spiraling labyrinth that winds a processional pathway along the grassy-green dragon-shaped Tor hill rising from the surrounding Somerset moors, and later spoke with us of the mysteries of Avalon over cream teas on High Street. I was about one month pregnant, and just beginning to get a bit green around the gills with morning sickness. In my mind I kept hearing the name Cerridwen, goddess of the Cauldron of Inspiration, over and over, feeling my body a cauldron, my womb a grail cup-full of life, and I knew the ancient goddess spirit was still strong in the land beneath the layers of Christianity and Arthurian legend.

Gaea Keridwyn was born at home in San Francisco, lovingly tended by family and midwives a few days after Mt. St. Helens erupted in May of 1980, the time of the baby rosebuds' blossoming. She was a faery child. Shortly after her birth we moved to a cabin in the redwood forests of Mendocino, where we lived nearly a year and a half in the midst of otter families, bear, rattlesnakes, and marijuana farms. In the late fall of 1981 we returned to England to research the Glastonbury Zodiac, or Temple of the Stars.

The Glastonbury Zodiac is a terrestrial star temple twelve miles wide, encompassing the land surrounding Glastonbury, Somerset, known more anciently as Avalon, the site of the Arthurian legends and Grail lore. The figures of the Zodiac, formed by the landscape itself—the streams, woods, hills, earthworks, and roads—can be seen from the air and maps. Like an image of heaven on Earth, when a planisphere of the stars is laid over a map of the area, the constellations fall accurately within the figures of the Zodiac. We initially settled in an old stone farmhouse in the moors just outside Glastonbury within the Zodiac, and weathered our first English winter. And so began a two-and-a-half-year initiation into the Star Temple.

At every new and full moon, solstice, or equinox, we would go to a site in the Star Temple that corresponded to that celestial time—to the eye of the phoenix of the Aquarius figure at the Tor at the Aquarius full moon, or to the breast of the Virgo figure, Wimble Toot, a mound surrounded by luxuriant wheat fields, at the Virgo new moon. Exploring the Zodiac in this way became a great adventure into the mythical landscape which took two-and-a-half years to complete, ritually journeying though the star-wheel of the year in the land. This outer experience reflected a far deeper inner transformation for me, and when it was finished my entire life changed.

Those years in England were some of the most difficult of my life. Whatever magic had held my relationship together with Gaea and Raven's father rapidly disintegrated under the stresses of the dismal English weather and our poverty. At one point, unable to find housing in Glastonbury, we were forced to stay several weeks in a friend's attic in Bath before renting a barely livable bungalow that had been previously condemned. I was miserable—teaching at a Montessori School in Bath, with no money, two little ones, and no help with all the domestic and childcare responsibilities—as my partner pursued his dream researching the Zodiac. While we continued to explore the stone circles and sacred sites of Avebury and Stonehenge, and roamed all of Cornwall and the southwest of England, the pilgrimage continued—yet our paths separated. As my connection to these sacred places deepened, so did my experience of the sacred feminine. I couldn't bear to live in such an imbalanced state or patriarchal relationship any longer.

We had met and become friends with many of the British geomancers also researching and involved with the Earth Mysteries during this time, especially Tony and Jan Roberts, who lived in a village just outside Glastonbury. They had invited us to meet their friend, sacred landscape artist Christopher Castle, at an exhibition of his work in Street, near Glastonbury, in 1983. It was a rare, hot, honeyed summer day for England when Chris and I met. Within a year we were madly in love. My marriage ended in a dramatic blow-out, and I flew back to California with the children to get a divorce. On the flight I noticed a passenger in front of me reading *The Mists of Avalon*, which friends had said I must read. When I later did, I felt as if I had lived it. I realized I had completed the circle of the Star Temple of Avalon, and now it was time to go.

Back in California, the children and I lived alone in the Sierra Nevada mountains the year of '84, before Chris moved from England to join us. The mountains and elements were healing and purifying. Gaea, Raven and I loved exploring places like the Stone Mother and Her Basket at Pyramid Lake, Crystal Peak, Campbell Hot Springs, petroglyph sites at Donner Summit, beaches along Lake Tahoe and, synchronistically, the nearest mountain we lived beside and the highest peak in the area, Castle Peak. I felt a new joy, strength, and freedom creating a fresh life with the children, and when Chris joined me after this year of solitude in the snow country, I was happier than I had ever been in my life.

We spent a blissful summer together in the Sierras before moving to a home overlooking the Valley of the Moon in the wine country of Sonoma. Chris set up a studio and began networking in the art world, while I directed a Montessori School. We were wed in the autumn of 1985, but our honeymoon was short-lived when a series of personal tragedies struck, including the loss of a pregnancy, our home, and my teaching position, a car accident that injured my neck, and the death of my adoptive father—all within less than a year.

That first summer in the Sierras a year before, I had had an unusual dream experience. As I dreamed, I heard a soft, dry rattling sound, like a rattlesnake's tail. I followed the sound in the dream, trying to reach its source. As I drew closer, the sound got louder and louder until it seemed as if I were the sound itself. At that moment I was shocked to realize that I was wide awake—eyes open—looking up at a masked Kachina figure standing over me and shaking a golden-colored gourd rattle. At the instant I knew I wasn't dreaming, he suddenly vanished, and I felt a great power whoosh out of the house. From this dream I knew that I would have to make a pilgrimage to the home of the Kachinas, the San Francisco Peaks in Arizona, to understand why I had been visited. So at the end of the summer, when we moved from Sonoma to Point Reyes Station in West Marin, we packed the kids and camping gear into our station wagon and drove down to the Southwest.

The San Francisco Peaks loomed magnificently purple in the sunset light, with blackening storm clouds gathering overhead as we approached from the west. Lightning began to sizzle between the earth and sky as we drew nearer. Planning to camp near Sedona that night, we turned south, looking for an exit we never found. Instead, we drove on—lost—into the heart of a ferocious storm crashing all around us. The road vanished in a deluge so heavy we could see nothing but torrential rain, illuminated by the flash of lightning strikes. Terrified, as I closed my eyes and prayed for our safety, I saw in vision an antlered man standing with his arms upraised in the midst of the storm, his arms and legs crackling with lightning running up and down them. I wondered who he was as we gratefully took refuge at a roadside motel we finally found as the storm thundered on.

Once settled into our room for the night, we phoned our friend, video artist Joan Price in Santa Fe, who told us we must visit a friend of hers at the Hopi mesas. We set out the next day for the Hopi land, stopping to explore the site Wupatki along the way. As I walked along the trail, I noticed the rich red color of the desert earth; it was the same color as the skin of a Hopi man I had passed nearby, and I understood there was no separation between the Hopi people and the land that is sacred to them.

We stayed in Hopi for several days over the August full moon and found Joan's friend. He and his wife were elders, living with their extended family in one of the villages. We were astonished and deeply moved by the grace, warmth, and open-hearted generosity with which they welcomed us. As we feasted together on delicious mutton, blue corn, vegetables, and herbs—all from their gardens—and later sat in a hut over a fire and stone, learning to make piki bread, they told us Hopi prophesy and stories of their people. To help replenish their daily water supply, we walked down through the dusty village to their sacred spring inside a cave lined with prayer sticks, then carried the full buckets back to their house. As we left, I prayed to know how I could help the Earth. This is when I heard clearly: teach your own people the way of balance.

Our pilgrimage led us into deeper communion with the spirit of the Anasazi, ancestors of the Hopi, so peaceful and reverent towards all life. We camped next at Canyon de Chelly, and then drove on to Santa Fe, where we visited our friend Joan. She told us about the Hopi image of the Earth, dappled with sacred sites— the Spotted Fawn—and that her Hopi friend was the Lightning Kachina in the sacred dances. Inspired by these experiences, when we returned from this journey to Point Reyes, Chris and I created Spotted Fawn, the organization we would direct together for the next four years to represent geomantic arts and to promote and increase awareness of traditions relating to the Earth and its sacredness.

We loved Point Reyes, with its wild beaches and mossy forests, and the children were especially happy here, with lots of friends and freedom to roam. During this time I went back to school, studying psychology and co-teaching a course called "Images of the Feminine," a cross cultural study of sacred feminine images and archetypes, at Sonoma State University. It was a very busy and fruitful phase for us, and we were pleased to weave our creativity together in such a partnership, which had been an unrealized dream for me in relationship for so long, although it was not to last … By the summer of 1990 we separated— symbolically, at Lammas, I found a dead fawn beside the stone labyrinth we had made together in the apple orchard.

One of my main spiritual practices for many years had been integration with the elements, and for several months I had worked with a different element each day. Floating completely relaxed in the hot tub outside at night and integrating with the sky was a favorite, or sitting with a fire. The following dream came during this time: Walking into a cavelike room, I see a Tibetan man sitting on a raised platform along one wall. He is friendly, smiling, dressed in ordinary Western clothes, and we seem to recognize each other. He shows me some things, then leans very close and says that he will now give me a certain teaching. He sounds a mantra, but what I experience is a wave of the most powerfully blissful, ecstatic energy moving through me, where everything—my body, the dream, his voice—is all the same, and made out of a rainbow light. I woke up wondering who on Earth he was, and what that was all about! I searched photos of Tibetan lamas, and asked Buddhist friends, looking for clues without success. Though I had not entered into any formal practice, I had attended Black Hat Ceremonies given by H. H. the Karmapa in the early seventies, and had seen other teachers. I knew the man in my dream was a real person, and that I would find him.

In June of 1987 we had an event in which Chris, John Steele, Feather Anderson, Steven Post, and I all gave geomantic presentations. The following day, several of us went for a walk on National Seashore land at Pierce Point. As John Steele, who had co-founded the Dragon Project that studied ancient sites in England, and I talked on the trail, he mentioned his dream teacher, Dzogchen master Namkhai Norbu Rinpoche, and I knew then that he was the man in my dream. When I learned he lived in Italy, I wondered how I would ever meet him, but as it turned out, he arrived in the Bay Area several weeks later, and I went on my first retreat with him. Tsultrim Allione, also a student of his, was there, and I felt such a profound and ancient connection with her, Norbu, and the teachings that I was deeply transformed.

Tsultrim and I corresponded, and we invited her to give an evening presentation of the Mandala of the Five Dakinis during a Goddess exhibition I had

organized which opened with a Bridgit ritual on Imbolc, February 1st, 1988 at
Spotted Fawn. After Tsultrim's presentation, I joined her for my first Dakini
Retreat at Bodega Bay, where she became my teacher as well as Norbu. Through
their blessings I discovered the unbroken lineage of sacred feminine wisdom
teachings transmitted within Tantra and Dzogchen.

By going to sacred places around the world doing dakini practices for several years, Tsultrim had been weaving what she called the Net of the Dakinis,
an energy web between sacred sites that is actually referred to in Tibetan texts.
Interestingly, the net as an ancient symbol relates to the lifegiving power of the
goddess in Old European imagery. It seemed especially auspicious to go with
her to dakini places in Tibet, the land of the women from whom the practices
had been born. I also saw this journey as a continuation of the work I had been
doing for many years to help restore the sacred feminine in the world, as a kind
of global geomantic tantric practice, in the sense of re-balancing the male/female
imbalance currently rampant within most human religion, culture, and relationship. The purpose, as I understood it, was to empower and re-honor the
sacred feminine energy that had been lost, diminished, forgotten, and destroyed
over the last 5,000-year era of a primarily patriarchal consciousness dominat-
ing the world, and to help heal the wounds caused by this devastation which is
resulting in the ruin of the entire biosphere on the greatest scale and is the root
of domestic violence on the most personal. I see now too that this is also an
inner alchemical process within myself. Put most simply, when the feminine —
as mother of all life — is harmed or devalued, so is the whole earth.

Many questions remain unanswered, such as: What caused the emergence
of patriarchal consciousness? When I asked Marija Gimbutas this question the
last time I visited her, she replied, "It was the horse," which presumably allowed
superior weapons capability — the quest for which holds the whole planet hostage
today. The horse may have made it possible to conquer, but the horse itself was
not the cause — it was the *intention* of the rider. Where in human consciousness
does this intention arise — from the egoic delusion of duality and the ignorance
of the interconnectedness of all life? How does the desire to dominate and control rather than collaborate or cooperate arise, and what is the cause of violence?

In my own observation and work with children, it seems to be either taught
by the adults and community surrounding the child or a response to abuse that
the child has suffered. It is a result of conditioning, not our innate nature. In

5,000 years we have created this global catastrophe as a species inhabiting Gaia. So what are the solutions? What does a postpatriarchal world look like?

I envision a world where children are born to loving parents who want and cherish them, who recognize their pure and divine nature; where all women and men are respected and honored as equals and cultures are based on the ecstatic experience, creative expression, exploration and protection of the interconnectedness of all life embodied within Gaia. Where the values of love, affection, compassion and kindness prevail, nurturing all beings, for it is ideally the tenderness and passion of this love that we are all born from and without which no life can survive. In my temple I worship this divine embrace, and my temple is at the same time the world, my body, and all phenomena. It is possible to create a realized world—a pure land—but we must all return to our primordial nature. That, my friends, is the pilgrimage we are all on. It is the sacred place from which all sacred places are born.

When I returned from Tibet, I began working on this book, which has come out of all these years of experience at sacred sites as well as out of friendships and collaborations with many of the women who have contributed their stories to this collection. I hope that by weaving these stories together, symbols and patterns reaching far beyond individuals, cultures, continents, and centuries will reveal themselves. I believe you will see that this does indeed happen as you read them, each written with no previous knowledge of what the other women were contributing and without strict guidelines from me as to content, other than requesting that each woman write what she felt were the stories the sites wanted to have told through her experience. The next section looks at the patterns of the weaving of these chapters in a more historical context.

DRAGON PRIESTESSES OF THE EARTH

THE PRIESTESSES OR ORACLES OF DELPHI—the Pythia—were known as Dragon Priestesses of the Earth. It was to the voice of the Goddess Gaia, mother of the oracle, that they listened, long before Apollo slew the Python, the serpent guardian of the oracular shrine. In the Goddess cultures of Old Europe, the snake was regarded as a guardian, a symbol of the life-force, immortality, rebirth, and the underworld because it shed its skin and emerged from the Earth in the spring after hibernation. The serpent and dragon, often synonymous, have represented the undulatory energy (chi) and currents of the Earth worldwide since the Paleolithic era.

In our own bodies, this energy, which rests at the base of the spine until awakened, is called the kundalini, or serpent power. When raised it signifies wisdom and enlightenment, like the uraeus serpent that crowns the foreheads of Egyptian deities. The cobra is the hieroglyphic image of Ua Zit, the most ancient goddess of Egypt. Delphi, according to Pythagoras—who lived and studied there under the Pythia (from whom he took his name, and whom he considered the source of his wisdom)—was founded by a lineage of Egyptian high priestess queens. He believed that the Pythia represented human manifestations of this serpent energy, which "belts the earth as currents that meet at sacred intersections" from which the source of true wisdom rises.[1]

Geomancy, or earth divination—knowing the language of the Earth—comes from the root *geo*, "earth," derived from "Gaia" and—*mancy*, "divination" or "intuitive knowledge." The connection between oracular tradition and snakes is very ancient, and seen historically throughout the Near and Middle East in the Sumerian Serpent Goddess Nina, esteemed as an oracular deity and interpreter of dreams; as Ishtar of Babylon, Lady of Vision, she who directs the oracles; and as Cassandra, whose ears were said to have been licked by snakes at Delphi as a child.[2]

It is interesting that the olfactory bulb, which connects directly with the limbic system—seat of memory, intuition, imagination, sexuality, and emotions and the oldest, reptilian part of the brain, our ancient serpent mind—is located at the position of the third eye, where the uraeus serpent symbol appears. No wonder the Pythia was said to have inhaled the vapors of the earth or the smoke of burning laurel.

Where are the dragon priestesses to offer wisdom to the leaders of nations today? Imagine listening to the voice of the Earth for guidance in matters of government! Yet this is an awareness preserved in the teachings of most indigenous people everywhere, and lost to Euro-American culture for centuries since the last of the witch-burnings that drove underground and virtually extinguished what is likely to have been the ancestral gene pool of seers, visionaries, and healers from thousands of years of priestesses. Even Paracelsus, the father of modern medicine, said that he had learned everything from a sorceress.[3]

With the loss of our ancestral wisdom teachings, we are fortunate to be able to reconnect with this ancient memory through our relationship with the Earth, most vividly with sacred places. This association between sacred sites and wisdom is found worldwide. In the Tibetan Buddhist Nyingma lineage there are *termas*, hidden wisdom treasures, stored at power places protected by dakinis and *nagas* (serpent beings) to be discovered by destined people, *tertons*, in order to benefit their particular time and culture. Dakinis, or sky-goers—enlightened female deities or women—are especially associated with sacred places, either living and practicing there or acting as guardian of a site. They often inhabit charnel grounds and pure lands, described as Lands of the Dakinis. As well as inhabiting these places on an outer level, they are connected to them nondually within the body itself.

In her book *Voices of Our Ancestors*, Cherokee chieftainess Dhyani Ywahoo speaks of the true history of North America as told to her by clan elders, describing the great dragons that once protected this land. They were "energy moving in the wave pattern of the Earth's energy," and worked with the medicine people as guardians. When the medicine people disappeared, so did the dragons, until the last one "was seen in the Smoky Mountains in the 1700s."

Chinese geomancy, or feng shui, meaning wind and water—the study of the chi of the land—utilizes the images of the azure dragon and the white tiger. Feng shui masters are called Dragonmasters. The practice of geomancy aims to create harmony between people and places, both in the land and within dwellings, to help people live in balance with the natural world. It seems likely that what we now experience globally as an increasing disturbance of the elements in floods, droughts, earthquakes, and tornados may be directly related to the destruction of the lineages of medicine people, shamans, and priestesses worldwide who were responsible for the healthy relationship of the people and the land, and kept the ancient knowledge of the *dragons*, of living in harmony with the Earth, alive.

If there was ever a time we need to remember this ancient knowledge, it is now. It may already be too late. We may have damaged the biosphere to such a great extent, from the ozone layer to plutonium waste, that all life within Gaia will be poisoned or altered in some way. The stories in this book are those of remembering, of listening to the Earth, of each woman learning to reconnect with her wisdom nature and the wisdom of the Earth. They are stories of contemporary priestesses of Gaia. Each chapter reveals different ways each woman has learned and been taught to reclaim her sacredness and the sacredness of the Earth through her pilgrimage to, and relationship with, sacred places. These experiences communicate patterns of similar themes and symbols that transcend time and connect us with the ancient knowledge of prepatriarchal Goddess cultures from sites all over the world today.

The themes that run through these stories are like threads that weave Ariadne-like through time, revealing a continuity at sites connecting us as contemporary women with the ancient women of the past. Many of us were seeking healing, following a dream or synchronicity, or were inspired by a vision as we entered the original altar, the body of the Goddess, in the form of a cave, mountain, spring, or tree—places of connection between the worlds. We died and were reborn in her womb-caves, and knew we were no longer separate. The death we experienced was the death of the ego and the loss of knowledge of the interconnectedness of all life. Our rebirth was to nondual awareness. We dreamed with the land and journeyed to the underworld, other realms and dimensions, to meet the spirits and ancestors of both blood and spiritual lineages. We were taught by sacred medicines and plants, by elders, shamans, and wisdom-holders and have explored nonordinary states of consciousness through entheogens, prayer, meditation, and trance, seeking guidance, communion, healing, and knowledge for ourselves, families, friends, and loved ones, for our communities, enemies, and planet. And we have been inspired to create *endlessly*—paintings, poetry, children, books, sculpture, music, song, films, videos, plays, photographs, projects, collaborations, conferences, rituals, celebrations, workshops, teaching, and retreat centers—to name a few.... All in the expression of and service to a love of the Earth and all beings.

There is a reciprocity between the sites and ourselves as we alternate in both creative and receptive relationship. They serve as transformational gateways, giving insight and healing, charging us with the creative power of the Earth itself, and receiving our sorrow, pain, and the ashes of our beloved as a comforting mother accepting our prayers and offerings, tears, and love. They are places of initiation as we enter into the *field*—the archetypal energy and living mythos associated with it. Here we can explore the sacred dimensions of relationship between the Earth and ourselves as we enter into the consciousness of a site. We may then be taught by the site itself, whatever is appropriate for us at the time or by a gradual unfolding. We can align ourselves with seasonal tides and celestial energies by observing the cycles of the Earth in connection to her vast cosmic family—the stars, sun, moon and planetary rhythms—and experience the whole Earth as a sacred site dancing in the midst of space.... Gaia, little sister of night, the Sky Goddess Nuit.

It is not easy to overcome or heal thousands of years of patriarchal conditioning and its influence and manifestations in our own psyches, lives, or world. But if we are to do this, we must integrate with the living Earth, the Gaia-field. The Goddess in all her manifestations is the symbol of the unity of all life in nature. The women who have shared their experiences at sacred places in this collection have walked the labyrinthine pathway to the center of the maze where the heart of the Great Mother still resides, and have returned to offer these stories to inspire you along the way.

EUROPE AND THE MEDITERRANEAN

The first site we visit is Delphi, in **Sensing Sacred Space** by Charla Devereux. Charla brings two very rich gifts from her experience there, which continues to work through her life. As a researcher in the Dragon Project Dream Program, she explores the documentation of dreaming, continuing Delphi's oracular tradition today, at sacred sites in Cornwall, echoed in many of the following chapters.

As an aromatherapist, she brings the fragrance of a site to the attention of our noses, as we breathe in the smoky green scent of laurel. A fitting start to set your feet upon the path of the serpent!

In **Red Eggs and Black Olives,** we journey next to Crete with Tsultrim Allione, author of *Women of Wisdom,* for the intimate sharing of her daughter Aloka's initiation into womanhood through a beautiful and very precious spontaneous ritual she created at a sacred site there at Easter. Initiation is a strong thread that runs through each woman's story, and in **A Woman and a Mountain,** poet and artist Jill Smith speaks to us of her initiation "by place, moon, Earth, and the power of all that is" as she describes her relationship with the Sleeping Beauty Mountain and integration with the body of the Goddess on the Isle of Lewis in Scotland. In **Well Worship: The Cult of the Sacred Waters** Swedish artist Monica Sjöö reveals many of her personal journeys, both tragic and healing, to Goddess sites, and the legendary women associated with them at holy wells in Britain, Wales, Germany and Scandinavia—"the very heart of the mystery of the Old Religion"—that have been the creative source of her painting and writing for nearly twenty years.

Another artist whose work has been inspired by her relationship with sacred sites is filmmaker Jo Carson. Approaching the entrance to the temples of Mnajdra, Malta to film her documentary, (and title of her chapter) **Dancing with Gaia,** she respectfully greets the spirit of the place—"I enter you, recognizing your power to transform me"—and in **Seeking an Oracle** she offers practical insights into the oracular wisdom learned through this transformation.

We travel next to the heart of Avalon as Serena Roney-Dougal, author of *Where Science and Magic Meet,* tells us what it has been like to live as **A Woman in Glastonbury,** learning to observe the seasons in ritual and her own alchemical relationship with the land over many years at a site that was sacred to the realm of the faery long before Arthur. The only fictional story of this collection, **Ancestral Voices of the Land,** is an imaginal and poetic visioning by artist Chesca Potter of the mare and deer cults and the rituals of their priestesses at the Vale of the White Horse in ancient Britain.

THE PACIFIC, ASIA, AND AFRICA

Hallie Austen, author of *The Heart of the Goddess* and *Womanspirit*, shares her experience of a place of the living goddess Pele, still honored in Hawaii, and the teaching given to her by a woman kahuna that continues to inform all her work today. She takes us to the Big Island of Hawaii, where we enter the underworld realm of Pele's cave in **Listening to Gaia.** Carole Nervig then tells the story of her longtime relationship with Nan Madol on the tiny Micronesian island of Pohnpei, where she experiences a deep, feminine, personal transformation in being "taken by a site" and actually becoming its protectress as founder of the Nan Madol Foundation in **Journey to Mu.**

From the ancient past to the present time, dakinis have been associated with sacred places. We climb the path of pilgrimage in Tibet to an 17,000-foot-high mountain-cave retreat of the great woman teacher Yeshe Tsogyel and meet one of her living incarnations, in **The Flesh of the Dakinis** by geomantic and fragrance artist Leila Castle. Bridging cultures between her Celtic ancestry and the Australian landscape of her birth, artist Lynne Wood writes of the Dreamtime teachings she has experienced with Aboriginal women, and how this has opened her connection to her own native European Goddess traditions and places in **A Cailleach in the Antipodes.** Uzuri Amini returns with us to her motherland in Africa, and shares the ritual she did with Luisah Teish to honor the ancestors at **Goree Island,** Senegal — the last place where Africans who had been captured for the slave trade were held before sailing to the colonies — at the beginning of her pilgrimage to be initiated as a priestess of Oshun in Nigeria.

NORTH, CENTRAL, AND SOUTH AMERICA

Southwestern video artist and producer Joan Price contributes her photo essay **Wuti Axis,** about the Anasazi site Wupatki near the Hopi mesas in Arizona, where she has learned ancient traditions "in which our own bodies reflect that of the Earth" from Native American elders as well as the land itself for many years. Claiming as her birthright the ancestral knowledge encoded in the landscape, sacred-land photographer Cindy A. Pavlinac then takes us to Death Valley, California, where she honors her father's death in a ceremony that emerged from the land itself in **Death Valley Journey.**

The power of listening and experiencing the sound of a site as an important aspect of our total sensory awareness in relationship to the Earth is the gift chantress and musician Ani Williams brings to us in **Her Song Changes Everything,** as we join her travels in the Southwest, Mexico, Egypt, and England. Many of these stories are those of coming home—of meeting with the ancestors—and in **A Personal Journey** Nancy Zak, who writes about and teaches Native American and Inuit studies, tells of her return to the Native American worldview through the power in the blood of her Inuit grandmother, and through visionary experiences of the Earth Mother in the Southwest that have transformed her life. Betty Kovacs then courageously shares the path of reclaiming her intuitive nature from the tyranny of academic training as a professor of mythology and literature; in **Journey of the Mothers** she describes her experiences at Machu Picchu, the heartbreaking death of her son, and her pilgrimage to a cave in Peru where his ashes were scattered. In our final chapter, **Earth as Sacred Space,** World Wheel artist and performer Vijali describes the process of being transformed by sacred places, and the art and creativity that is born from them as she creates sculptures in the landscape at sites from southern California to Tibet.

May the wisdom teachings of the Great Mother through her sacred places continue to help all beings remember their true nature.

NOTES

1. Norma Lorre Goodrich, *Priestesses* (Harper Perennial, 1989).
2. Merlin Stone, *When God Was A Woman* (Harcourt Brace Jovanovich, 1976).
3. Barbara Ehrenrich and Deirdre English, *For Her Own Good* (Anchor Books, 1979).

Barbara T. Myman, *"Sea Mysteries"*

EUROPE
AND THE
MEDITERRANEAN

Codrus Painter, Vulci Cup. Reproduced from Edward Gerhard, Auserlesene griechischen Vasenbilder. Berlin, 1858. (Shows Aigeus before the Pythia called Themis.)

CHARLA DEVEREUX

SENSING SACRED SPACE

THERE ARE KEY AREAS scattered around the planet that we recognize to be sacred space. What is it that makes these places so special?

To a degree, a sacred space can be created anywhere. It is a place where you feel comfortable and protected. You are free from outside influences to meditate, pray, or just sit quietly and be. Through continued use over time, a kind of "etheric fingerprint" can be established at such places.

Tribal societies shared a special relationship with nature, so their special places were located in the forest or wilderness, where the elemental presence of nature is strongest. Sometimes, it almost seems possible to reach across time and touch the souls of the people who used such sites.

My first journey to Britain in 1984 introduced me to the concept of sacred sites in the landscape. Until then, I was very much a part of the New Age scene in the States. I did the usual round of workshops that a well-paid staff assistant at a major corporation can afford to do—on astrology, crystal healing, herbs, reflexology, shiatsu, etc. Each one of these areas can be a lifetime study, and yet people were literally hanging out their shingles and going into practice after a two-week course—and in some cases shorter. Indeed, some of the workshops that I attended seemed to be run by just such people. I became disillusioned. All too often I came away having learned nothing, knowing full well that I knew more about the subject than the person running the workshop!

In 1984, I spent two solid weeks on a carousel of sacred places, visiting a variety of ancient British sites with a tour group. It was impossible to absorb what was happening at the time due to a kind of megalithic overload. On one occasion, the group had to send out a "search party" to find me after I had wandered off alone across the wild, prehistoric landscape of Dartmoor, Devon! I was inwardly working through some changes in my life, and the atmosphere of that granite upland encouraged me into a walking meditation so deep that I became totally oblivious to time and my companions. The overall exposure to the stone and earthen monuments of past ages changed my life:—six months later, I was living in Britain, in circumstances where attendance at and attention to ancient sacred sites became an integral part of my life and work experience. One of the things that I have come to understand over the years is that these places demand nothing and everything at the same time. And they cannot be rushed.

DELPHI

Of all of the sites I have now visited, none has made a greater impression on me than the temple complex at Delphi, Greece, which pushed me into a specific area of research. This is currently a work-in-progress, so I can only give background to it at this time.

My first encounter with Delphi was in late April, 1990 when, on short notice, my husband, Paul, and I had to visit Greece in order to obtain photographs for his book, *Secrets of Ancient and Sacred Places* (Cassell, 1992). Neither of us had been to Greece before, and we arrived in Athens on a bucket-shop flight in the dark, wee morning hours, leapt into a hired car, and drove through the night to get to Delphi, our first site to photograph. Hermes must have been in the back seat, because even though we had only the vaguest notion as to the direction we needed to take, we never became lost. We arrived at Delphi in the gray, drizzly morning.

Delphi is dramatically situated on the southern slopes of Mount Parnassus. In legend, the site was discovered by Koretas, a herdsman, who saw fumes issuing from a fissure. As he breathed them, he went into a trance in which he saw visions of the future. The spot became the location of a series of oracle houses from about 500 BC onwards. Tradition says the first one was built of timber and dedicated to Ge or Gaia, the Earth Mother Goddess.

Two other specific legends are attached to the place. One is that when Apollo arrived there he slew a she-dragon, Python, who dwelt in a cave. This smacks of a male-deity religion taking over Bronze-Age Goddess worship at the site. Python lived on, however, in the form of the oracular priestesses at the Temple of Apollo on the site. These women were given the title "Pythia."

The other legend is that Delphi stands at the center of the Earth. Zeus sent out his two eagles from the ends of the Earth, and Delphi was where their flight-paths crossed. This mythic central point was marked by a "navel stone," or omphalos. Two are visible at Delphi, in fact—a remarkable, ornately-carved stone now in the site museum, and another smooth cone of gray stone on the Sacred Way that winds up through the ruins of the various shrines and temples within the precincts of the hillside complex.

The key site, though, is the Temple of Apollo, where the priestesses uttered their oracles after taking large draughts of water from the springs at the site, notably the Kastalian spring. The temple's remains stand on a platform made from irregularly cut stones. This is an ancient Greek anti-seismic platform, that could rock and roll during an earthquake without collapsing! This points to the fact that the site is subject to earth tremors, one of the powerful, chthonic aspects of the place which Python doubtlessly symbolized.

We discovered another elemental aspect of Delphi shortly after we arrived. Exhausted from our flight and night drive, we made only a cursory initial visit to the temple complex, and then found a hotel room and collapsed. We awoke late in the day, and as we were having a meal a tremendous thunderstorm erupted. As the hotel clung vertiginously to the hillside, we had a splendid view of the storm, rolling through the valley beneath us. Lightning tore through the clouds, seemingly at the level of our knees! It was an exhilarating and extraordinary spectacle; never have I felt so close to thunder and lightning. It was indeed a visitation by Zeus, and I understood why scholars credit the weather and the geology for much of the mood and power of Delphi.

HALLUCINOGENIC PLACES

Joseph Fontenrose, who studied the site for forty years, felt that the references to Delphi in the classical literature with phrases like "pneuma ethousiastikon" and "atmos entheor" related to the numinosity of the site, to an "Earth Spirit" or particularly powerful *genius loci* inhabiting the place and inspiring the prophetesses.[1]

Julian Jaynes, a psychology professor at Princeton University, goes further, claiming that Delphi had hallucinogenic powers for the people of the time: "Oracles begin in localities with a specific awesomeness, natural formations of mountain gorge, of hallucinogenic winds or waves, of symbolic gleamings and vistas...."[2]

Jaynes believes that up until 2000–3000 years ago in Europe, and later in the New World, people had a different structure of consciousness than the one we have today—one in which the left and right brains had more differentiated functions. The left brain heard "voices" from the right brain, which were taken to be deities or ancestral spirits, who told them what to do. This became a highly socially-organized system of hallucination in which idols played an important role. To such a "bicameral" consciousness, to use Jaynes' term, the rushing sounds of wind or water, or evocative sights, could readily trigger visionary states and inner auditory phenomena, as can be the case today in unmedicated schizophrenics. If Jaynes is right, then we have "lost the soundtrack of prehistory," as Paul Devereux puts it.[3]

LOST SENSE

As we wandered up to the Delphi temples early on the morning following the storm, I realized we had lost something else too. The sun shone down, casting that brilliant Greek light, and everything was fresh from the rain. The combination brought forth powerful scents from the surrounding vegetation. The smell of the cedar trees was rich and strong, and at every turn there were different smells from the local flora. It was as if Gaia herself had swung her censer over the temple complex.

I realized that we had lost the odors of sanctity that were an integral part of ancient holy sites. Only our eyes and sense of touch visit the original essence of such places, while our ears and nose never do.

In the case of Delphi, this is a particular loss. After all, the site was identified in legend because of its fumes, and the Pythia was said to inhale the smoke of smoldering laurel leaves to enable her to enter prophetic trance. Recently, Christian Ratsch has suggested that the hallucinogenics hemp (cannabis) and henbane may have been used as well.[4]

HOLY SMOKE

Throughout the human record, fumes and scents have been used to aid the aura of sanctity in a holy place, to help meditation, and perhaps to alter states of consciousness. Indeed, the word perfume comes from the Latin *perfumum* which means "through smoke." Frankincense, for example, has been used as an incense in places of religious sanctity through the ages. Its first known use was in Egyptian temples some 5,000 years ago. Wars were even fought over access to frankincense.

The fumes from certain plants were also used to dispel evil spirits. During the Middle Ages, juniper branches were burned to rid habitations of demons, devils, and the like. A number of shamanic cultures inhale juniper smoke to help induce trancelike states of consciousness.

Cedarwood, and especially its oil, was revered in ancient Egypt and Mesopotamia as a magical substance. It is used by South American Indians, and chips of cedar are burned in all peyote ceremonies in the North American Peyote Church, where its fumes are thought to ward off evil spirits. Throughout the world, shamans inhale the smoke of plants, especially conifers, for intoxication leading to trance states.

One only has to visit the archaeological museum in Athens and see the dozens of ancient pottery oil containers and lamps there to appreciate the scent-sense of sacred places, which has been lost. This is ironic, as odors have an especially powerful effect in stimulating memory.[5]

The mind-altering effects of inhaled fumes of incense, oils, and wood terpenes has not been systematically studied in modern times. We know that camphor was highly prized, which is known to have a powerful effect on the central nervous system. Nutmeg oil contains myristicin and saffrole, which can aminate within the body to form MDA and MDMA respectively, heightening the effect of dreams and even encouraging lucid-dream states.[6]

REAPPRAISAL

Archaeologists such as Andrew Sherratt[7] have been reconsidering prehistoric pottery artifacts found across Europe as various forms of burners for producing fumes for mind-altering purposes. For example, 6,000-year-old ceramic dishes with three or four feet, found around the Baltic Sea, have long been described as "ritual items" or "altars." Sherratt gives evidence that they may have been used for burning aromatic substances such as pine or birch-bark resins. Early Bronze-Age Kurgan "pipe cups" containing charred hemp seeds have been found on the steppes and it is documented that the ancient Scythians used to throw hemp on hot rocks and inhale the fumes which caused them to "howl in pleasure." Prehistoric pottery bowls found in the Ukraine may have been braziers for cannabis, and only recently cannabis and opium resin was found in ceramic artifacts in La Houge Bie, a Stone Age chambered mound currently undergoing excavation on the island of Jersey in the English Channel.

That gloriously scented morning at Delphi brought home to me the importance of the missing element, the missing sense, in our appreciation of ancient holy places. This, plus the fact that I research and write[8] on the subject of essential oils as well as supply them to therapists, prompted me to start researching scent at sites, although in a somewhat unusual way.

DREAMWORK

For many years the Dragon Project Trust, of which I am a trustee, has been studying possible energy effects at prehistoric sacred sites.[9]

The current program of research involves a transpersonal dream experiment at four sites in the U.K., chosen for their special geophysical properties. The program pursues the basic idea of the classic "dream-incubation" or "temple sleep" practices carried out by many ancient peoples and brought to its greatest sophistication in the Greco-Roman world. Participants would retire to a temple (usually dedicated in Greece to the Healing God Asklepios) in order to seek a divinatory dream, often to seek a cure for illness. They slept in special cells and were aided in the dreamwork by temple helpers or "therapeutes."

In the Dragon Project's modern version, a volunteer sleeper goes to one of four selected sites with a helper. This therapeute watches over the sleeper, looking for the rapid eye movements (REMs) that denote dreaming sleep. The dreamer is then awakened, and any dream material recalled is immediately tape-recorded. These tapes are later transcribed onto a computer database. Eventually, the dream records will go to Dr. Stanley Krippner at the Saybrook Institute in San Francisco, where they will be cross-referenced to see whether the many dreams at the sites will show any patterns of content, type, symbols, imagery, motifs, etc.; thus revealing site-specific material. The dreams remain the personal property of the volunteers themselves, as the project is only looking for transpersonal elements that might yield a new way of responding to ancient sites, letting them "talk" to our subconscious Dreamtime minds.

This intensive exposure to ancient sacred space provides an ongoing inner process; it is curious how the properties of certain places can so deeply interact with one's psyche. This process takes time, something not fully appreciated by our modern ideas which too often seek the "quick fix."

I have found myself spending many nights as a therapeute at the first three sites, and the following sense impressions come from these silent, protracted night-time periods.

THE DREAM-PROGRAM SITES: PERSONAL IMPRESSIONS

Carn Euny, Cornwall: An underground passage and "beehive" chamber, dating to the Celtic Iron Age, about 2,500 years ago. Purpose unknown, but communal ritual use strongly suspected. A radon zone.

There is always a sense of comforting protection here. For me it is the womb of Earth. It allows a space where it is safe to come face-to-face with oneself.

On a clear night, the light of the moon penetrating from either of the opened ends of the fogue (as such chambers are called in Cornwall) can almost seem like an intrusion, as it forces remembrance of the outside world. Very often a local farm cat visits and curls up on my lap. It finds comfort in the warmth there, just as I find comfort in its warm fur and gentle purr.

Madron Well, Cornwall: A holy, healing well. Celtic Christian, probably a Christianized pagan spring. Since medieval times the water from the spring has been diverted to a (now ruined) baptistry, where many healings have taken place over the centuries. Mildly radioactive water.

The gentle "pink-noise" background of the trinkling water allows one to easily slip into a meditative state of consciousness here. On one occasion, when I visited this site during the day, I listened to the buzzing of insects. The more deeply I listened, the slower the sound became, until I felt I could understand what they were saying, although it was impossible to express in words! Perhaps it was my vibration that somehow quickened—I really cannot be sure. I simply felt in tune with them as I drifted into a half-sleep state. For me, Madron Well is a place to explore other levels of being.

Chun Quoit, Cornwall: A stone chamber composed of uprights and a huge capstone dating from the Neolithic period, about 5,000 years ago. More than a tomb—perhaps a shamanic place for "showing the bones." High natural radiation.

Sitting high on the wind-swept moor, Chun offers a place of protection from the sometimes raw climatic conditions, as well as a vast vista that stretches to the sea on one side.

The quoit acts as a sort of storage heater, with the warmth from the sun stored within the stone. Even in the cool midnight air the stones are often warm to the touch. I find it to be a secure, friendly place, where a sense of kinship with the remote past comes readily. People have reported unusual, small, flickering lights inside the stone chamber from time to time.

I have visited the following site, the fourth of the selected dreamwork locations, on a number of occasions to set up volunteers there for dream sessions: Carn Ingli, Preseli, Wales, a holy hilltop. The Celtic anchorite St. Brynach often meditated here in the fifth century A.D. He spoke with angels, hence *Carn Ingli*—the "Hill of Angels." Prehistoric people draped the hill with stone walling. This peak has powerful magnetic anomalies—compasses spin. Strange lights and sounds are often reported in the vicinity.

This spot is detached from the everyday world and totally exposed to the elements, mainly wind and air. Newport Bay and the sea are in visual reach, and on a clear day it is said that the distant shores of Ireland can be glimpsed. Newport—Dylan Thomas's "Under Milk Wood"—is stretched out below the hill on the edge of the little bay. In a way, we are doing our own "Under Milk Wood" mindwork here on the peak, under the modern, waking mind—deep mind, linking with place, raw and elemental.

Descending the craggy and sometimes dangerous slope, it is easy to lose one's way after nightfall. There is no clear path. Space is somehow distorted, and even a normally keen sense of direction can be affected. Distant noises can seem disturbingly close, and not so recognizable. It is like descending from another world. A dreamer is left on the peak, close to the stars.

MAKING SENSE

I am now setting up my own research framework to study the nature of the aromatic plants and other scent sources in the vicinity of these four dreamwork locations. I am also studying what is known of the paleobotanical situation of the places, and even any references to vegetation in the dreams at the sites.

Beginning with myself and extending to other volunteers, I hope to study sleep at the same dreamwork sites, but with the addition of aromatics that may have been available when the sites were originally in use. I will see how sleep states at these places may be affected by switching on that missing sense—the olfactory sense, the direct link to the brain.

Perhaps the combination of sacred site, sleep, and scent can open a super-highway into cellular memory—or, if the theories on "morphogenetic fields" and "morphic resonance" are correct, into place memory.

NOTES

1. Joseph Fontenrose, *The Delphic Oracle* (University of California Press, Berkeley, 1978).

2. Julian Jaynes, *The Origin of Consciousness in the Breakdown of the Bicameral Mind* (Houghton Mifflin, Boston, 1976).

3. Paul Devereux, *Symbolic Landscapes* (Gothic Image, Glastonbury, U.K., 1992).

4. Christian Ratsch, "Der Rauche von Delphi. Eine ethno-pharmakologische Annaherung," in *Curare*, Vol. 10, No. 4, 1987.

5. A. Puharich, *Beyond Telepathy* (Picador edition, London, 1975).

6. Paul Devereux, "An Apparently Nutmeg-Induced Experience of Magical Flight," in *Yearbook for Ethnomedicine and the Study of Consciousness* (VWB, Berlin, Germany, 1992).

7. Andrew Sherratt, "Sacred and Profane Substances: The Ritual Use of Narcotics in Later Neolithic Europe," in *Sacred and Profane: Proceedings of a Conference on Archaeology, Ritual and Religion* (Oxford, 1989, Oxford University Committee for Archaeology, Monograph No. 32, 1991).

8. Charla Devereux, *The Aromatherapy Kit* (Headline, London, 1993).

9. Paul Devereux, *Places of Power* (Cassell, London, 1990).

Aloka in the Circle of Stones in Crete. Photo by Tsultrim Allione.

RED EGGS AND BLACK OLIVES:
A DAUGHTER'S INITIATION IN CRETE

ONE COLD JANUARY DAY when my middle daughter Aloka was fifteen, she told me she needed a day off from schedules and school. We decided to be truants and go into New York City, a half hour's drive down the Hudson River. We went to the Metropolitan Museum, and wandered through the rooms.

After lunch at the museum cafe, we found ourselves in the small room containing Neolithic clay and marble goddesses from the Greek islands. The clay vases had breasts on them, the silent marble Cycladic figurines looked as though they would be wonderful to touch. There were clay animals that made us laugh, and our adventures tracking the Goddess in Greece came rushing back. During our seven years of living in Rome I had researched power places of the Goddess in Italy and Greece as part of a personal journey in search of the sacred feminine.

Aloka looked at me and said, "Mom, let's go back!"

I looked at the light in her slate-green eyes, her eyebrows raised expectantly, lips parted in excitement, waiting for my response. She had grown from a tow-headed child into a beautiful maiden, her face had graced the covers of magazines, and she was about to become a woman. I made some quick calculations in my head.

"Okay. Let's go in the spring," I said.

Surprised, she looked at me closely. "Really?"

"Yes, we can do it. I have some money saved. We'll go for Easter."

Convinced, she grabbed my shoulders and said, "Yes! We're going!"

A few months later, in time for Greek Easter, we flew to Athens. The first night, we stayed with Carol Christ, feminist theologian and author, who was living in Athens. Our conversation centered around a rite of initiation into the mysteries of Aphrodite that she had created for the daughter of a friend and described in her book *Laughter of Aphrodite*.

That night, lying on Carol's living-room couch, Aloka asked me if I would do such a ceremony for her. I agreed, knowing how important it is for ritual to mark the stages of life. I wished that my transition from maiden to woman had been marked by a ceremony. . . .

The next day, before our flight to Crete, we visited the museum of Cycladic Art in Athens. The cello-shaped marble goddesses, some four feet tall, were intimately displayed, creating the atmosphere of a Goddess temple rather than a museum. We were transported into the peaceful Neolithic culture, imagining moonlight ceremonies occurring around these beautiful marble goddesses. The idea of temples containing beautiful female imagery was healing for us, mother and maiden seeking resonance and reflection for our spiritual and physical lives.

Without any definite plan for Aloka's ritual in mind, I secretly bought a small white marble copy of one of the goddesses, along with an alabaster cere-monial cup and two golden pendants in a spiral form. I knew they were for her ritual, but not how they would be used.

We picked up a rental car and headed out of Heraclion toward the south. When we stopped for lunch, we found they were selling eggs dyed red, the pagan symbols of fertility and spring connected to the Neolithic goddesses Ostarte, Astarte, Ishtar, and Ashtoreth. We bought woven bread with a red egg in the center, the fabric of life cradling the egg of rebirth, some small black olives in oil and oregano, some blood oranges and a hunk of feta cheese. As soon as we were beyond the confines of the city, the light rain we had encountered stopped; we turned off the road past a nunnery and stopped the car.

Finally we were back in Crete again. Aloka was now a beautiful young woman, glossy flaxen hair tied back loosely, naturally golden-brown skin, a sen-sitive mouth, the whitest teeth I've seen, and a clear rosy complexion. I reflected on the myth of Demeter and Persephone, realizing the depth of Demeter's loss in her daughter's disappearance, just at the moment when they could begin to share the mysteries of womanhood together. After eating our picnic under lemon trees glistening from recent rain we continued driving south, following precip-itous cliffs through fields of red poppies, daisies, and hundreds of yellow wild flowers arching to the sea. We ended up in Levantes, a tiny fishing village.

We rented a room, and after settling in Aloka took a rest and I went out for a walk. On the stone path I met an old widow wearing black, with bags of strong-smelling herbs in one hand. She invited me to her house. It was a small, low building facing the sea. The single bed was covered with gray blankets, and herbs in plastic bags were under a piece of cloth under the bed. She wore black-rimmed glasses, and short white stubble covered her chin.

I thought about the crone, the old woman who holds the mysteries within her. Instead of being honored by her community, however, she lived alone, cut off. With her our female triad was complete—maiden, mother, and crone, all looking for connection and for a way to find ourselves in our world.

I bought four bags of her tea, and one of thyme, and gave her some extra drachmae as an Easter present. Delighted, she rushed over to her little single gas-burner and poured water, sugar, and coffee into an aluminum pot. I never drink coffee, but there was no question about not drinking her coffee, made with such sparingness and pleasure. It was thick and grainy, served in a small cup jiggling on a saucer.

As I sipped it, she showed me pictures of her dead husband, son, and grand-children wrapped in cracked plastic bags. When referring to her dead husband she looked out the window to the sea. Doves sailed above us, bellies struck with afternoon light. She shook her head, and told me her legs ached and she was waiting to die. We spoke without the frivolity of many words, communicating the essentials of our lives as women.

At forty-three, my lunar cycle was already becoming less regular, my hair had turned silver, and I was realizing I would conceive no more babies and was at the edge of becoming a crone. I thought about the maiden, mother, and crone triad that symbolizes the Goddess. I realized how, in some way, each phase of being a woman needs to be reclaimed through honoring and celebration. No one would do it for us; we had to do it for each other.

I felt blessed to give my daughter the gift of marking her transition with a ritual, but I wasn't sure exactly what form it would take. I trusted the goddess to guide us, that once we had stated our intention, it would happen. I wished I could do something to honor the crone, but she seemed warmed by our meet-ing and walked me home.

On Easter Monday we left Levantes. As we drove along the small coastal road, we stopped for a drink in a roadside cafe. The hillside sloped in a poppy-covered meadow to the sea. A mother and her daughter were baking Easter cookies in an outdoor oven next to the road. As we got back in the car Aloka said, "I wish I could have a cookie, but they're just for the family."

As we started to pull away, the older woman pulled two hot cookies from the oven and passed them into the car. The hot, lemon-scented ricotta-like cheese, delicate and sweet at the center of a buttery crust, melted on our tongues. It was the best cookie either of us had ever eaten. We marveled at the blessings of our lives.

That afternoon we visited the cave of Saint Sophia in northwestern Crete, south of the small, picturesque mountain village of Topolia. We parked the car in the ravine and saw the star on the small chapel in the cave above the road. As we climbed the steep path toward the cave, the perfume of wild spring orchids and thyme wafted up the hillside.

Easter is an important holiday in Greece, more important than Christmas. Everybody goes back to their homes from Athens. Walking up the hillside, I understood why. This time of year is the pinnacle of beauty in Greece; flowers carpet every patch of land. Even the rocks themselves grew small flowers from their crevices. Easter marks the return of warmth, when the life forces are rising. Ancient spring rituals honored the Sky God coming and fertilizing the Earth Mother at this time. My body longed for these ancient rituals celebrating the erotic nature of all life. Ancient images were of a sacred sexuality, the embrace of male and female creating new life.

> Smooth, big Earth made herself resplendent, beautified her body joyously,
> Wide Earth bedecked her body with precious metal and lapis lazuli,
> Adorned herself with diorite, chalcedony, and shining carnelian.
> Heaven arrayed himself in a wig of verdure, stood up in princeship,
> Holy Earth, the virgin, beautified herself for holy heaven,
> Heaven, the lofty god, planted his knees on the Wide Earth,
> Poured semen of the heroes Tree and Reed into her womb,
> Sweet Earth, the fecund cow, was impregnated with the rich semen of Heaven,
> Joyfully did the Earth tend to the giving birth of plants of life,
> Luxuriantly did Earth bear the rich produce, did she exude wine and honey.
> from *History Begins at Sumer*, Samuel N. Kramer

I entered the cave alone as Aloka ate lunch below. It was huge and awesome, peopled with stalagmites. In the corner there was a small chapel built into the wall, dedicated to Saint Sophia. On the other side of the cave, bees-wax candles burned in homage to Sophia. There was one six-foot-high candle, set in a huge brass holder hanging on chains.

Saint Sophia is the descendant of the Cretan Goddess who wears doves in her headdress. She is called God's female soul. As I climbed behind the chapel, I raised my eyes and saw a stalagmite with a large round eye and a beak on a pointed head. I understood where the pointed heads or even headless goddesses from Neolithic times came from: they descended from the stalagmites in the caves which were the earliest cathedrals to the Divine Mother. . . .

When Aloka arrived, breathless from the steep climb, we explored deeper in the cave and found a small pool of water. I felt again the profound spiritual energy of caves. We sat under a little overhang, a cave within the cave, look-ing out towards the entrance. Laurel branches had been left in the area around us. A big white dove flew out of the cave. We talked about the real meaning of Easter as a resurrection ritual symbolized by the dove flying out of the dark.

I said to her, "The dove, for gypsies, was the soul of the ancestors who lived inside hollow mountains. After death, men were changed to snakes and women to doves. The miniature shrines found in Crete show doves resting on the God-dess's sacred pillars, or on her head. Doves are a symbol of the Goddess, repre-senting the cyclic nature of life and death, the sacred cycle of life. The dove was also connected to Aphrodite, and later to Christ, as a symbol of love and resurrection. It's amazing to be sitting here in an ancient cave on Easter and to see a dove fly into the light."

Following the flight of the dove brought my gaze to something green grow-ing in the cave. Thinking this strange, I looked at it more carefully and saw that it was a spindly fig tree. The fig tree had appeared in all the Goddess sites that we had explored in Europe. It had become a game to try to locate the fig tree at each site. At Eleusis, where the Kore-Demeter mysteries took place, we found one growing upside down in Pluto's cave! The fig tree represents the Goddess, the figs bear a resemblance to the womb, and the generous spread of the leaves suggest the bounty of the feminine.

After leaving Sophia's cave, we stopped in a small town where there was only one cafe. We sat outside on the gravel at a small table. We were offered more Easter cookies as we sipped our drinks. Then we traveled down to the sea and got a hotel room in Paleochora. We spent some days relaxing on the roundstone beaches, soaking in spring's warmth. The days slipped away and as the time for our return approached, we hadn't found the right place for Aloka's ceremony.

On our last day, I awoke from an urgent dream about Aloka's ritual. In the dream I was told to just go into nature and not to worry about finding a special place—just do it under some olive trees if necessary, but go! We had been thinking that we had to find an archeological site, but didn't know how to find one not swarming with people.

We decided to trust the dream. I packed the car with provisions for the ritual. We headed up the mountain road from Paleochora. After a few minutes of climbing up, we passed a small road on the right.

We looked at each other; there was something about that road that spoke to us both. Simultaneously we said, "Let's go up that road." We laughed because we had the same thought at the same time, and slapped palms.

When we turned around, and headed back, we saw an old, rusty sign full of bullet-holes, indicating an archeological site up that road. It rose steeply, a narrow track passing through olive groves and past several white houses clinging to the side of the mountain with buckets of red geraniums outside their doors. Above the level of the houses, lupines and irises dotted the mountain pastures.

We kept going higher, encouraged by occasional rusty signs. We were above the olive trees and still climbing. I thought it must be a peak sanctuary, a common place for temples in Crete. We went as far as we could in the car and then, taking our things, we got out of the car. We realized we were in a spectacular place. Wide views surrounded us, hawks circled, and bees buzzed in a profusion of flowers at our feet. We decided to climb to the top of the nearby peak.

We walked through grass and wild orchids. Crete has many varieties of orchids that aren't found anywhere else in the world. Between them were poppies, dandelions, large, smooth rocks, and spiky thyme. As we reached a knoll beneath the peak, Aloka stopped and gasped.

"Look, Mom," she said, pointing down to a small plateau underneath the peak. There was a circle of stones with a small bush in the center. She had found her place. We marveled at the perfection of the circle of stones, each fitted tightly against the other, several feet above ground, perhaps used for similar purposes in ancient Crete. How had we found this ancient healing circle, with incredible views in all directions? Even if we had planned and researched a ritual site for weeks or months, we could not have found a more perfect place.

We walked to the circle joyfully, and decided to do our ceremony immediately.

———

I took Aloka behind a clump of bushes and rocks and said, "Aloka, take off all your clothes and put on my white dress. I have worn it for seven years. I wore it the first time we were in Crete, and on all our explorations of Greece. It is a Goddess dress."

I pulled the dress out of my bag. It was loose, soft, and cool, made of thin diaphanous layers of white cotton, with a wide, square neck.

"Then sit alone for a while and make a drawing; I will prepare the circle."

"Do I have to take off all my clothes?" She looked a little dismayed.

"It symbolizes letting go of the past and opening to the new."

"Okay," she said, hesitating a little, but willing to go along with me. . . .

After changing, she touched the dress and remarked how good it felt against her skin.

When I had set everything up inside the circle, I went to get her. She'd made an abstract spiraling watercolor.

We returned to the circle of stones, and I took her to the center. "Kiss the Goddess, and as you kiss her know that you touch the Goddess in yourself." I gave her the small statue of the Cycladic goddess I had bought in the museum in Athens.

She looked at the little statue, slowly picking it up and touching her delicate lips to the surface of the smooth marble face with its closed eyes and crossed arms.

Then I handed her the alabaster cup full of wine from Athens: "The wine is the fermentation of the sweetness of life that becomes spirit. In the Tibetan tradition, the wine represents the energy of the dakinis."

She took a small sip of wine and put it down next to the goddess. Everything she did, she did a little timidly, but wanting to trust the process.

"The red triangular stone next to the goddess represents female blood mysteries, the power women have to transform and be transformed by the blood mysteries. We have the power to transform blood into babies, and each month our blood transforms us, giving us emotions and special dreams, reminding us of our connection with the moon and the water of life."

I continued, "On the other side is a white triangular stone, an opaque white crystal I found on the beach yesterday. It represents death and old age, the wisdom of the crone. The triangle is the oldest symbol of the feminine, the womb from which all life comes, the cosmic cervix."

Next I took her to the eastern edge of the circle, toward the peak. Here there was a candle, incense and tahini.

"Light the candle; it will ignite your passion with fire."

She lit the candle, but it went out in the wind. Maybe it was not yet time for her passion. Then she lit the incense and I explain, "Loki, everything that you experience with your senses can bring you liberation. Unite with the object of your perception and lose the barrier between yourself and the object of your senses. Let the incense, the smell of the incense, and you as receptor of the smell become integrated. In that moment you will find liberation."

She closed her eyes and smelled the rope incense I had brought from Nepal. Her eyelashes fluttered. She smiled.

Then she tasted the tahini. "This tahini represents the richness of life, the nourishment and sustaining qualities that we need to keep going in the face of difficulties."

Then we moved to the south side of the circle, the direction of the sea. A flock of birds flew by. I told her, "Close your eyes and feel the direction of the south—how different it is from the east."

I handed her a cowrie shell. "This is the shell that represents the vulva. I give it to you so that you claim your vagina as the gateway to pleasure and birth."

She giggled and took it.

Next I gave her a small crystal. "The crystal is for clarity and spirituality. I give you the shell and the crystal together to remind you that your spirit and your sexuality are not separate, but go side-by-side."

Then we moved to the west, facing away from the peak to the open sky. In the west I had placed a cut lemon and oil.

"Here, Loki, taste the lemon," I said. "It represents the sourness of love, how it stings and sometimes grows bitter. But after the lemon taste the olive oil; it is the antidote, and stands for communication."

She picked up the juicy lemon and scraped her teeth across it, making a face. Then I poured some oil into her hand from a bottle. It was a rich green shade, with gold tones in the sun's rays. She licked the oil from her palm and closed her eyes.

Finally we were in the north, the fruit of the journey through the circle. Here in the north I'd placed apples, oranges, and red eggs.

"The fruits of love are sweet and must be eaten when they are ripe, or they will rot. The apple has my blood on it because I cut myself when I sliced it. All the fruits of your womb will be touched by my blood."

She shook the ant off her apple slice, and bit into a piece smudged with my blood.

She said, "It's true; all of my fruits will be connected to you, and my fruits will be connected to my children."

Then we went back into the center, she kissed the Goddess and had another sip of wine. I gave her the golden snake ring of the Goddess.

"As you wear this, remember that the snake symbolizes the ability to go between the worlds of above and below. It sheds its skin, as in your moontime when you shed the lining of your womb."

Then I gave her the golden pendant with interlocking spirals. "One of these is for you and one for me, so that we can remember this day and your initiation into the wisdom of Aphrodite."

"We sat and ate the rest of the offerings, leaving for the ants and vultures what we did not consume, and pouring a libation of wine onto the Earth."

The next day we drove back to Heraclion. Aloka stared at her new ring, twisting it on her finger and saying, "I like this ring. It's not something I would ever buy for myself. It's bigger and more wild than what I would choose, but I like it."

When we stopped to pee in a silvery olive grove, I realized I'd begun to bleed, and welcomed this sacred shedding of my womb. My blood was coming less frequently, signifying the end of my time of fertility. Each time it came I was not sure whether it would come again.

The moon was full as we were going home. Having shed one skin, we were already growing a new one.

Jill Smith, "Lammas Moon, Achmore"

JILL SMITH

A WOMAN AND A MOUNTAIN

They rose from the magma at creation
The great women
Strode the earth
Strong limbed, fine bodied,
Long hair wildly flying,
Moving the Dreamings,
Marking the paths
Work done
Journeys made
The great women lay to rest
To sleep
To wait.
Great mountain women everywhere
Sleeping
Waiting
Will they rise again?

I WAS BORN IN LONDON and lived a lot of my life there. Since 1986, however I have lived on the bare, rocky, windswept Island of Lewis in the Western Isles of Scotland, out in the Atlantic—a very long way, in every sense, from London.

I have no "roots" here, at least not in this life, but this island is home in a way no other place has ever become to me. I feel that, no matter what happens, it will be impossible for me to leave. This seems to be very much because of a mountain—an incredible mountain that lies not far from where I live, though I can't see her from here—the great figure of a sleeping woman known locally as "The Sleeping Beauty."

Sacred Woman, Sacred Place

This is the telling of a story—the story of the development of a relationship between a woman and a mountain.

In 1980, some artists, writers, and photographers I knew spent several months at Callanish, on the Isle of Lewis. At that time I did not know any of them very well, and though it seems strange that I did not go with them then, I knew the time wasn't right for me, nor the circumstances. Things had to change in my life before I could make my own way, in my own time, to the island.

Several of those who made that journey later became friends, and although I now rarely see them, I feel bonded to them in a strange and powerful way. Though we have perhaps little in common in our daily lives, there is a sense of deep kinship that will not go away. I feel that somehow we are brothers and sisters, bound by some connection through place. One in particular, Australian artist Lynne Wood, has understood and supported me in all I have done in the last decade, comprehending its meaning more clearly than I.

That first summer, those people returned to England. I sat one day in a tipi-like structure at a faire in Norfolk in the east of England, with my daughter Saffron, listening spellbound as one of them, Keith Payne, told me of this mountain—the Sleeping Beauty Mountain which lies to the south of the Callanish Stones. Something happened to me that day.

From that moment she exerted an irresistible pull on me, but it was nearly two years before I was to stand gazing up at her in physical reality. In those two years, my life turned upside-down. I began a process like a total breakdown and re-assemblage of every atom of my being, which went on for several years. It began very suddenly and threw me onto a deep spiritual path and contact with the Goddess, land, and magic. It was like a form of shamanic initiation—but it was place and Earth and moon and the power of all that is, that initiated me, and I had to make some sense of it.

At one point I had on loan in my possession a piece of crystal rock which I was told came from the mountain. Through this I had the most profound connections and visionary experiences, shattering in their intensity. On another occasion I seemed to fly over the mountain—the mountain I had never seen, the mountain of which I had never even seen a photograph.

In the spring of 1982 I knew that many people were going to gather at

Callanish for the summer solstice. I knew that this time I must be there. I also knew that I could not just simply go, but must make a pilgrimage to reach her. A journey through the whole sacred land of Britain—Albion—she who I saw and felt to be Goddess/Mother, truly Mother-land, the sleeping giant woman whose body stretched from the feet of Land's End to the brow at the far north of Scotland, and the islands beyond.

I had been receiving Dzogchen teachings from the Tibetan master Namkhai Norbu Rinpoche, and had learned a practice of purification in which one purifies certain places in one's body. In talking with friends, it seemed there were major ancient sacred sites throughout the body of the land which corresponded to the places in one's own body.

I knew that the journey I must make was through these sites, toe to brow. So I left the life I had led for decades—family, and possessions—and with just an old rucksack made my way to Land's End. I did not walk the whole way. I hope one day I will. I got to perhaps twenty miles of each site, then walked in pilgrimage and lived a few days at each place. I did the purification practice at each site, and somehow these ancient places integrated with the corresponding places in my own body. Slowly, as I rose through the land—feet, genitals, navel, heart, throat—I became integrated with the body of this being, this mother, my birth-land, Britain. I became the land, lying in the sea with these ancient sacred sites on my own body.

It was an extraordinary experience. I slept out, with no tent, under hedges, in forests—wherever I could—often in the ancient sites themselves. I truly nestled down to sleep each night into the soft comforting body of my Mother.

At last I crossed for the first time the water to the island where the mountain lies. As I stepped onto this land without preconception, I utterly felt that I had come home with a sense of total relief I never could have anticipated. I knew from that moment that I could never live anywhere else.

My first view of the mountain was overwhelming. I could hardly believe the life of her, the reality of her, the perfection of her. Lying there so alive, sleeping, seeming to be at the very moment of waking, waiting to rise, to stand and walk the Earth once more.

Sometime later, with a group of others, I walked the body of the mountain, the ultimate pilgrimage. It was wild, ecstatic, windswept. Each step was a sacred caress, until at last I stood on her crystal brow. I lay, my brow to her brow, the brow of Albion. As I lay there the journey I had made from Land's End snaked up her body, my body, like a living line of light. I lay there in a state of absolute union—of land, of mountain, of me, the pinnacle of lifetimes.

I watched her and watched her during that unbelievable summer. I could hardly bear to return to England, and over the months she called me again and again to sit and gaze at her, in all weathers, at all times of the year.

In 1986, after many more adventures, I drove my few remaining possessions and my little son Taliesin, then aged two, onto the ferry and over to our new home on Lewis. It had to be. I had no choice. There was never any question.

Sacred Woman, Sacred Place

So who is she, this mountain? She lies by Loch Seaforth, near the border between Lewis and Harris. Seen from close by, she is stunning in her perfection. To see her face etched dark against the sky is breathtaking, but it is when she is seen from farther away that more of her mystery unfolds.

As one moves along the road from Liurbost to Garynahine and Callanish, one sees her form change dramatically. There is a mountain—Ben Mor—behind her, and as one's viewpoint moves this mountain appears to move in relationship to her. As it moves, it changes her shape. Seen from Achmore, she appears to be pregnant, from farther back to be giving birth. From Callanish she lies free of the mountain, which has moved beyond her head.

There is a ridge running alongside this road, and at key points on it are places which seem to be there to view the mountain at particular times of the year. At one point there is a balancing stone. From here the mountain behind her appears to lie between her thighs in the acts of both impregnation and birth. Where one views her in her pregnant form, there is a stone circle, the stones now lying flat, like a flat platform on a hillside. Were they ever erected, or were they deliberately flattened? They do not just seem to have fallen.

This is a wonderful place where my son and I always try to go for Lammas. Here all attention seems focused on the pregnant mountain. She fills the skyline, drawing one's whole consciousness to her. It is the place for celebrating her ripe harvest. This place feels more ancient to me than the other circles that form the Callanish complex, as though they belonged to a more ancient race. These are my own feelings about the place; as are my feelings that a ritual journey was made along this ridge to celebrate the four quarters of the year and the changing form of mountain and Goddess as the year's circle turned. The mountain becomes truly sacred in her manifestation of the changing aspect of Goddess.

Sacred Woman, Sacred Place

The mountain reaches her peak from the main Callanish circle. From here, once every 18.6 years, at the major moon standstill, the moon rises from out of her body with an intense and erotic power. The Sleeping Beauty is kissed, and the energy of her awakening flows through the land. The last major moon standstill was in 1987. It was the June full moon which was lowest that year (though I believe the late September half-moon was the very lowest and the actual point of standstill). It is the lowest full moon that seems to hold the power.

Night after night that June, a group of friends and I sat and watched the moon rise, lower and lower, until the full-moon night. We sat spellbound as the blood-red orb rose at her feet, slid up her legs, her thighs, her belly, then rose a little above her, moving slowly over breasts and throat until it seemed to pause to look down on her face in a wonderful act of love. I have never known anything like that night. Due to my journey in 1982 and my integration with land and mountain, as I watched this coming together of moon and mountain, I also experienced it as though it were happening to me.

When one stands at the end of the northern avenue of the Callanish main circle at the standstill, when the moon has left the mountain, it then appears right in the center of the circle. This must be one of the main reasons why the stones were actually situated at that place. I felt strange that night, awed by the sense that I had actually stood there to watch the same thing, long, long ago. For tens of thousands of years people sat watching that low moon rise from the mountain, long before the stones were erected. Who then came to put the stones there, to capture that moon energy, to channel it . . . where?

One of the mountain's Gaelic names is Airghid, which means silver. That night in 1987, the moon was blood-red. Maybe in past times the atmosphere was clearer. Maybe the moon rose silver and turned the mountain silver also. . . .

That year, I felt the moon's focus rising up the body of the mountain each month, maybe purifying it as I had done on my journey through the land in '82. It seemed to be rising through the chakras of the mountain, awakening her kundalini.

Sacred Woman, Sacred Place, Sacred Mountain

I now live down the glen, at her feet. I cannot see her from there, but every time I go to town to do my errands, she is there to greet me, to remind me. Often she disappears into cloud or mist, seeming sometimes to choose who sees her; but then she reemerges, her dark blue-black profile gazing ever skyward. I cannot leave her; however hard my life on that island may be. I am hers forever.

Sacred Woman, Sacred Place, Blessed Be

This is written in the fond memory of the late Annie Macleod of Callanish, who brought the Sleeping Beauty to the attention of many people I know and offered warm firesides, tea, and gentle kindness to many, many visitors.

Jill Smith, "June Moon and the Mountain II"

MONICA SJÖÖ

WELL WORSHIP:
THE CULT OF THE SACRED WATERS

MY FIRST REAL AND POWERFUL EXPERIENCE of Earth Mysteries and Earth as the living Mother was at Avebury and Silbury in the autumn of 1978. This is no coincidence. Wiltshire, in the south of England, is the home of Avebury stone circle (the largest of the 900 or so stone circles in the British Isles); Silbury mound, *the* pregnant womb of the Earth, from which all of creation takes place and where the spirits emerge from the Otherworld; and West Kennet long barrow, one of the most ancient Neolithic womb/tomb/temples of the Underworld Dark Mother in existence (from the fifth millennium BC). This is altogether perhaps the most powerful ancient Goddess center in the whole of the northern world.

It was my ecstatic as well as very painful experience there, and sacred mushrooms that helped me "see" with my third eye, that altered my perceptions and made it possible for me to truly encounter the Goddess of the land at that time,[1] setting me on my journey since then, to Her sacred places in and out of Britain.

I also moved to a cottage in Dyfed, Old Pembrokeshire, near Fishguard/ Abergwaun in Celtic Wales/Cymru, where I learned to grow a garden and to live under the vast night skies full of stars, and with the luminous light of that windswept land by the sea. This was the first time since my early childhood in the north of Sweden that I experienced the darkness of the night sky without the artificial electric lights that always keep it distant and banished from the cities, the first time I was truly able to live with the radiant moon in her changes. As a result the skies, the land, the sea, the standing stones came into my paintings as never before, and I did many powerful and beautiful images during the five years that I lived there in the early 1980s.

I lived in the little cottage called Dwr Bach, or Little Water, with a lover, my mixed-race son and assorted friends. My son Leif was tragically killed by a car in the Basque country while we were visiting a friend in the south of France in August, 1985. His ashes are now buried, sewn into an African drum, in the center of the Medicine Wheel in the Tipi village, in a valley of the Black Mountains near Llandeilo in Dyfed, where many of our friends live and where I feel he is happy to be.

Monica Sjöö, "Sheela na gig as Gateway to the Faerie Realm, St. Non's Well"

That same year, my oldest son was diagnosed as having virulent cancer, and I chose to return with him to live in Bristol, my home during many years before going to live in Wales/Cymru, while he was in chemotherapy and other treatments. He died in the summer of 1987.[2] It had become impossible to stay in that cottage in Wales filled with painful memories and grief at the loss of my vital and beautiful young son, only fifteen years old.

This is the background of the sadness with which I write of my experiences in Wales, a country that I love so much and was prematurely torn away from. I have found myself often returning there in the last few years, and the magic continues for me in visions and dreams at Her sacred places.

ST. NON'S WELL

The area of Pembrokeshire where I lived, not far from St. David's Cathedral, has always in the past had strong links with both Ireland/Eire and Brittany/Bretagne, also Celtic lands, and has a powerful Faery tradition. During the late seventies there were many so-called UFO sightings within the "Dyfed Triangle" that also took in the Long House Farm cromlech situated near the village of Trefine on the coast, not far from us. A cromlech (or dolmen) is a Neolithic enclosed chamber of upright stones, capped by a huge stone. The capstone of this cromlech weighs about twenty five tons, and some of its stones are full of large chunks of quartz. It is believed that the Neolithic sacred structures were deliberately placed near fault lines in the earth's crust which act as a sort of window area or gateway to other states of consciousness and realities, where shamanic trance states and out-of-body journeys were undertaken by the ancients.

It is possible that what is now thought to be UFOs are in fact Earth lights—conscious energy forms or entities that emerge from deep within the hot belly of the Earth Mother at these fault lines, and in the past were perceived of as Faeries, the Shining Ones.[3]

Some of the rock formations along the Pembrokeshire coast are composed of the purple pink Cambrian sedimentary rock which is seven to eight million years old, amongst the earliest rock known in the world. In it there are caves that look like vaginas, which is as it should be, since the Paleolithic peoples experienced their cave homes and sanctuaries as the womb of the protective and all-powerful Mountain Mother.

Only half a mile up the road from our cottage in a farmer's field there was a large earthwork that felt like a vast, circular dance floor . . . peaceful and meditative, with panoramic views of the mountains and sea in the distance. We used to go there often to center ourselves, to commune with the Lunar Mother on full-moon nights. We felt very blessed to have this place so close to us, and so hidden away.

It is believed in Pembrokeshire that at some places along the coast one can see enchanted islands in the Irish Sea—the Blessed Isles of the immortal and shining Faery women—especially if one is standing on turf taken from the yard in front of St. David's Cathedral.

St. David was originally a Welsh Sea God worshiped as Dewi. His symbol was the Great Red Serpent, which became the Red Dragon of Wales. The whole of St. David's Head area was an ancient pagan sacred site called Menevia, which means Way of the Moon or Lunar Paradise, and it was an oracular holy well, now called St. Non's Well, that originally gave sanctity to this place. The well lies a mile to the south of St. David's, overlooking the bay which is also named after St. Non, one of the numerous bays forming the ten-mile stretch of St. Bride's Bay along the coast.

St. Non, the mother of David, according to legend, was a holy and learned woman and the daughter of Cynys, chieftain of Menevia. She became pregnant after being raped by Sanctus, King of Ceredigion. Barbara Walker writes in *The Women's Encyclopedia of Myths and Secrets* that St. Non, like the Virgin Mary, was the same "temple maiden who gave birth to every ancient god," and that *Nun* was the Egyptian word for the primal ocean, the Mother of us all. As applied to a religious woman, *Nun* originated from *Nonne,* a nurse, because in the ancient world priestesses were practitioners of the healing arts.

The Bretons claim that St. Non was born in Brittany, and there are many wells and chapels there dedicated to her. The Welsh say that St. Non went to Brittany shortly after David's birth, taking the child with her. It is also said that David, or Dewi, grew up in St. Non's residence, "The White House," and was educated in Old Menevia. St. Non is the matron saint of Dirion, in Finistere, where there is a chapel and a well dedicated to her, and where she was said to have been born. The chapel is thought to contain her tomb and is one of the historic Breton monuments.

I had known of holy wells and of the ancient well worship before I came to live in Wales, and of their great and mystical significance in the ancient religion of the Goddess. The waters of the miraculous springs emanate from deep within the body of Earth, holding the memory of its internal heat, crystals, minerals, and ores. They have the powers of creation. The underground serpentine waters are the blood arteries of the chthonic Mother, the Dragon Earth spirit; and the wells are the vaginal openings from which flow the blood/waters of her womb. Some wells, such as the Chalice Well/Blood Well in Glastonbury, flow with red waters. Wells are at the very heart of the mystery of the Old Religion, but we have forgotten, and many wells have been destroyed, covered or built-over, have been ill cared for and even poisoned by herbicides and the deadly chemical fertilizers used in factory-type farming. The Irish believed that Summerland, or the Sidh, the world of the Spirits or Faeries, could be reached through the wells.

In the Celtic world some of the holy wells are still honored and used, and some have been taken over by the church as places of pilgrimage, dedicated to saints. This is so with St. Non's Well, and for this I am grateful. It was only when I started to visit this well that the powers of the sacred waters became a reality to me.

One day, soon after we had moved to the cottage at Dwr Bach, I went for a walk with one of my sons along the stunningly beautiful coastal path high on the cliffs above St. Bride's Bay, when we happened to stumble upon the well. It is clearly sign-posted from St. David's, but we had not been aware of this and were delighted with our "discovery." Since that first time I have visited it frequently over the years, at different seasons, in daylight and night-time, in the different lunar phases, often bringing friends with me to be blessed and healed by its powers. I have had many strange, wonderful, eerie experiences at St. Non's Well—a visit with a friend who submerged herself naked in the extremely cold waters and reemerged shuddering, looking for a split-second like the very indwelling spirit of the well ... being there with another friend, Lynne Wood on an equinox full-moon night when the sky became absolutely still and clear after two whole days of pouring rain during which we had been drenched at various times ... slithering down the muddy path in the rain of a thunderous night and being given the vision of the marble-white statue of the Virgin in her niche, in the beam of the torch light, flashing out at me, looking like the White Lady, the specter of the great Goddess Bride/Brigid herself, to whom so many of the wells in the Celtic world are dedicated. It is visions such as these that have inspired so many of my paintings.

St. Non's Well has trance-inducing powers, and its still waters can act as a scrying mirror. Many a time I have sat there by the well dreaming and meditating.

St. Non's Well was thought to cure illnesses of the eyes, and sick children were submerged in its waters. Restored in 1951 by the Catholic Church, it is now a Catholic retreat. The same year, a shrine to the Blessed Lady, St. Non's Chapel, was built adjacent to the well using stones taken from the ancient buildings all around. The present barrel-vaulting covering the well replaced the ruins of a more extensive medieval structure in the eighteenth century.

An early eighteenth-century description of it says: "There is a fine Well . . . cover'd with Stone roof, and inclo'd within a Wall, with Benches to sit all around the Well. Some old simple people go still to visit this Saint at some particular times, especially upon St. Non's day (March 2nd) which they kept holy and offer Pins and Pebbles at this Well." In 1811 it was noted that the fame of the well was incredible, and that it was still resorted to for many complaints.[4]

Naturally I became curious as time went by about who St. Non actually was, and what her connection was with the well. According to legend St. Non, also called Nonita, found herself in the last stages of pregnancy and about to give birth out here on the wild coastline on a thunderous and stormy night. Where the child David was born, a spring emerged miraculously out of the ground, which is now St. Non's Well. To relieve the agony of the labor pains, it is said, Non supported herself on a nearby stone. This stone retained her fingerprints, and when St. Non's Chapel was built the stone was said to have been included as the altar table. The birth was accompanied by a golden light from heaven that surrounded mother and child and protected them from the storm and the wind. This is the Welsh version of the story of a virginal (not owned by a man or married) mother giving birth in miraculous circumstances to a divine and special child/savior/religious teacher.

Somehow it didn't ring true to me that this learned, well-off, and saintly woman, daughter of a local chieftain, would find herself about to give birth out in a storm on this wild coastline. If she was out there, it must have been for a reason, and that must have been because this holy and healing well has always been there and sought out by birthing women. This became clear to me when I found myself doing a series of paintings that included images of embryos and new life around the time I started to visit the well regularly. The waters of the well have in my experience a pulling power that would be helpful in childbirth. Perhaps the stone that Non gripped when in labor also had some such energies. This may have been a woman's only sanctuary, where a priesstesshood of shaman women dwelt who were midwives, astronomers, healers, and oracles.

I have wondered if St. Non's Well also had a connection with Rhian/non, the magical Welsh Faery-Queen Moon/Sun/Sea Goddess. She is the shamanistic white mare on which one travels into the Otherworld. Living in Wales/Cymru, within her domain, I have found myself under her spell. Her counterpart south of England was Epona who, traveling on her white mare, carries the solar disc in her arms. The White Horse/Mare is carved on many hillsides, the turf cut out to reveal its body in the white chalk in Wiltshire and Berkshire. The White Horse/Mare at Uffington is particularly ancient and sacred. I have had many dreams and visions of my young son riding on a white mare in the Otherworld, an African drum on his shoulders, proudly naked, his afro-curls flying in the wind.

BRIDE/ST. BRIGID—FROM GODDESS TO SAINT

Brigid/Bride was the Great Goddess, probably pre-Celtic, of fire, waters, poetry, smithcraft, healing, and inspiration. Her serpent/dragon sanctuary at Kildare was originally a wattle enclosure into which no man was allowed to enter. A sacred place of origins, like Delphi in Greece, it was oracular and perceived of as the navel of the world, with its sacred flame, its healing, birth-giving, and trance-inducing waters, and indwelling spirit. Waters move everywhere across and under the land in serpentine formations, and ancient women as well as animal mothers came to give birth over powerfully spiraling underground "blind springs," and by the wells. Brigid is also the Goddess of crops, cattle and vegetation, and appears in the form of a white cow. She is called upon by women in childbirth and by the sick. She was so beloved that her worship continued well into Christian times, when she lived on as St. Brigid.

St. Brigid of Kildare, known as Mary of the Gael, was the most popular saint in Ireland next to St. Patrick. Her eternal fire was still tended by nineteen nuns in the monastery enclosure from which men were excluded. The fire was said to leave no ashes; miracles were performed here, and it remained a center of pilgrimage and healing. In 1220, however, the archbiship of Dublin decided that the fire cult was pagan, and it was extinguished. But after his death, the nuns relit the fire only for it to be finally put out at the Reformation when the monastery was also shut down for good. St. Brigid was said to have been a fifth-century holy woman who performed healing miracles and was the Matron saint of the hearth, home, and sacred wells. She was said to have been born at sunrise on the 1st of February, which is Imbolc or ancient Bride's Day. She was spoken of as a priest or bishop, and this in a church that claimed never to ordain women. By the Druids she would have been seen as the living reincarnation of the Goddess.

Brigid was worshiped all over Europe under the names of Bride, Briginda, Brigidu, and Brigantia, "the High One."[5] The Sanskrit word *Brhati* means the Exalted One. She was depicted as triple, one aspect concerned with healing, one with divination and prophesy, and one with fire and iron-making.

Bride/Brigid's particular sacred islands are the outer Hebrides (He-Bride-s). I have made journeys up to these remote islands off the northwest coast of Scotland, to visit Callanish stone circle, to walk the Silver Maiden mountain, to welcome in Bride at Bride's Well. I have stayed with Jill Smith who lives on the island of Lewis and with her I have explored many hidden-away and difficult to reach ancient Celtic chapels and sacred places of the Old One, Caillech, the Dark Hag Goddess on Lewis and Harris many times, in storms, rain, and howling wind sounding like the Banshee herself.

Bride's Well is situated on the northwest coast of Lewis, in a field close to the wild sea. We arrived there late on a cold and stormy night and slept in the car overnight. At 5:00 AM we were up and warmly dressed, and sat meditating by this beautiful little well in the early dawn light. At an earlier visit I had felt that I was entering a state of out-of-mind, or beginning madness, when by this well. It is only at holy wells on Lewis that I have had this particular, almost fearful experience.

On Lewis I have had strange dreams, been inspired to write poems, and returned to Bristol with my mind full of visions and images that have materialized in powerful paintings. There are some strange energies or powers at work on these isles that are so barren, since no trees grow there, and so primeval. Many people of the Hebrides are known to have the "second sight."

When we left Bride's Well on Imbolc morning in 1989, we also visited

Callanish stones not far away. The graceful, silvery-streaked stones, looking like hooded crones or trolls, felt especially intense and vibrant that day. At night we saw the Northern Lights flashing like great pillars of light across the skies or, as I thought then, like burning candles of Bride's crown. It brought back

Monica Sjöö, "Bride's Well on Lewis"

memories of my childhood in Sweden of the feast of the Queen of Light (Freya) that is celebrated every 13th of December; of young women in long white gowns carrying crowns of candles on their hair, celebrating the new birth of light out of the mothering and nurturing darkness. We felt truly blessed by Bride that day, and we were welcome on Her land.

Bride inspires poetry in Her devotees. This poem is dedicated to Bride/Brigid, and was written at Chalice Well/Blood Well in Glastonbury on the full moon of July (the anniversary of my oldest son's death from cancer) in 1990.

Full Moon July 1990 at Chalice Well
—for Sean

Sean, my son, are you joyous
in your Otherworld?
Do you hear me now from the Spirit realms
you who I no longer can touch or see . . .
Watching the Full Moon
slowly slowly emerging
this night of July
three years after your "death" from cancer.
Silver dragons, fishes & birds . . .
Moonlight playing behind gridwork,
dark webs of clouds.
Lunar beams subtly seeking pathways,
reaching us where we waited a long time
on Glastonbury Tor enfolded
in the darkness of the night.
Great joy, excitement
as She shows Her radiant face
for a brief hour . . .
an eternity.
Sitting by the Blood waters next day
(menstrual flow of Mother Earth)
singing, dancing, rushing, falling
at Chalice Well.
Trance gardens where Spirits dwell
Bride's Well by the Mother Tor

Ancient Dragon ... living now & living then,
with us always ... always was,
is & will be.
Goddess rising within us,
was there in the beginning
& awaits us now.
Sorrowing Spirit
Grieving Mother
forgive us for we know not
what we do ...what we do.
Brigid of Waters
serpentine Spirit
Mother of fire ...
Fire of belly
Fire of hearth
Fire of Earth
Mother of Spirits
living Earth
Holy waters
sacred places.
Caillech and Bride
Mother and Daughter
Dark and Light ...
White Lady spectre
of Earth lights and Astral realms
Dark Earth Spirit
of Black fertile soil and life giving waters
Be with us now
Be with us now
So mote it be. Blessed Be.

There was originally a White Well at the foot of the Tor. It was destroyed when it was made into a Victorian waterworks in 1872, and now there is a cafe where the waters still flow. So here emerge the bloodwaters and the white ovulatory waters of the Goddess, by the sacred Tor with its indwelling ancient Mother Madrona, later known as Morgan. The Tor itself, with its wells, might be the cauldron of Cerridwen.

To the Celts it was the entrance to the Other/Underworld of the Dead and Faeries, and it was known as the Isle of Avalon. It looks like a huge, humped dragon, and is a three-dimensional labyrinth.[6] Terraces cut by the Neolithic peoples on its slopes create its serpentine and winding paths. One can see the Tor from miles around in the green, rolling, and lush Somerset lowlands, where apple orchards abound. The tower on its pinnacle, the only remains of the church of St. Michael, the dragonslayer, looks distinctly like a nipple on the Tor-breast of the Goddess of the land.

The Chalice Well garden is full of spirits, and a great peace reigns there. Its red-colored waters originate from within the Mendips hills far away and have a high content of iron oxide.

Monica Sjöö, "The Cauldron of Cerridwen"

I find myself deeply inspired when meditating by the Chalice Well waters, and have returned from there with images, poems, and new visions and dreams coming into my mind, as well as a sense of being healed and protected. It is thought to be very beneficial to drink of the waters, and I do this as often as I can since Glastonbury is close to Bristol.

YEWS: SACRED TREES OF THE DARK/LIGHT MOTHER OF DEATH AND REBIRTH

Yew trees grow in the Chalice Well gardens, giving sanctity and power to the place. A yew can live for several thousand years, and the "flesh" of its body is flamelike red. Like the Goddess who eternally gives birth to Herself parthenogenetically (without fertilization), eternally dying and returning like the moon, the yew has the ability eternally to regrow itself from inside out. Along with the sacred redwood trees in California they are perhaps the most ancient living beings on Earth, the Trees of Life indeed.

It is now thought that Yggdrasil, the World Tree of Norse religion, was not an ash but a yew. Yews are now very rare in Scandinavia, but sacred yews might have grown in the past by an ancient well at old Uppsala, the old Pagan center of Sweden.

The Nevern Church of St. Brynach, with its grove of yew trees—yews gave sanctity to places later taken over by the church—and its Celtic cross, one of the finest to be found, was one of the stations of the pilgrimage from St. Winifred's Holy Well in the North of Wales to St. David's Cathedral and St. Non's Well. There is still a pilgrim's seat and a cross, carved in the rockface overgrown with greenery, just beyond the church on the path the pilgrims would have taken when leaving for St. David's.

St. Brynach was supposedly a hermit, a contemporary and friend of St. David. Many miracles are associated with this god-turned-saint. He reputedly carried the large and extremely heavy Celtic cross on his shoulders and placed it there. The cross is about thirteen feet high, with a glow given it by the pollen from the yew trees, and is carved in the Celtic eternity knots. In the present-day church, which otherwise is of no interest, there is the Maglocumus stone, dating back from the fifth century, and is carved with the secret Druidic Tree-Ogham alphabet as well as with its Latin letter-equivalents.

The graveyard has an extremely ancient and sacred feel about it, and has reputedly been the setting for ghost-lights/candles and phantom funerals. As recently as March, 1991, a man was frightened because he found himself pursued by some globes of light when he was going home from a pub early in the evening. He called them UFOs but they seem to have been much like the Faeries/Earthlights/entities of old.

One approaches the church through a tunnel of yew trees that feels extremely old and underneath which there is eternal darkness. One of these venerable beings is the Bleeding Yew. I first experienced the Bleeding/menstruating Yew Mother when I spent a truly magic day, March 9th, 1983, on pilgrimage to Nevern and to Pentre Ifan. I set out with a friend on a mild, early spring day and hitched along the beautiful coastal road towards Cardigan, the ancient "Bay of Rhiannon." The smaller road branches off on one side up to the cromlech and on the other side down to Nevern, which lies in a valley by a river. It turned into a day when nothing could go wrong, and we felt guided all the way. We walked the three-mile-long lane and paths leading to the cromlech and found ourselves "by mistake" taking the wrong path, one leading to the farm of Pentre Ifan.

We both became convinced that this was an ancient Faery path snaking its way through the forest, here and there crossing a winding, serpentine stream. The atmosphere was such that we both felt in an altered state, and our hands tingled as if from hidden energies. The mood became meditative and trance-like. We had, however, to return down the path to find the road to the cromlech, which is placed on high with a view of the Preselau Mountains beyond and the sea below. I later learned that *Pentre* means "village" and there was formerly an ancient settlement where the farm now stands.

It was this experience more than any other that convinced me that how one travels to a sacred place of the Goddess is as important as reaching one's destination or, rather, it is the journeying, guided by the Spirits or Faeries, that decides what the experience will actually be at the sacred site. One has to be open for the unexpected and have no preconceived notions. Dreamtime cannot be programmed, and the Faeries coexist with us in other realities. The powers of the Goddess are a reality in the sacred landscape, and one has to come to her with love, awe, and respect.

After having spent some time at Pentre Ifan cromlech, we made our way down to Nevern. It was getting towards dusk when we finally arrived at the graveyard which, within the embrace of the yew trees, is eternally dark even on a sunny day. This is truly the abode of the Dark Mother. I felt the place even weirder and more eerie than I remembered due to our heightened state. We thought that we would like to return here again at the full moon, bringing candles, and later in the summer we did so.

I again felt the wonder of finding the amber glowing Celtic cross by the church wall. It is extraordinarily powerful, and its carvings very delicate as well as brooding and barbaric. We went searching for the Bleeding Yew tree among the dark, gnarled, gigantic tree trunks. I had not seen the tree when I had visited the graveyard once before. But now, as I turned around one of the trunks, I found it!

I wasn't prepared for the impact of it, and my reaction was one of amazement and wonder; my hair was standing on end. I had a chill up and down my spine, a split-second feeling of unreality, as I saw the dark red, tacky, blood-like substance seeping out as from a cunt or a wound in the trunk of the tree. It was truly astonishing! I feel this is a place of trance states, and that she "speaks" to one here. These experiences at the Nevern yews opened me to the sacredness of ancient tree spirits everywhere.

PENTRE IFAN

On a mystical, magical, journey I did with three women from Bristol in August, 1990, we arrived at Pentre Ifan in the dark, the night after the full moon night we had spent in tents by St. Non's Well. It was a very dark and overcast night, but in spite of this we decided to sleep under the capstone of the cromlech, hoping that it would give us some protection from eventual rain. It did soon start to pour, and continued until the next morning. Our sleeping bags and everything else got sodden-wet, but in spite of this we managed to actually sleep awhile. I sat up part of the night, and tried to do a drawing in torchlight of the stones looming around and above us. This eerie image stayed with and haunted me for a long time to come. When back in Bristol I dreamt about cromlechs many times, and did some powerful paintings as a result. When I finally went to sleep that wet night, I dreamt that I met some women who enthusiastically told me of UFOs and Faeries they had seen.

Pentre Ifan is a gateway cromlech, and was the entrance in Neolithic times into an oblong earthmound, the outline of which can still be seen. This womb/tomb/temple of the Goddess was still used by the Druids as a place of initiation, when initiates would stay in the darkness of the chamber undergoing days and nights of death and rebirth, vision quests and out-of-body journeys, and was called by them the Womb of Cerridwen.

A few stones still remain of the original lunar and horned enclosure at its entrance. This is the abode of Cerridwen, magical Dark Mother/Crone of the Celts, to whom the cauldron of transformations, inspiration and rebirth belongs. The whole of the Preselau mountains were sacred to her, and the Bronze-Age Great West road that connected the south of England with Ireland went past here in Wales/Cymru.

We walked many hours on the Preselies, a few days after our night at Pentre Ifan, on a gloriously sunny, clear and windy day. It was breathtakingly beautiful. These mountains are sacred indeed; everywhere there are remains of small stone circles, cairns and dwellings here, high under the skies. We reached Carn Menyn with its blue stone outcrops of spotted dolerite, and it looks indeed as if many of those beautiful and delicately colored stones were almost freestanding and didn't need quarrying. We sensed a great power at this place that stayed with us for the rest of the journey.

VISIONS AND DREAMS

Several years I have slept on Silbury mound, the Earth's womb, on some full-moon nights in July and August, in the company of other women. Silbury is to me an awesome place, ever since my first initiary experience there on sacred mushrooms in 1978. I also feel that my young son's death is somehow linked to her, the Lammas Mother of the Harvest, since he died on the very Lammas full moon in August, 1985; so it is with a mixture of great pain and fear as well as incredible love that I go there.

I have found, these last years, that to sleep and dream at the sacred sites is something else altogether than just visiting them. After all, the sacred Neolithic places are gateways to other realities, where the energies are heightened, the spirits communicate, where Dreamtime becomes a reality in trance states, visions and dreams. I have had a dream of meeting ancient, barely human ancestors when sleeping within West Kennet long barrow on a dark-moon night in July, 1990.

The crop circles that now appear so frequently during the summers in England, and especially so near the sacred Neolithic places in and around Wiltshire, also induce dreams and altered states in those who visit them with open minds and respect. People are changed by them. No one knows from where they come or what powers or energies create them. Is it Earth herself who speaks to us, is it the Spirits or Faeries warning us? It is interesting that some linguists have thought they have recognized ancient Sumerian pictograms in some crop circles, and that one message says, "The wells are drying out. Take care of and uncover the wells"—or some words to that effect. This would be very apt indeed, and certainly peoples of old would have thought that if the wells are dishonored and dry out that would spell the end of the world, the death of Gaia, the Earth Mother, and cosmic, conscious spirit.

Sacred sites were situated by wells, springs and rivers, encircled by serpentine underground water formations that fluctuate according to the lunar phases and are particularly healing on certain nights of the year. There is constant presence of magnetic underground water currents at the center of earthworks and circles. Stones that are placed above streams that cross each other come to act as amplifiers for these energies.

The most universal legend is that of the power of the Serpent/Dragon, the magic powers of water. She dwells in rivers and seas, in pools and wells, in the clouds above the mountain peaks, in caves and underground caverns; she regulates the tides, the menstrual flow, rainfall, thunder, and lightning. Her energies are mostly beneficial, but they embody powers for both good or ill. To the Christians, however, she came to represent the devil, and the women and men who still communicated with and were consciously in tune with her energies were vilified as witches and said to be in league with evil powers.

Holy wells and some stones, drunk of, touched, or embraced, especially on certain days of the year, were seen to heal and prolong life. Natural crevices, caverns, and caves, the vulva and womb of the Goddess, were powerful spirit realms and givers of immortality, healing, and rebirth. People living under patriarchy have lost the abilities to absorb these powers due to suppression of the lunar mind, our Dreamtime consciousness. According to patriarchal science there are no spirits of nature, and it knows no curative properties of stones and little enough of the healing mineral waters of the holy wells.

THE CULT OF THE SACRED WATERS
WAS NOT EASILY DEFEATED

The Church fought well-worshipers, and forbade divination by trees and stones. Both King Kanute in England and Charlemagne in Europe campaigned against the pagan beliefs. The second Council of Arles stated, in 452: "If in the territory of the Bishop, infidels light torches, or venerate trees, fountains, or stones, and he neglects to abolish this usage, he must know that he is guilty of sacrilege." In 640 it was decreed: "Let no Christian place lights at the temples, or the stones, or at fountains, or at trees, or enclosures, or at places where three ways meet.... Let no one presume to make lustrations, or to enchant herbs, or to make flocks pass through a hollow tree or an aperture in the earth; for by doing so they seem to consecrate themselves to the Devil."

But when such beliefs could not be defeated or destroyed, there was placed an image of the Virgin, Our Blessed Mother, or of some saint, in a sacred tree or grove, over a holy well or fountain, on the shore of a lake or a river. A transformation was made, and the country folk beheld in the brilliant images new and more glorious dwelling-places for the spirits which they had long venerated. The church slowly got people accustomed to praying to the saints at the sacred water places instead of to the spirits residing there. This is the reason for all the statues of saints placed in niches at so many wells and fountains.

Just as the cult of the fountains and wells was absorbed by Christianity, so was the worship of the sacred trees, for example, "Our Lady of the Oak" at Anjou. Sometimes a whole tree would be enshrined in the wall of a chapel in the same way that standing stones and whole cromlechs were included in some churches. There were haunting images of the Virgin, often shown standing on a lunar crescent, deep within grottos, as at Lourdes where there is also a wonder-working well.

I was at Lourdes on Maria's Ascension Day, the 15th of August, 1985, with my son, only eleven days before he was run down by a car. It was wonderful to behold 40,000 or so people in the darkness, with lighted candles in their hands, singing "Ave Maria." There was such a feeling of love all around us, and such a reverence of the Goddess in spite of its Catholic setting. Many sculptures of Maria, Mother of God as she is called, are to be found far out at sea or high on mountaintops, in trees and in caves.

There were pilgrimages held to the Fountain of St. Anne of d'Auray in the Morbihan, in Brittany, with a pardon ceremony lasting three days and torch-light processions at night. At the time of the Eleusian Mysteries in Greece the initiates searched for Persephone by torchlight and visited the seashore and sacred well. In the same way, sacred processions carried the image of St. Anne with the child Mary in the night, and all night services were held in the dimly lit church of St. Anne, where special masses were held for the saints and the dead. Offerings were given to the sacred pools and lakes; rivers in Europe were named after the Goddess as in the Danube or Donau (Danu of the Celts).

St. Anne is a derivation of Ana/Inanna, Sumerian Goddess of the cosmic waters and of childbirth. Is she the mysterious and particularly powerful mira-cle-working Black Madonna found in sacred caves, where there are also heal-ing and wondrous wells, in mountains and mounds across Europe? It was Inanna that gave birth to the sun at the midwinter solstice, and hills where beacon fires were lit were called St. Anne's hills.

BLACK VIRGIN

The Catholic church co-opted and took credit for the healing powers of the wells. Under many of the Gothic cathedrals of Europe dedicated to Our Lady/Notre Dame there is a well in a crypt which gives sanctity to the place. The Black Madonna (Black Isis) is Lady of the Underworld, Queen of Night, Dark of the Moon. She is connected in folk tales to her healing powers, her love of waters, and the dark. Her shrines are often in underground grottos close to water sources.[7]

I visited La Vierga Negra, the Black Madonna of Montserrat, in the winter of 1983. She is a wooden carved sculpture that was found, according to legend, some hundreds of years ago by shepherds in a cave in the sacred white Montser-rat mountain, and is now the matron saint/Goddess of Catalonia in the north of Spain. She might have been left there by the Moors when they were driven out of Spain in the end of the fifteenth century by the intolerant fundamen-talist Catholic church of the time. The mountain, inland from Barcelona, is truly beautiful, with extraordinary rock formations that look like gigantic, lean-ing crone figures, women trolls casting strange shadows in the bright southern light. Many rare herbs and plants grow there. It must have been a very sacred place to the ancients, but was taken over by the Catholic church and its orders of monks. There are now innumerable hermitages and cloisters on its pinnacles. Thousands pilgrimage to the huge cathedral in the mountain where the Black Madonna is housed; to touch her image works miracles. I experienced this for myself, and I hold her in great reverence.

In 1957 I encountered the Black Sarah of the Gypsies when I visited their yearly festival in May in Les Saintes Maries de la Mer in the French Camargue by the sea. The encounter with her was traumatic, and haunted me for a long time.

The Cathedral of Notre Dame de Paris, which stands on the mandorla (vagina)-shaped island in the river Seine, is also built where there was formerly a temple of Isis. I have entered a trance state there while standing bathed in the multifaceted blue light emanating from the three absolutely magnificent and beautiful circular stained-glass windows.

HOLY WELLS IN SCANDINAVIA

I was asked by the Danish Women's High School, situated near the German border in Jutland, to teach a course in Women's Culture and Art for two weeks in August, 1983.

Before going there I had inquired whether there were any holy wells in the vicinity, but to my surprise no one knew anything about it. So we decided to go to the local library to see if we could find any books or information on the subject. We found that there is a holy well in a village only a few miles from the school and that the directions to find it were set out in detail.

So we set out, three women, on what we were to experience as a mystery journey, a pilgrimage, with powerful effects on us and other women. We drove off to the little village and found the old white house with the garden and well. When knocking on the door we were told by the old man who answered that we were to go and talk with his wife in another house nearby. He said, "She knows all about the well; you go and talk to her." And so we did.

Again we knocked on a door, and an old and very dignified woman appeared. We said, a bit feebly, that we were interested in the holy well, at which she looked us deep in the eyes and said, "I believe in its powers!" When we said that we did too she relaxed, smiled, and asked us in for a cup of coffee. Then she talked to us for hours, about her family, the history of the village, and so on. She brought out a big old scrapbook in which she had collected a lifetime of information, both handwritten and in newspaper cuttings. She finally told us that we could borrow the book for a couple of days to photocopy some very old newspaper cuttings telling the extraordinary story of the holy well. We felt very honored that she trusted us with this precious material, and the women at the school were amazed and delighted when we brought it back. It was greatly admired and read. We found out that the well is simply called Helligkilden (Holy Well), and that the old house was named after it. The white house and its garden have been in the old woman's family for 300 years.

There were indeed many stories of miracle healings—of the blind who could now see again after visiting the well, and of crutches thrown away by people who had once been disabled. Some of them went back to the eighteenth century. The waters of the well were known particularly for bringing down high fevers, and the old lady said that there are still people who sneak into the garden to drink of its waters, even though nowadays its mouth is covered with a heavy concrete lid.

In the 1920s, someone from the village thought of sending a bottle of well water to a lab in Copenhagen to be analyzed. It was found to be radium-active. A company was formed to bottle the water on a large scale and sent samples far and wide by train, even as far as Switzerland, to sell it at high prices. After awhile the costs involved in transporting the bottled waters got too expensive, the family lost money, the men involved quarreled, and the well fell into disuse and was slowly virtually forgotten. We thought to ourselves that this economic failure and ruin happened because greedy men tried to exploit the waters.

We returned on Saturday to give the old woman back her book. Again we listened to her talking for a long time, sitting in the old house surrounded by beautiful old furniture and long-cherished family possessions. Now at last we had proved our sincerity and genuineness to her and she allowed us to go to the well and fetch some of its waters back with us. In the morning, when leaving the school, we had not been able to find a glass jar, so we had brought a large plastic container to collect the water in. It took us awhile just to move the very heavy, large concrete lid inch by inch, but at last we had a clear crescent opening into the well and could see into the dark waters. Because it had been built up and a pump put into it, the waters were far down and difficult to reach. Also they didn't look very clean at first sight, but then I saw a frog in the water and knew that such creatures will only live in healthy waters.

We then had a difficult time trying to submerge the plastic container long enough to fill it with water. At last we managed to fill it almost half full. Quite miraculously the opening that the lid and the well structure formed was that of a large, perfect, silvery crescent moon reflected in the mysterious black waters below. We all felt that we were taking part in something very special and sacred, like an ancient ritual.

We proudly brought the waters back to the high school. Never before had there been a plastic container in the school fridge on which it said "Holy Water"! We found over the next week that just about every woman in the school went there to take a sip or to wash her aching limbs in it. From some old books in the library in Tonder I pieced together the following account of wells and well worship, practiced until fairly recently all over Europe by the common people.

During the summers in olden times (long before there were any fridges), when all the water from rivers and lakes was lukewarm to drink, it was only the clear and cold water from the wells that was refreshing and exhilarating, that made you feel high and heady. (I remember my own delight as a child when coming across some cool, clear well deep in the Swedish forest on a hot summer afternoon). A holy well is one that is powerfully and miraculously healing at some certain time in the seasonal year. People would have noticed that animals came here to be healed, and that the grass was greener and the Earth more fertile in their vicinity. Some holy wells have also sprung up in particularly strange and special places, such as from an ancient mound, from within a hollow tree trunk or on the seashore.

In Scandinavia the wells were considered miraculously healing on May Eve and Midsummer's Eve, close to the solstice. On Bride's Day or Imbolc, in early February, when so many wells are magically powerful in the Celtic world, snow still covers the ground in the northern lands, and it is not until May that the Goddess dips her finger or throws a stone into the waters to warm them. Then Nerthus rides across the land in her solar wagon drawn by she-oxen, and the new life of spring begins to bud. The spring festival was celebrated some time between April 21st and May 11th, when the cows were let out to grass.

Beltane or May Eve, is called Valborgsmasse Eve in Scandinavia and Valpurgisnacht in Germany. This is the night when the witches/wise people of the

Craft were thought to fly or ride to Blakulla in Sweden, Bloksbjoerg in Denmark and Brocken in Germany (all of them sacred mountains), for this Great-Goddess lunar and fire cross-quarter day celebration. Sacred fires, called "witches' fires" in Germany, were lit to guide their way. Valborg was Valuburg, an ancient Vala or sibyl, who might have been an aspect of Nerthus, or of her daughter Freya herself.

Many fires were lit near the wells on Valpurgisnacht (or Maynight), and rituals were performed there. Peoples everywhere believed in the cleansing, renewing, and protective powers of the sacred fires, and cattle were passed through the flames for protection and healing. The Midsummer Festival was always held on June 24th in Scandinavia, and is still popular as perhaps the greatest feast day of the year, together with Yule at midwinter. In Denmark Midsummer's Eve is called St. Hans' Eve, after John the Baptist, who was conveniently born on this day just six months before the supposed birth of Jesus at midwinter. In many parts of the world this night is celebrated with sacred fires (in Germany called Johannesfeuer), and is famous for its well journeys. In Denmark alone there are 200 wells known to have been visited by great numbers of people on Midsummer's Eve.

In Sweden all of nature is in her most wonderful bloom on Midsummer's Eve, and the nights are light. Many plants are then in fruit and animals pregnant. Flowers and herbs that bloom then, and early potatoes, are named after St. Hans, and nine of these plants were collected and kept for protection. The early morning midsummer dew was thought to have particular healing powers, and if one treads in it barefoot one absorbs its powers and recovers life energies. The sick rolled around in the dewy grass, and clothes were rinsed in dewy water to protect their owners from ill-health in the coming season. Dew was of the very essence of the lunar light and the life-giving waters of the Mother.

The most famous and most visited of the midsummer wells in the whole of Denmark was St. Helene Kilde (Well) at Tisvilde, in Odsherred on the seashore of North Sjaelland. Helene Kilde is situated on the seashore, the especially sacred place where sea and land meet, and where sometimes the sea waves caress the well. Associated with the holy well appears to be a strangely shaped stone with markings on it as from a recumbent woman's body. It is situated, along with two other wells, also named after holy women, in a large cleft in the seashore hillside. Nearby is Helene's grave and the remains of an old well chapel, and three miles inland lies the ancient Tibirke church. There are wells with similar legends attached to them and dedicated to women saints in Skane, in the south of Sweden.

There are many versions of the legend around these wells, one of which says that a holy woman called Lene was murdered in Sweden, and that her dead body sailed across the sea on a stone. When her body reached the island of Sjaelland the hillside burst open to allow her to enter, and where her body came to rest a well sprang forth. People tried to bury her in the nearby churchyard, but the body could be neither moved nor carried. So her grave is here on the seashore, which in fact was seen as particularly protective of the dead and where many ancient burial places are to be found. The drowned were always buried by the sea.

Another version of the legend goes that Helene, a Swedish princess, tried to avoid the clutches of a lovesick king by throwing herself in the sea. She was rescued by a stone that floated on the water, and on it she sailed to Denmark. The well sprang forth where she set foot on the land, and she lived here as a holy woman for many years. Yet another version has it that three holy sisters wanted to sail across the sea but died on the way, and were brought by the waves to different places where wells burst forth. There appear to be a number of Helene Kilder (wells) in Sweden and Denmark, and they obviously relate to the Goddess in her midsummer aspect. Is she the Helene of the ancient winding tracks that the British dowser Guy Underwood writes of in *The Pattern of the Past*,[8] the Earth Spirit that journeys across the landscape sanctifying wells, stones and mounds?

Helle-Lene was transformed into a Christian saint, St. Lene, in medieval times. The Catholic church built special well-chapels, to divert the people from the actual well and its indwelling spirit, where they could pray to Maria, God's Holy Mother, for help or in thanksgiving. Some of these chapels were later extended and became parish churches, but most of them fell into ruin. Many cloisters were built by the wells.

In Germany the Goddess was called Fau Holle or Holda. Her name also means holy, heal, hallow, hole, and whole, as well as all, halo, and holly. In the Nordic sagas I learned about as a child, the Huldra was clearly both the Goddess of the forest, of animals, and of death. She was portrayed as a beautiful, naked woman with long blonde hair, but her backside was like a hollowed-out tree trunk, and she had a tail like an animal. The sagas told that she lured lonely men to their deaths.

In Neolithic times, circular well-shrines were built in Sardinia actually enclosing the sacred waters, and reached by climbing rockcut steps far below.[9] In many countries even today there are still well-chapels where people pray, hang up their crutches if cured after bathing in the well water, discard their old clothes as offerings and leave money in the trough for the poor. The water from the wells was collected and kept all year round as medicine.

From time immemorial, until around 1900, the Danish people visited their holy wells and the church could do naught to stop it. Here is an example from Ireland which could just as well be applied to Danish wells: "At the well of St. Declan, Ardmore, County Waterford, about a century ago, masses of people assembled annually on December 22nd, crawled beneath a hollowed stone and then drank of the well. It was surmounted by the image of a female figure which is described as being like the pictures of Calee, the Black Goddess of Hindostan. The Catholic priests actually whipped the folk away from the spot, but to no purpose."[10]

At many wells, far into medieval times, there was still the ancient memory of the association with women's blood, but the blood they were now connected to in legend and myth was blood unwillingly given from the bodies of murdered women. It was now said at the many Maiden Wells that the water had welled out of the ground where the blood from a murdered or raped virgin had fallen, where a woman was killed by her husband or by robbers, or where a mother cried for her murdered children. One story says that a woman was murdered by her husband because she had shown disrespect in church — she had burped during a sermon!

For the Midsummer Feast the wells were decked in flowers and garlands, and in green finery. This custom is still alive in the small towns around Sheffield in England where, at the end of June, the whole church congregation follows the priest and the church choir in a round of well-blessings. The most famous holy wells are in Tissington, where beautiful, vibrant images are created with entirely organic materials like flower petals, leaves, moss, wool, and sand (although sadly, of mainly Biblical motifs), and raised above the wells. It is mostly girls and women who spend the months making these short-lived images. When traveling to a holy well on St. Hans' Eve, one had to come in silence and not even greet friends. No bustle of noise was allowed; however, many people were waiting their turn by the well, and if the peace was broken the waters disappeared and only returned when it was restored. The water was thought to be most powerful after sundown or at midnight.

Everything had to be ritually repeated three times: One walked three times around the well or jumped over it three times, drank three mouthfuls or glasses of water, fetched the water for three Thursdays in a row, bowed three times to the rising sun, and bent three times over the well. The sick person walked three times round the well-chapel and shouted her or his illness three times at its altar. Witches walked three times moonwise around the well to undo some magic.

The water was to be drunk for internal illnesses and washed with for external ones. Old clothes were thrown away, along with bandages and crutches. Many beggars came to the well-markets to ask for the discarded clothes. The new clay mugs bought in the market were thought to possess healing powers even when ordinary water was used in them. To be entirely effective as a cure, the sick should revisit the well nine days later and then again nine days after that, and to wash themselves in utter silence. Those who drank from the waters of a holy well on Midsummer's Eve together with their beloved would soon be married to each other.

It was thought that droughts were caused by badly kept wells, and that when a well was cleared it would rain. The farmers in Scandinavia continued the tradition, until quite recently, of honoring the dead at the seasonal festivals and making sure that the peace of the dead and of the Faeries was preserved and protected within the mounds. On the festival night a bowl of porridge or an offering of milk was brought to the burial mound that shared the name with a farm nearby. The milk was for the serpents, who represented the spirits of the dead and were the totem animals not to be harmed. It was thought that without the milk the serpents would not successfully shed their skins to renew themselves.

The dead and the serpents are of the nature of the Dark Mother of the winding underground waters, of the sacred stones and mounds. As the serpent sheds its skin and is reborn anew, so the moon eternally waxes and wanes but never dies, and so women shed our womb lining in our monthly menstrual flow. We bleed, but we live and we create life; we are of the nature of the Goddess of the holy wells.

NOTES

1. I have written of this, my experience at Avebury and Silbury, in the anthology *Voices of the Goddess: A Chorus of Sibyls,* edited by Caitlin Matthews (1990, Aquarian Press). My section is called "Tested by the Dark/Light Mother of the Otherworld." Also see my book *New Age and Armageddon: The Goddess or the Gurus, a Feminist Vision of the Future* (Women's Press, London, 1992).

2. In the same book I have written of my son Sean's illness and death from cancer.

3. See *Earth Lights Revelation* (Blanford Press, London, 1989) as well as *Places of Power* (Blanford, 1990) both by Paul Devereux on Earth Mysteries.

4. Informational leaflets for tourists in St. David's.

5. Much information on Brigid/Bride in Janet McCrickard's *Eclipse of the Sun: an Investigation into Sun and Moon Myths* (Gothic Image, Glastonbury, 1990).

6. Read *Avalonian Quest* by Geoffrey Ashe (Methuen, London, 1982). He lives in the skirts of the Tor, and has explored the labyrinth fully.

7. Books on the Black Goddess are: *Sophia: Goddess of Wisdom* by Caitlin Matthews (Thossons, London,1991), *The Cult of the Black Virgin* by Ian Begg (Arkana, 1985) and *The Black Goddess of the Sixth Sense* by Peter Redgrove (Bloomsbury, London, 1987). All worth reading.

8. Guy Underwood, *The Pattern of the Past* (Abacus, London, 1974). A book that was very important to me when I discovered it in 1976.

9. Sibylle Von Cles-Reden, *The Realm of the Great Goddess* (Thames & Hudson, London, 1961).

10. Lewis Spence, *Irish Goddess and Kali* (1948).

Mnajdra, Malta. Photo by Jo Carson.

JO CARSON

DANCING WITH GAIA
AND SEEKING AN ORACLE

WHAT DREW ME TO THE GODDESS? A deep love of mother and Earth? I don't really know why I responded so strongly to the first Goddess images I saw, at the home of artist Fred Adams; it was too many years ago. It had a profound effect on me as a filmmaker, and today I find myself in the process of making another film devoted to exploring and celebrating the Goddess and the Earth. *Dancing with Gaia* is an educational documentary, mostly made up of interviews with authors and artists. To complete it I knew I needed footage of ancient places with visual evidence of how closely people used to relate to the seasons and to the currents of Earth energy.

During my research, I discovered that the world's oldest buildings were built in the shape of the body of the Goddess. These temples are on the islands of Malta and Gozo, about sixty miles southwest of Sicily. Obviously, I had to go. So I flew there, alone, with all my equipment and a little trepidation.

From the air, Malta looks dry and rocky. In the distance was the walled city of Valetta, whose buildings have stood for many hundreds of years—its walls date back to the 1560s. Beyond, there are ruins from the Roman era, but even these pale by comparison to the 5,000-year-old temples I came to see.

The temple called Mnajdra is on the south coast of Malta. I rented a motorcycle and found it, following maps and an occasional Maltese road sign. I only got lost once. Mnajdra is one of about thirty known megalithic temples in Malta, all built between 3600–3100 BC. They were constructed of enormous stones, with a single stone often weighing fifty to one hundred tons. How they were made and what happened to the early temple builders is still unknown, for they vanished around 2000 BC.

Nearby, on higher ground, is another temple called Hagar Qim, where I began my exploration. I felt Hagar Qim to be huge, and public-oriented toward big festivals and ceremonies. I left it, carrying my cameras and tripod over my shoulder, and walked down the long, perfectly straight pathway that connects the two. Heat waves shimmered around me. I wondered if this could have been an old processional way. Did people walk toward Mnajdra then, as I was now, eagerly looking to the smaller, more intimate temple, seeing the flowers along the way, the winged island of Filfa in the distance?

Approaching the open-topped temple, one door invites me. The heat is almost overwhelming. My head aches from the blinding sunlight. As I approach I do a small honoring ritual, just a simple recognition: "Hello, entranceway. I enter you, recognizing your power to transform me...." I go in.

I want to experience the place first, to see what draws me. Video and photography will wait. Past the first doorway I see another one, very similar, in front of me; on either side there is a rounded room—the one on my left has a low stone bench at the back. I walk around, checking it over like a dog preparing to sleep. I sit on the bench, awestruck by the realization of how many have sat here before me. I look at these huge, cream colored walls. Over five thousand years of visitors....

The rock slab is the perfect size and height to lie on. Protected from the sea breezes, it would be comfortable at night, if softened by cushions. It would have had easy access to glorious sunrises and views of the sacred island of Filfa. Shrines have been found on Filfa, but being so tiny, it doesn't seem to ever have been settled. To see it, one is reminded of a bird in flight. Perhaps the sight would encourage the soul to fly off in search of a vision, while the body rested on this rock.

The inclination to lie down is overwhelming. I am alone with these walls that have seen so much. Initiations, births, deaths, weddings, trysts, declarations of love, pilgrims of every color, and now tourists, archaeologists. I feel the miracle of this space being held sacred for so long. Finally following the urge, I lie down, the sun bright red through my closed eyelids. Hard hand-hewn rock supports my back, hips, shoulders, and skull. I feel my body relax, absorbing the sense of this sacred place around me. I open up to images, messages, dreams.

There is a small statue called The Sleeping Lady in the museum at Valetta, the capital of Malta. Archaeologists have speculated that she was demonstrating dream incubation; the practice of sleeping in a sacred place to cultivate a healing or prophetic dream may have originated in Malta.

I realize that this is what I am doing as I lie here. Who is so lucky that they don't need to be healed, physically or emotionally? I realize that I have made a pilgrimage here; now I am fully present, alert, and open to the possibility of healing. I think of the many reasons people seek out the sacred places of the Earth and make pilgrimages to them—healing, inspiration, atonement, and renewal; connection with ancestors, the Goddesses and Gods, and with the Earth itself. Of these, I believe most people seek personal healing. But what is that? Here, lying in this temple built in the shape of the body of the Goddess, I feel the peace of being within the Mother—my mother, all mothers, and the Earth Mother.

I am experiencing a brief return to the womb, intimate and perfect, like the care received by an unborn baby. A memory of my own basic innocence and freshness comes over me. Stone walls surround me now, visibly, here in this temple. But the truth is that these stones are the bones of our mother Earth, and they are never far away. Not even when I work on films back in California, where everyone I see is so alienated from their roots. The Earth is still there, beneath the floors. She is always supporting us. Her minerals come to us through food, even in workday lunches, and persist in our bones. It is good to feel these connections as my body lies on the hard rock, to see the interior of her body with my own eyes.

The thick walls of this temple separate me from the concerns that brought me here. I've been working hard on *Dancing With Gaia*, shooting ancient religious sites all over Britain and the Mediterranean. Protected now, in the body of the Mother, I lie, sunlit and dreaming, in her embrace. My loneliness, deeply felt as I traveled for so long, drops away in the pure joy of being present. I feel honored to be here, and honored that I am able to see it, feel it, and record it for others to share. I only wish that their experience could be as complete as mine.

When I think back on Mnajdra, I know it makes all the difference actually to have gone there myself. If I am depressed or in pain I have the memory of it in my body to draw on. I've seen photos and film of many sacred caves, temples, and mountains, but the connection is not alive—I haven't breathed that air, walked that ground, or found a personal moment of inspiration there. I believe that we need to physically experience a place to be healed by it. Then later, when we need it, our bodies can call on their cellular memories to re-create the healing energy of the place.

Mnajdra and Hagar Qim are a pair of temples, a common siting plan in Malta. Some scholars have speculated whether the relationship between the two might parallel the mother/daughter relationship, with the two temples each representing one aspect of the Goddess. Another view, which I mentioned fits my feeling about it, is that the larger temple was for public rites and festivals, while the smaller temple was reserved for intimate ceremonies and initiations.

Hagar Qim is larger and more complex than Mnajdra. The typical ground-plan has been altered, over the course of time, for enlargements and for other reasons that we can only guess at. Seen here for the first time is a stone phallus, shown in conjunction with a "female" downward-pointing triangle. Hagar Qim is also the site of some of the first separately carved statues. Archaeologist Veronica Veen sees in this a newly emerging male influence, "demonstrated by a tendency toward grasping reality instead of symbolizing it."

Mnajdra is alone among Maltese temples, so far as we know, in being aligned with the solstices and equinoxes. Its architects were agricultural people, who needed like most in the Neolithic world an accurate way of forecasting the seasonal changes. It seems likely that even the first planters and harvesters had methods of keeping track of the year's progression but their methods are unknown to us. Those first Maltese temple builders did not apparently think it important to include methods of solar tracking in their architecture. Mnajdra was not constructed until the middle of the temple-building period. Only at this point did the stone re-creation of the body of the Earth Goddess show the integration of a new sanctity accorded to the sun's movements.

I loved going to Mnajdra. It spoke to me more deeply than many other sacred sites I visited. I also felt clear as to the purpose of the temple. It provided a separate place, dedicated to the purpose of reflection and connection with the greater powers. These powers were understood to be the mysteries of birth, growth, and death. Growth was indicated by the spiraling outward of the plant forms seen endlessly repeated over the arches and rock walls of the temples. Growth of the person who came to the temple would parallel that of the plant world; birth and death were part of the endlessly repeating spiral. The sanctuary of the temple, the earthly body of the Great Goddess, provided for both.

THE TEMPLES OF GOZO

Many archaeologists believe that the Maltese temple culture began on the nearby island of Gozo. Gozo is tiny compared to Malta, yet of the thirty known sites, at least ten have been found there. While few facts are clear regarding their construction, there is a legend of a giantess on Gozo who carried the huge stones all over the island. One of her creations was the Stone of Qala, which we now know to be a remnant of a Goddess temple.

Oddly, from the Western point of view, the villages of this era were often on higher ground than the temples they constructed. As the people looked down to the Earth as a life giving Mother, so they were comfortable looking down to their temples. In contrast, our culture tends to erect cathedrals on hilltops—we expect to look up to divinity.

The pots found there, from around 2800–2500 BC, were baked a bright red on the inside, probably produced with red ochre. On the outside, they were a fleshy cream color. Cooking pots were thought to be like wombs, where, as in life, a transformation could occur; thus their tools of everyday life also reveal an integration of spiritual awareness.

The temple builders were apparently a social people who needed to stay in visual contact with one another. We see this in their choice of village and temple locations: they were always constructed in sight of other settlements and temples. Other choice sites were thus passed over in favor of those that were visible, but there may have been additional reasons for this unusual siting plan, such as a possible relationship between these sites and the ley or energy lines used elsewhere in Europe.

As connected as I felt to the place and culture of these sites, I found that I was not alone—a pretty German woman, Sylvia, was staying at the same hotel. She was on her way to Gozo to visit a girlfriend who had moved there two years earlier. After moving there, her friend had found that her new home was only ten minutes away from Gigantija, a megalithic temple said to be the oldest free-standing building in the world.

When she went into the temple she felt like she had come home after a long absence. At the full moon she would sometimes sneak in, either alone or with a few of her close women friends. She always felt a desire to lay down on a certain stone in the fetal position, and later she found out that in the ancient past women used to die in that position in the temple. In one corner of the temple there is a stone which has a very smooth shape. It was her favorite corner of the temple, because she always felt very protected when she leaned her body against that stone.

She was back in Germany during the Gulf War, but by remembering the Gigantija temple she wasn't afraid at all. She said if people around her got too nervous, she would think of being in the temple, and it gave her a lot of strength. Sylvia told me she had once gone to Gigantija with her friend. While they were wandering around it, her friend explaining the construction of the place to her, she also felt very calm and protected.

After hearing this story, I was eager to experience Gigantija for myself. It takes quite an effort to get there. First there is a long, dusty bus ride across Malta, then a ferry crossing to Gozo. Another bus takes you to Victoria, the main city and finally, a local bus, found after much questioning and waiting, takes you to the town next to the temple. From there it is a short walk. The ancient, craggy stones rise up, unmistakably, as you round a walled corner. I was disappointed to see that the road was now filled with tourist buses; most of Gigantija's visitors arrive via prepackaged tours. Guards and guides greet them, and give them a well-rehearsed history of the temple. I found that by waiting through several waves of tours, a short time would occasionally open up when I was almost alone there. This was precious, but all too brief.

I got one of the guides to tell me about the place—he was dark and slender, like many Maltese, and despite being young, he knew his history. He was intrigued by my video camera and description of the documentary I was shooting, and by the fact that I was traveling alone. He showed me the best angle for shooting an overview of the two paired temples.

It was exciting to be in this ancient place. As at Mnajdra, there are intriguing details that hint at some of its past. One is the presence of small holes made in the huge stones which link one area of the temple to another; referred to as "oracle holes," it is speculated that they were used by hidden priestesses to answer questions or deliver oracles to those on the other side. There are also slots in the doorway stones between sections of the temple which apparently held barriers; thus the inner sanctum was reserved for special uses, perhaps only by the leaders of the religion.

Still, I found it impossible to feel a real connection with the site when there were so many people around, and it was not just the number of people, but that so many of them seemed completely ignorant of the place. There was a lot of shouting and children playing whenever a new bus would unload and when they reloaded there were always stragglers buying T-shirts in the last few minutes before the bus would roar away. I am sure that when Sylvia's friend went to Gigantija in the full moonlight, she was able to experience it in a profound way—I would love to meet her and hear firsthand what she has learned, or perhaps accompany her some moonlit evening.

THE TEMPLE OF DEMETER AND PERSEPHONE IN PRIENE, TURKEY

Priene is an ancient Greek city on the west coast of Turkey. In ruins for many centuries, Priene was moved from an earlier, unknown location and rebuilt in 350 BC where it thrived as a trading city until about AD 100. By that time patriarchy was well established throughout the area, although Goddesses were still worshiped.

The grandest temple of Priene is the one dedicated to Athena, a Greek goddess who is often shown with many "male" attributes. She is said to embody dispassionate wisdom and wears armor, shield, and other implements of war. The temple is massive and the view commanding; countless huge column stones are scattered around the foundations. The atmosphere is severe, stark. The strong wind almost blew my tripod over when I was shooting there. Most visitors consider this temple to be the main attraction of Priene. I felt exposed and bare there—the place felt majestic, but not healing.

Higher up the hill, hard to find and virtually ignored by tourists, is the Temple of Demeter and Kore, the Mother and Maiden Daughter Goddesses. It feels older, by far, than the larger temple to Athena, although the literature claims that both were built "at the founding of the city." It might have had the same magnificent view—there are distant hills in three directions, though now trees are blocking them—or it just might have been established in a sacred grove.

It took close attention to the hand-drawn map, several false tries, and considerable legwork to find. Finally I saw a rusty metal sign in French, "Demeter et Persephone." It was too faded to be sure, but I knew this was the place.

I approached slowly, warding off the thought that the only bus back to the city would leave very soon. Too many times on this trip I knew that I was experiencing something I would never come back to and that each moment was precious. I had to breathe slowly, letting the place speak to me. So many generations of women have come here, honoring the connection of mother to daughter, to all women, to the larger cosmos. I am struck by the value of likeness, the similarity of wombs, my mothers', her mothers', and on back through time for millions of years; they are all our mothers.

There are low stone walls still in place, showing the layout of the temple and sanctuary. The map led me to notice the placement of a water basin on the right, after entering the temple. It immediately brought to mind images of women washing their hands and faces as a purification before approaching the place of the Goddesses; I went to the back, where stones marked the place of their statues. A profound peace settled over me as I sat crosslegged there in the central sanctuary.

There was something incredible for me, as a woman, about being in a place where the Goddess has been honored for so long. I felt a deep "thank you," a feeling of gratitude and rightness as I sat there. Had women built this place? Or at least come here, for years, before there was a stone temple to mark it?

I wanted to stay there, just to remain in that communion. But I knew I couldn't. This had been an ongoing conflict for me, as a filmmaker, to find a balance between wanting to shoot as many sites as possible—after all, you never know ahead of time which one will "work" on film—and my personal desire to experience some of the places deeply. Often, I wanted to throw the schedule out. Maybe my fear of doing just that was what led me to buy all of the airline tickets ahead of time, before leaving the States—at least I knew I would cover something in each of the far-flung countries of my destination that way. The truth is, when the three-month trip was done, I was amazed to have succeeded in actually shooting all of the sacred sites that I had hoped to cover, and without any major problems. Many times I felt I had been unusually lucky, or blessed by the Goddess, in being able to find and shoot some of the more inaccessible places.

I have close to three thousand slides and twenty-three hours of video tape now, and need only the time and opportunity to edit them. Most of the rest of the project has already been shot. I have interviewed about a dozen authors, artists, and philosophers about their ideas on the reemerging Goddess, Earth energies, and sacred sexuality. The documentary will explore the area where these three things converge—the way the feeling of sacredness can infuse our bodies, our lives, and our perception of the living Earth. I can't help but feel that a similar convergence is taking place in my own body, since I am pregnant as I write this.

It seems clear that if people felt this kind of connection on a daily level, life for all of us would be vastly different. Our actions, reflecting this kind of awareness, could create a world of kindness and beauty that would make a nurtured, centered life possible for future generations.

At the ancient sacred sites I went to, I made an attempt to feel the past. I waited until images came to me, visions of people moving in sacred space, or just doing their work. What was their experience? What is my relation to them? What happened to their culture, their beliefs? Perhaps more important, did they have knowledge or ways of being that we need to be aware of now?

It is exciting to me that many ancient sacred sites are receiving new energy, being brought back to life. Not that the Earth ever died in those places, but our connection to Earth did. Right now, when we need it so much, attuning to the power of these places can give us strength as we move into the future.

SEEKING AN ORACLE

Spending time at a sacred site can be a healing experience. The profound harmony of the place seems to entrain the body and mind, to pattern them into harmony.

It can also be like consulting an oracle, such as the *I Ching* or the Tarot. This is easier if you have some knowledge of symbolism and geomancy, but it is enough to use your own intuition.

Observing the site from a little distance, a shape will become apparent. How does this shape relate to the surrounding landscape? Does this shape define a relationship of support, domination, or harmony? Does this reflect a relationship in your life? This might be seen as the theme for your experience.

Are there peaks, canyons, or bodies of water in sight? Does their shape remind you of anything? What position are they in, relative to the site? How do the site and the land/water forms align to the compass directions? If you are familiar with the traditional associations of directions with the elements, the seasons, and psychic/emotional states, you might find that the location of the site begins to make a statement now.

As one approaches the entrance to a sacred site, it is good to address the place in an honoring way. Some kind of recognition of the place and the energy unique to it creates a conscious relationship for you. State your intention and wait until you feel an opening—a receptiveness to your presence and your purpose—from the place. Then enter. Slowly is usually best, allowing impressions to come from all directions. Open your senses. Be aware of the smell in the air, the quality of dampness, the texture of the earth underfoot.

These conditions, which probably change over time, are specific to this time that you are here. Like readings of the *I Ching,* they can be seen as unique to the moment, and your reading of them will reflect the state of being that you bring here now.

It is ideal to spend enough time at a place that you can watch how the light changes through the day. Look for shapes in the stone or shadows. Qualities of the beings you might see may be experienced as the gifts you need now, or as the challenges you are confronting.

Events may occur while you are there—a sudden heavy gust of wind, a rainstorm, a bird landing in front of you, the far cry of a wolf or owl—all can be experienced as messages to us from the natural world. Use your intuition or the same set of symbols and correspondences that you used to explore the site in your thinking about the meaning of the event.

If you have time to spend the night there, watch the position of the sun and moon rise and set. If you are there near a solstice or equinox, or a day halfway between one of these (called cross-quarter days in European traditions), you may see an alignment between the site, some more distant marker or landform, and the setting or rising. This can reveal that the place has a special relationship to that time of year. For instance, a winter solstice alignment would remind us of the importance of the return of the lengthening days, and give promise of the days of spring and growth.

Watching the star constellations wheel through the night sky might inspire other ideas. Certain stars, like Sirius and the Pleiades, have long been associated with star people or advanced beings who have a special relationship with Earth. For example, seeing Sirius rise in the north as you sit in the mouth of a sacred cave could lead you to feel a message from the ancestors about your place in the universe, or it might refer to your life path in relation to your family.

If you dream while you are there, you are participating in one of the oldest forms of healing and divination known. We know that dream incubation was practiced in the temples of Malta and Greece, perhaps longer than five thousand years ago. If you want to try this, state your intention first. When you say it out loud, the sound waves touch the place and set up a stronger connection than if you only think it in your mind. Then focus on your goal as you go to sleep, using whatever dream incubation techniques you may know.

Going to a sacred site for guidance can be an incredibly rich experience. It is by far more complex than reading an oracle, and can address life on a more profound level. Since it usually requires more effort and time, one's involvement is deeper. It is more personal than going to a reader or psychic, because the process is interior. You are consulting your own knowledge of symbols, personal analogies, and intuitions about what is going on.

Occasionally no "thought" will be required at all. Sometimes the message or healing process will come instantly, in an overwhelming fashion. But a certain readiness is always there, when this happens. . . .

A few places of power have been polluted by people with negative intentions, so I can't recommend going with your heart completely open at all times. Take your sensitivity with you, and tune in to what you feel from the place. Then open up if it feels right, and meditate, sing, chant, or just listen for what comes to you. A chant or small organic or appropriate item left there can be your gift to the place as a thank you.

As you leave, again turn and address the place; recognize the site and its special powers. This will give the experience a sense of completion.

You may soon want to write something about what happened, but it is often good to wait for a little while. The experience is not necessarily over, and it may be too soon to subject it to the limits of the linear, rational mind that are used in writing. Let it seep into your life first, and look at it from several directions. Now when you write about it, you may be surprised to see how far the tentacles of the experience have reached.

Glastonbury Tor, England. Photo by Cindy Pavlinac

SERENA RONEY-DOUGAL

A WOMAN IN GLASTONBURY

I HAVE LIVED IN GLASTONBURY for eleven and a half years now—since September 1980. This is my home, my hearth, my heart, my earth. I love the land here deeply. I live high up on the north side of St. Edmund's Hill, otherwise known as Windmill Hill. Every morning I look out my bedroom window and think, "Aaah, how beautiful it is," and my heart flies out over the apple orchard at the bottom of my garden and ten miles over the levels to the Mendip Hills and on another twenty miles to Brent Knoll, ancient sacred hilltop temple of the Celtic people. On clear days I can just make out a dim blue line in the distance, which is the hills of Wales.

I've never had a home before. My father was in the army and so from birth I'd traveled, never living in a house for longer than three years. Here, I've planted a wild cherry tree by the front gate and have been here to watch it grow. I've planted a hedge of hawthorn and blackthorn so that there are flowers from early March to May. Flowers, herbs, and fruit are all becoming familiar as the seasons turn. What joy to create a garden and see it mature—I had never done that before.

I've learned to make wine from the flowers and fruits of the countryside (one wine for each of the festivals). There's blackberry for Samhain, ginger for winter solstice, parsnip for Imbolc, dandelion for spring equinox, May blossom for Beltane, elderflower for summer solstice, nothing as yet for Lammas because I'm always away, and elderberry for autumn equinox. I have made each wine with the flower or fruit of the season and kept it a year so that we enjoy it in season. The flavor and quality of the wine is just perfect for the time of year: root in the winter, flower in spring and summer, and berry in the autumn. I've begun to learn to live in rhythm with the seasons, letting the rhythm of my life echo the rhythm of the land here. I've started to learn the rhythm of the moon, beginning to get to know the nineteen-year cycle, seeing the moon high in the sky or low over the tops of the houses up the hill to the south of me.

For fourteen years I've been making herb teas from loose herbs initially bought from old glass jars at Baldwin's medical herbalists in London. Now I'm growing my own herbs, or going out into the country and picking them in season (for example, there are the early spring celandines that are like drops of sunshine after the winter), drying and putting them into jars and making up my own mixes according to the need of the person, time, or season. It gives such satisfaction to drink a tea you've grown or gathered. And vegetables—there are now some seasons of the year where I hardly need to buy vegetables or fruit—we're nearly getting self-sufficient and that feels very important to me. I don't know what effect that ozone depletion and the greenhouse effect will have on world food supplies, but I'm feeling concerned, and to have learned how to grow my own food feels very good, satisfying, real. It's not trendy, yuppie, New Ageism; it's real, honest, hard work, a good life.

There are five hills that make up this island of Avalon. In the winter there are times when it returns to being an island, when the rains come down and flood the moors (known also as levels, which are at sea level a bit like in Holland). They lie for weeks under inches of water that doesn't drain because all the rhynes (drainage ditches) are full. If it freezes there is an enormous ice skating rink. The five hills are Wearyall Hill, Chalice Hill, the Tor (Tor is an old word for hill), Stonedown Hill, and St. Edmunds Hill. I think where I live is the old beacon hill—you can see all the other beacon hills—Dundon Beacon, Crooks Peak, and Penn Hill—where fires were lit on Midsummer Night.

The children still build a fire on the top of this hill every November, the old Samhain fire. They spend a month doing it and it can have flames thirty feet high when they light it. The feeling I have as I come round the corner and see the circle of people round the great fire on the top of the hill is how ancient this custom is, going back through the millennia. I keep stepping out of time on this hill. I walk down Whiting Road, which leads into St. Edmund's Lane and down the footpath to the old coaching inn, the Wagon and Horses, and on across the levels to Godney Church. I am walking physically down a modern road with modern houses and I don't see the houses; I see the trees. I've been here before and there is no change in the spirit feel of the land.

When I lived out in Barton St. David, a village south of Glastonbury, in the zodiac sign of the dove, the five hills would be spread out before us as we drove across the moors into town. My eldest daughter who was then six years old saw them as the body of a woman with the head at Stonedown Hill, the Tor as her breast, the tower being an enormous nipple as a breast-feeding mother, Chalice Hill her pregnant belly, and Wearyall and St. Edmund's Hill her outstretched legs, which means that the Lady Chapel in the Abbey is her vagina and the towns High St. and Bove Town are her groin. This vision has remained with me ever since.

In this vision, Chalice Well with its blood red water and the White Spring with its limestone water, are at the left hand side of the rib cage just below the breast where you can feel the heart beat and where the myths say Jesus was pierced and blood and water flowed out. They say Joseph of Arimathea brought two cruets to Glastonbury containing the blood and sweat of Christ from the crucifixion. This myth was already embodied in the land except that it is the Goddess and no one is crucifying her for her blood and water, she gives it freely with great beauty and peace.

Perhaps it is the blood of menstruation and the milk of ovulation, for to sit by Chalice Well is one of the most healing experiences you could ask for, with the old dark yew trees, the sound of the ever-running water, the light dancing birches, all the birds, and the hump of the Tor sheltering you. Many a time when its been bad for me, I've gone to sit in the gardens and I always feel better for it. They say that when the White Spring ran there was the most beautiful limestone grotto with fantastic shapes, but the Victorians filled it in and built an ugly reservoir so all that beauty is now lost, and we have to rip out the old reservoir and refind the spring with its limestone sculptures.

We have had to remove the sewage works from Bride's Mound, as well. Imagine, they actually put sewage works at the foot of the mound where for centuries women kept a sacred Chapel of St. Bride with a perpetual fire. Even the old well of St. Bride is gone with nothing but intuition to tell where it was. They say St. Bride herself came to found that chapel, which is by the end of Wearyall Hill just where the baby's head would be if the mother hills of Avalon were birthing a baby, the most beautiful spot for gazing on the Isle of Avalon. You can feel the sacred processional way up to the Isle from there except now this sacred way has been covered with houses, a secondhand car yard, a timber warehouse, coal yard, enormous smelly sheepskin factories, and other industries. The place has been totally desecrated and my heart bleeds whenever I go that way. It's a place of visions, most times when I take people there we just lie on the earth and dream. The dreams are often sad and painful, but when I went there this year I dreamt of a wise young child. It feels like a new birthing is happening. The whole area called Wearyall Park was so sacred that in ancient times the road had to go over the other side of Wearyall Hill for nothing was to be built between Bride's Mound and the Isle of Avalon. This was the chapel you came to from over the Perilous Way. You had to spend a whole night in vigil here before you could go up to Avalon by this processional route, and I know why—the view of Avalon from here is breathtaking.

One Imbolc, a group of thirteen women with five girl children, a pony, and a dog walked this way with drums and a pipe playing. We went to Bride's Mound through all the factories, past the stinking canal and sewage works. On the Mound we sat or lay quietly breathing in the feeling of the place while the children played, and the time must come again soon when we reclaim it. The factories are beginning to become disused and will soon start to crumble and fall.

The Neolithic people, who built the great stone circles of this land, laid an oak track across the marsh between what is now called Street and Glastonbury. The Pons Perilous is the old way that was dangerous because when the area was tidal marshland and at times would be flooded, the track would be under water so people would have to know their way or would step off the old oak beams into the peaty marsh.

This is a land of myth, a force to use to its full potential, while being very aware that every molehill here becomes a mountain. If there is a flaw within it will be cracked wide open and you will go through a difficult time. I went through four years of sheer hell—I came out of the worst of the trauma feeling like I'd just been through the heavenly blacksmith's forge. All the dross had been burned out of me in the furnace and I became like tempered steel. Some people get spun right out again while others, like myself, live through the dark and come out the other end much stronger and clearer. It is a wonderful place for growing.

When I came here, I was leaving London because my eldest daughter was turning five years old and I didn't want her to go to a city school. I left the Ph.D. experiments that I had spent three years doing at the University in London, moved to Glastonbury, and carried on my work here. Six years later I got my

Ph.D. in Parapsychology, having studied the similarities and differences between telepathy and subliminal perception. Those were the years of trauma because my flaw had to do with relationships; I suffered hell and just managed to keep my work going by a slender thread; my work helped to keep me alive and sane through all the nightmares and ensuing depression. I was so damaged that I lived completely alone with the children for four and a half years; then for the next four years I slowly came alive again, very gently, with intermittent part-time relationships. Through that time I learned how to relate to women, and my bonding and friendships with women grew stronger and stronger. My ability to love and feel warm affection was taught to me by my second child, who was conceived and born during that time, now a beautiful nine year old, strong and wise. I look at the women of Glastonbury and our children because St. Edmund's Hill is a women's community and I feel that something very strong and beautiful is slowly growing between us.

We've a good women's community up here on the hill. When I first moved into my house most of the people living up here were local folk, husband and wife and their children. Now nearly every other house has an incomer, younger people with children drawn to Glastonbury like iron filings to a magnet. Most of them are single parents, with or without temporary or permanent lovers. The community spirit is definitely growing: practical things like sharing slices of bread or cupfuls of milk, sharing car lifts to take children out to a village school that is preferred over the town ones, sharing meals together, babysitting, cups of tea and gossip. I'm learning what friendship with other women is, never having had it before. Now here is Juliet with the kids coming back from school—it's her turn on the rota!

After I got my Ph.D., I was asked to write a book, which took me three years and came out last year. I called it *Where Science and Magic Meet*. It is about my fifteen years of study, learning, and experience—from my Ph.D. work through all the magic I have grown into living here in Glastonbury, all the ancient sacred ways of living and relating to the land, and earthed through my scientific discipline (which I love because for me it helps to see clearly what is, as opposed to what people believe). Now I am teaching in the local schools, teaching parapsychology and yoga, as well as lecturing around the world and doing workshops. There are so many of us here in Glastonbury whose creative gifts are flowering.

What struck me when I first came here was the quality of the people, such creative people—artists, musicians, and actors abound, along with writers, sculptors, psychics, healers, and teachers. Glastonbury seems to do something to people because of its intensity, so many things start as seeds here, and then go out to other places. The Assembly Rooms are down in the heart of the town just by the Abbey, and is a true community center where the local dramas occur and everyone gets very hot and bothered about it. There we work out just how we want to interact with each other and what our way of life really is—do we or do we not accept drugs, dogs, smoking, drinking, playing, children, straight exhibitions for the tourists. What is our level of tolerance, intolerance, flexibility; can we work cooperatively or do we need some form of hierarchy? How do we share responsibility, blame, and all the other questions between families and friends that come up here at the community level. We have all bought the building together, people on very small incomes paying £3 (about $4.60) a week as their share for four years—that is the degree of commitment to the building. Now musicians can play for us and we can dance and dance and dance, the local theater company rehearse and put on their shows, local people come together to put on a pantomime which is always such fun, and local artists have their exhibitions. Such a wealth of talent.

There is never a dull moment in Glastonbury. The best street theater in the world is to be found in the High Street with the travelers juggling or busking, playing their digeridoos or sitting round with their dogs and Special Brew in St. John's churchyard, a green place with trees on the High Street where the holy thorn tree lives. Its blossom is picked every Christmas to be sent to the Queen— the children from the local primary school stand about and sing, while the vicar performs this lovely custom marking some of the myths of the land. They say that the tomb in St. John's church is the sarcophagus of Joseph of Arimathea because it's got "JA" carved on it. Others say that it's the tomb of James Austin, whose family owned the Abbey during Victorian times and who then sold it to the Church of England (who own's it now), and whose family built the Assembly Rooms. There's a stained glass window in the church showing Joseph with the two cruets of blood and water.

I've learned all about the festivals while I've lived here and about the newly growing pagan religion, Gardnerian and Alexandrian witchcraft, Aleister Crowley, and Dion Fortune, whose house on the side of the Tor is now lived in by Geoffrey Ashe. Most especially I've learned about the quarter and crossquarter day festivals—magic moments watching the dawn come up on Chalice Hill or the Tor, getting out of bed at 3 A.M. while it's still dark, packing a bag with blanket, thermos of tea, biscuits, and the chalice and bottle of wine that I've made the previous year with the flower or fruit of the season, and which is now to be opened to mark the moment. As the cock crows we leave the house and bicycle in silence to the hill. Bicycles in the cold air and silence of predawn do not disturb as cars do; on a bike you are one with the land. We climb up in the dark, find a spot, settle down with blankets, and sit in silence watching, listening to the cock crowing. Then a bird sings and gradually the first hint of light appears; slowly the stars dim and the birds get louder as one by one they all add their song to the chorus. The sun comes and we get up and dance or chant or weave a labyrinth, or just stand and greet the sun marking the turning of the seasons. At the equinox, when watching from Chalice Hill, the sun rises at the foot of the north side of the Tor. As it rises, it follows the line of the Tor until it is over the top of the tower. If there is a mist, as there often is, the shadow of the tower then makes a shadow bridge from Chalice Hill to the Tor.

What nights we've had up on top of the Tor at a full moon or Beltane or just for the fun of it, as on 8/8/88, with a fire flaming up from the top and loads of people singing, drinking, dancing, and drumming—a whole night party. Every festival there's someone who spends the night up there, often a whole group of people, whatever the weather, dreaming the dreams that come when one sleeps on a sacred spot. I've heard of many stories of weather on the Tor giving people just that touch of magic in the moment—as when Linda, who lived in the house just below Dion Fortune's, died, and there were the most incredible rainbows.

So many festivals shared with so many people that they all merge into moments, images. Meeting in a quiet circle of women down by Chalice Well with the sound of the water gurgling and rushing, the beauty and peace of that incredible space with the yew trees, birch, flowers, and birds. Three women and my youngest daughter lying up on Chalice Hill watching the sunset on autumn equinox with a large bottle of elderberry wine that had popped open a circle of glass from its side in a most startling manner so we had to drink it all as we walked up the hill. Finally when it was dark we wobbled home, or at least my daughter on her bike wobbled, while we laughed and felt such joy and merriment—an image never to be forgotten.

I recall Imbolc ceremonies in the Assembly Rooms, that beautiful hall with its fine west window built in the proportions of the golden mean on a very strong ley line. The energy of that place is intense, it's either magic in there or dire, but when it's magic, it's spine chilling. To stand in the dark in silence and have the pure sweet voices of the Glastonbury women singing a Celtic song to Bride is a magic moment never to be forgotten. Some years back it was a place where a whole weekend would be spent at the quarter or crossquarter days for people to come together to talk, to learn about the mysteries, and listen to fine music and see slides. Or to watch Kathy Jones's mystery plays, which use ancient myths at one level with its modern equivalent being played out at another level, as with the myth of Inanna and Dumuzi contrasted with Greenham Common, or Lysistrata connected with the war between local councils or landowners and the travelers.

Or I can recall meeting with a small group every dark of the moon and going to a part of the zodiac whose moon and sun time it is, and finding a well or spring and sipping of the clear water, with a song and a prayer and a picnic for the children. What a beautiful way to get to know the earth zodiac in the land round here. Finding areas of land I'd never known before and feeling the connections between the different signs, seeing the bowl of Avalon from many different views.

Just recently I've started celebrating the lunar cross-quarter days, so at sunset when the moon is in her last quarter closest to October 31st we celebrate Samhain, and when the moon is dark at midnight we celebrate Imbolc, or rise at dawn when the moon is in her first quarter to celebrate Beltane, and of course, full moon at midday for Lammas. This means that day, moon, and season all meet at the same point and it's quite something to feel the cycle of day, moon, and year in this way.

And there's Glastonbury Fayre, or Pilton Pop Festival as it is known locally, a once-a-year at summer solstice local industry that provides work for many, for several months in the summer, organizing the children's area, building all the structures, organizing the theater field, the circus field, the Green fields, and King's Meadow. A city of tents arrives at Pilton just six miles from Glastonbury to celebrate the summer solstice; tens of thousands of people watching films and theater; musicians sitting in the sun or in the rain, living outside in a few fields in Somerset with a silver pyramid as the main stage. Mind bending in its vastness, there is no way you could walk all round the site, too much to do. So much happening—from the labyrinth and sacred circles of King's Meadow where the day starts with yoga and chanting, through the green fields with musicians from all over the world. At the One Earth arts tent there is alternative technology, Greenpeace, Oak Dragon, and Rainbow Circle camps. Down through the circus field with clowns, jugglers, and acrobats. There are thousands of tents everywhere—tipis, benders, buses, trucks—and a multiplicity of lifestyles and people.

I've tended only to go to the festival when I've got something to do. I've probably missed as many festivals as I've been to because I find that it's all too much. I hate the market with its litter, cheap junk, and rampant consumerism, and I hate the drunks. There are people who just cannot take the energy and end up flipped out in a mental hospital. I find that about Glastonbury as well, and I'm glad to live up on my hill in peace and quiet, out of the maelstrom of the town and the surge of energy.

It's important to have a safe base living in Glastonbury. It's so easy to get spun out on the heady atmosphere of people and things going on, all the workshops and classes, it becomes quite ridiculous. What I call "flavor of the month" happens here, with God Training, Immortality seminars, American Indian gurus and EST training jostling for people's momentary interest with rebirthing, star journeys, African dance, drumming, crystal visions, ecology seminars, Earth First!, shamanic journeyings, hypnotherapy, and regressions to past lives. And all the different shops: Starchild with its herbs and incenses, Gothic Image with its books and New Age gimmicks, Little Gem which is all gimmick, Pendragon with its Celtic-like stuff, Dragons with its more Eastern Indian flavor, Margaret Kimber with her clothes from Bali and India, the Goddess and the Green Man with statues and books on that theme, Art of Africa with its African stuff, Shambhala with its New Age books and crystals, Unique Publications with recycled stationery, Phoenix, the wholefood shop, Top of the Crops with local organic vegetables, and the Food Co-op, which runs as a true co-op—everyone is responsible to make sure it runs okay—so we have good organic wholefoods at cheap prices.

The good with the awful side by side, all the froth and glamour of the so-called New Age is to be found in the town with channelers, charismatics, and Goddess gurus. I've met at least six reincarnations of Arthur and Merlin, although Guineveres and Morganas are thinner on the ground. In general women seem to be stronger than the men, more earthed, more grounded, not so badly affected by the intensity of this hothouse spiritual center. In fact it seems to be a good place for women to live. We become strong, more centered and clear. I think that's what is meant by women's sacred space. It's an energy women can cope with better, we get more positive. Not quite so many end up as alcoholics, or flipped out in the local mental asylum, or on the streets, though of course some do. Perhaps it's a women's sacred center in that the woman side of nature thrives here, and so men who have a strong woman side also thrive here, while those, both men and women, who deny that aspect of themselves are the ones who do not grow true.

The number of spiritual centers here is quite remarkable. When I first came, I was told that Glastonbury had more spiritual groups than London, and I laughed, but it's true. Every corner has another church, every other house has another center, meditation group, or healing circle. The list would probably take up two pages, and that's just at present because they come and go: the British Israelites, the Dutch Israelites, the Druids, the White Eagle Lodge, the Ramala Center, Shambhala, the Anglicans, the Baptists, the Bahais, the Roman Catholics, the many fundamentalist and evangelical Christian sects, the United Reformed Church, the Krishnas, the Essenes, the Alfred Orthodox, the Swami Barmi Ashram. You just have to take your pick—whatever suits your spiritual style will be found in Glastonbury—and if it's not there, then the land is fertile and ready for yet another variant on the essential human urge to adore another and create a dogma out of it.

The cauldron is not yet full. When I first came here I got ill and spent ten days in bed; during those ten days I read Cowper Powy's *Glastonbury Romance*. When I was well enough, I stumbled out of the fifteenth-century cottage built out of Abbey stone in which I lived, at the foot of Dod Lane, right on the beginning of the Glastonbury/Stonehenge ley line. I walked down to the Rifleman's pub mentioned in *Glastonbury Romance* as St. Michael's Inn. I sat in the rocking chair by the enormous old Inglenook fireplace with a huge log burning in it and I sipped my ginger wine and watched the people. I was living a Glastonbury Romance and it never dies—it just changes as the years change.

CHESCA POTTER

ANCESTRAL VOICES OF THE LAND: REAWAKENING ITS ANCIENT GUARDIANS

THE FOLLOWING STORY is an inspired and fictional description of the cult of the horse (mare) and deer. Although the story is focused upon a specific place, the Vale of the White Horse, southern England, their importance was worldwide.

The Vale of the White Horse contains prehistoric sacred sites of various ages, the most famous being the elegant Celtic chalk hill figure of a white horse-mare, cut in the late Bronze or early Iron Age. It is approximately 365 feet long and can only be viewed fully from the air. The prehistoric chalk pathway of the ridgeway (c. 2000 BC) unites the horse carving to a stone-chambered long barrow, built on the site of an earlier earthen barrow (c. 3600 BC). It is now called by its Saxon name, Waylands Smithy. It is probable that barrows of this period held bones that were buried, after having been stripped of flesh by carrion, the bodies having been placed on mortuary platforms.[1]

Horse cults are very ancient, wild horses being once an important source of food. One of the oldest carvings in the world is of a horse's hoof (c. 30,000 BC, France) considered to have vulvic associations. Horses are also the animals most often painted in the caves of Paleolithic Europe.

Reindeer were the main meat source for Paleolithic Europe, and it is probable that most of the earliest tracks used by humans were those used by migrating reindeer. Female reindeer are antlered. Herds of wild horse and reindeer roamed over what is now southern Britain. When the ice melted, forests of mixed oak sheltered herds of red deer. In Neolithic Britain, simple agriculture was combined with hunting and gathering, and the primal totems of the land were not forgotten.

In the indigo darkness of planetary space, a vast and ancient being hovers. She reaches for the Earths sphere, the wisdom in her touch feeling its suffering. It shudders, unaligned, torn, dying. So tired.

I was there at its creation. Then the molten fire was creative, the primal oceans cleansing, the air golden and vibrant, the greens rich, damp, and fertile for the emerging life forms. Grim scavengers scratch and flap at the edges of the Earth, feeding on its weakness.

"Begone lost souls," I call, with a voice that echoes into the recesses of space. I cast the ancient protections around the Earth. "Sad world, the greatest evil of humans is to force your destruction, then call it predestined. I challenge that destiny. I, who witnessed your beginnings, formed from the flames of primal chaos, call for your re-creation. Be still Earth and rest in my wings." And with a touch that is both all-compassion and all-power, she cleanses this planet. Holding its sphere protectively in the immensity of space, she calls the guardians of inner Earth to awake.

In the remains of what was once a prehistoric wildwood, ancient oak spirits are stirring, eyes dew webbed and heavy with memory, deep rooted in a primal pre-human past. Water beings form from mists and shimmering springs. Guardians of the deep are rising from cracks in the loamy soil. Everything is shuddering into life. Honeybees, oracular sisters, swarm through the dense undergrowth, humming; "She is coming." Some humans may only sense her presence, the parting of trees, the shaking leaves that welcome her, the golden deer prints half-seen, pressed into the old green tracks.

The Green Woman stands strong as the oaks, in the forest's central stillness, at a place where eight paths converge. Gold green leaves stream from her, generating a primordial wildwood potency. She is antlered with burning green eyes. Herds of deer have gathered around her, and she calls deep into the heart of the land. "This is the re-empowering. Mine is the love that awakens the forgotten, breathes life into the unborn, and gives peace to the undead. I am the vitality of nature. I call the primordial ancestors of this land. I am your remembering."

———

Scattered across the landscape, giant mare bones lie buried unmarked, unmourned, dislocated. Bleached skull, cracked, infested, has eye sockets without vision. Spine broken, white segments spiked into white chalk. Jaw shaking, teeth chattering, endlessly chattering. Frost splits the bones. Decayed skin, hide rotten, unable to move. Hooves hung up, feet cannot touch the ground. Spectral horses gallop above without purpose. Heart, ice shrunk, calculates coldly; broken legs—whose legs? So many shards of ice in flayed flesh. Horse whips cannot raise the half dead.

The Green Woman calls "Remember," Green words seep into the blood-stained, bloodsoaked land, and the mare eats them, for her hunger is ravenous. Surprisingly they calm her tortured nightmares. "Yes, rest but remember," the green words soothe. And the Green Woman lays a cloak of green and growing things over the bones without skin.

Then the Green Woman rides the ridgeway across the mare's broken back, knitting bones, banishing ravaged specters. Finding her hooves hanging at Waylands Smithy, newly shod, she gently binds them to the bone mare's legs. When the nights inside the barrow are restless with the mare's whinneying, the antlered woman sits beside her, transforming eyes that are staring with terror, into those that are dreamy with vision. She begins to remember when the humans came here.

———

Screeching, scratching, screeching
Carrion flock, black wings flapping,
Sharp claws stained red.
Pecking and cawing
Frenzied by blood
Gorged on the body of the dead.

Raven woman Anna drops her arms, tired by the summoning. Satiated with human flesh, the black wings fly off and the cackling subsides. Anna walks to the wooden platform and looks at the body of her friend Heli, now still, fragile, skeletal.

Deft from experience, Anna dislocates the bones of the skeleton. Setting some aside, she throws the rest on a heap at the center of the mortuary enclosure. These are the bones of those in the tribe who have died this year, and lie waiting for their burning at the harvest moon. Then they will be ploughed back into the earth.

Anna lifts her friend's skull, major bones, and heart into a basket. Relieved the rite is over, Anna walks through the gateway of the palisade, honoring the horned skulls that hang above her. The bones shine a milky blue, for some of Heli's spirit still clings to them, although Anna had cut her spirit threads as she sadly watched her friend dying.

She is taking the bones to the chamber of the stone barrow, the place where the ancestors of her clan hover on the edge of worlds. It is a starry winter's night, and the chalk path gleams white in the moonlight. Behind them the white horse carved into the hills watches over her, guarding this sacred landscape.

The entrance stones of the barrow recognize her presence. Resting the basket beside them, Anna marks the X of life and death upon the key stone. "Protect us from any unwanted presences, great stones." It is cold inside. The small stone chamber is damp, and Anna lights a small fire in the sacred hearth.

Anna unwraps the bundle she has been carrying on her back, and lays out the ancient mare's skull, decorated with chevrons of red ochre. Older than she could imagine, it has always belonged to the clan of the wild horse.

She takes off her black-dyed clothes, and marks her naked body with red ochre on her heart, palms of hands, soles of feet, and the three lines of knowledge on her face. "May our hearts beat with the heart of the land," she chants. Anna wraps her sacred mare skin around herself, shivering with anticipation as she feels the beginning of the contact. She stands and marks the red ochre X on the end wall, opening the gateway, then raising her hands in invocation, calls; "Ancient mare, guardian of this land, of places seen and unseen, of bones and of blood, shine through me now." Sitting cross-legged behind the skulls, Anna shudders as the power of the mare totem enters her head. Her eyes gleam emerald with vision, her hair becomes a plaited mane, her face is no longer

Chesca Potter, "Reindeer Shamaness"

human. Her body shakes with emotion, for she loves this ancient spirit. Anna's hands reach out over the skulls, but the green light that streams out of them forms crescents upon the skulls in the shape of mare's hooves. The green shimmers over the white of the skulls, just as grass plays over the chalk of the land.

Before her, with vision eyes, Anna sees Heli's spirit merge with the shining mare. "Great Mare, please watch over Heli. May she run beside you down the ancient paths, protected." They spirit walk through the stones of the gateway, gone to other places. Anna, grieving but radiant, seals the gateway.

She wraps Heli's heart in leaves, and sprinkles her bones with ochre and charged water, then buries them in the corner of the chamber. Her skull will remain beside the ancestral stones along with the others of her extended family for some time yet. The rite is complete.

PRESENT DAY: WAYLANDS SMITHY LONG BARROW

The antlered Green Woman sits weaving in the winter darkness of the barrow. From holly, fir, berries, ivy, moss, hoarfrost, and sun dew, she is making a cloak. She looks down affectionately at the sleeping mare, and knows that her quickening is near. She wraps her cloak around her, and sweeps the forecourt of the barrow with her birch broom. Then she stands amidst the trees, spreading her cloak, in the thin icy light of the approaching solstice dawn. The cloak seems to root itself into the land, its rich greens and reds flashing out across the landscape, reactivating the deep green-fire currents of Midwinter.

Inside Waylands Smithy the mare has remembered. Blazing eyes, visionary, with knowledge. Golden hoof prints shall mark out ancient paths. Past and present will be one. From the tree, dead wood, rotten wood is removed. From the green growth the drum is framed. Her skin is stretched over it bound by the soul. When her mouth opens, so long closed, engraved teeth fly out. They fall in a pattern. The drum's destiny is read. The drum shall not be painted, for its summonings shall be everchanging. The bones shall be its resonance. Her ochred tail shall be plaited around it, and it shall beat with her heart.

The mare carries her drum outside. Reconnected, she is radiant. Her antlered friend, who has watched over her healing, gently marks the drum with her hoof print, for they shall always walk the land together. The mare sits beside her on the cloak and in the dawn sun drums the land alive.

NOTES

1. A. Burl, *Prehistoric Avebury* (Yale, 1986).

THE PACIFIC, ASIA, AND AFRICA

Pele cave. Photo by Leslie Miki.

HALLIE IGLEHART AUSTEN

LISTENING TO GAIA: PELE AND THE HAWAIIAN ISLANDS

"Go to this place and listen, just listen."

In 1976, a friend urged me to look up a woman kahuna, or Hawaiian priest, in Honolulu. Even though I had planned to go to Kauai for my vacation and had no other reason to go to Oahu, I felt the rightness of my friend's advice. I called the kahuna and asked if I could come see her. I took a bus to her neighborhood from the Honolulu airport. I walked along the streets to her house, lugging my backpack in the searing heat. When she asked why I had come, my only response could be that I had been told to see her. After considering me for a moment, she gave me an assignment, an assignment that I would practice and teach for the rest of my life.

She told me to go to a very large banyan tree at a big hotel in Honolulu and listen to what the tree had to say to me. I thanked her and set off, wondering about going to a fancy hotel as a sacred site. I learned later that, consciously or unconsciously, people are drawn to sacred places and make them into their own kind of pilgrimage center, often of their own religion, which in this case was commerce and luxury.

I found the hotel and sat under the banyan tree. I was dressed in white yoga pants and a white top. Even though I felt out of place, I sat there with my hands on the tree trunk and my eyes closed. Soon a group of men came by. They started laughing at me and making nasty jokes and comments with an ominous tone to them. I could hear them very clearly even though I was trying to listen to the tree, something I had never done before. I felt threatened by these men, but I persisted. I kept focusing on the banyan tree, remaining open, listening to the tree, and letting the threats remain on my periphery. After about fifteen

87

minutes, one of them said to the others, "Oh, just leave her alone, we have to get out of here."

This was my first conscious experience of listening to Gaia, even though I didn't call it that then or "hear" an actual voice. Because I was focused on listening, I could hear what the banyan tree had to tell me—how to focus in the face of fear. I have come to learn that there are many ways of listening. One may hear an internal or external voice, feel a body sensation, or simply just "know" with that intuitive understanding that is beyond words. However, I continue to describe this experience as "listening" because we have forgotten how to be silent and listen to ourselves, one another, and the earth. Sometimes I "hear" Gaia's cries of pain as she is wounded by her children. Sometimes I hear her asking me to do particular actions for her. Sometimes she gives me personal advice. We can all come to hear what we recognize as the authentic voice of the Earth, in whatever way it manifests for each of us. In order to do this we must learn how to get past the mental chatter and the busyness of our everyday lives—and even our fantasies of what the Earth has to say.

Over the years since I went to the banyan tree, I returned to the Hawaiian Islands whenever I could, usually about once a year, and had a series of intense experiences. In retrospect, I realize that I was being initiated into a deeper relationship with the Earth through one of her most dramatic expressions—Pele, Goddess of the Volcanoes, creatrix of the Hawaiian Islands. This deeper initiation led me to experience the Earth at a cellular level. I believe that this transformation was necessary in order for me to be able to guide others in listening to Gaia. In learning to listen, I could open all my senses—indeed, every part of myself—to the plants, rocks, water, and air. I began to allow my usual barriers to fall away, so that I could feel myself to be a part of these elements and them as part of me.

The most powerful experience I had with Pele came at a time of upheaval in my life. As is often the case at such times, my life pattern was torn open, so that I was more open to other people and circumstance. I have found that when I am receptive like this, whatever the reason, my life becomes full of synchronicities. These synchronicities, which are part of the flow of life known to the Chinese as the Tao, happen all the time. We are more open to them whenever we get out of our usual patterns. The challenge is to make our daily lives a pilgrimage, so that we can be open all the time to the guidance of the blessed spirits that surround us and want to help us.

The more I learn, the more I feel that life is a vast mystery: Forces are working on us and through us, and we are an integral part of them. We may have very little, if any, awareness of these forces. And so it is for me with Pele. She is a powerful and mysterious force and, particularly as a non-native Hawaiian, I invoke her name with awe and respect. Yet, she has called me and I have learned much from listening to her.

In all my travels, the Hawaiian Islands is the only place I have ever been where a living Goddess is widely recognized. As a male tourist I once briefly encountered on a remote hiking trail ecstatically exclaimed, "She's everywhere! Pele is everywhere here!"

Indeed, Pele is everywhere in the islands and people report seeing her in human form as well as in the volcanoes that created the islands. She is sometimes seen as a beautiful young woman and Her unmistakable image has appeared in erupting lava columns. I have heard stories of people giving a ride at night to an old woman only to find after a few miles there was no one else in the car. Her magic continues—there are numerous stories of Pele's lava flow dramatically altering its course so as not to harm her sacred shrines. She also manifests herself through the native Hawaiian organization, the Pele Defense Fund, which works to prevent planned geothermal drilling on Kilauea, the world's most active volcano. Both native and non-native Hawaiians work in Pele's name to protect the environment from destruction and this manifestation of the Goddess from desecration.

Without Pele, the islands themselves would not exist. Bringing up her great flow of red-hot magma from the deep core of Mother Earth, she created the land out of the ocean. According to ancient legend her first home was in the northernmost islands of Ni'ihau and Kaua'i. She gradually moved southward and finally settled on Mauna Loa, Earth's largest mountain, which forms part of the island of Hawai'i, also known as the Big Island. This myth reflects the geological history of Hawai'i in the sequence of the volcanic activity and creation of the islands.

Interestingly enough, my own journey through the islands over the past twenty years has followed Pele's path. From 1975–1981 Kaua'i, the oldest and greenest island, was a powerful source of nourishment for my spirit. During 1982–1988, I traveled once a year to Maui which seemed a place to strengthen and enjoy my body. Finally, in my thirteenth year of visiting the Islands a series of synchronicities, beginning on a plane flight to Maui, led me to meet Pele in one of her most sacred embodiments—the Pele cave.

I'd heard stories about the Pele cave on the Big Island. The cave is a twenty two-mile long lava tube, an underground tunnel formed by the cooling of a river of molten lava. Near the beginning of the cavern, the lava has cooled in the exact shape of a seven-foot long yoni, or female genitalia—complete with finely detailed outer labia, inner labia, and clitoris. I had heard that the Pele cave held ancient Hawaiian shrines, sacred art, and burial canoes. The cave was discovered only recently by a man who owned the fields under which it lay. Word spread of his discovery and he removed the artifacts to safeguard them. But he could not remove the most precious of all, the yoni formed by Pele herself. Pilgrims, both Hawaiian and non-Hawaiian, came to pay their respects.

Unfortunately, in their eagerness to honor this delicate self-formed lava sculpture, the visitors were unwittingly damaging the shrine. By the time I got to Hawai'i in the fall of 1988, the owner had erected a fence made of heavy steel bars inside the opening of the cave with a heavily padlocked gate set in the fence. When I heard this, I thought that the Pele cave was to be only a tantalizing legend, and I let go of my desire to visit it.

Yet it seems the Goddess had other plans. On a flight to Maui, I met a woman who gave me the name of a friend of hers she thought I'd be interested in meeting. When I did finally meet Lucienne, we spent a long afternoon talking in her studio while she made a pendant of semiprecious stones set in silver. I told her of my work with the Goddess.

"You should go to the Pele cave on the Big Island," said Lucienne.

"I'd love to, but it's closed."

"Oh, but I have a friend, Leslie, who has a key to the gate. She's the only person besides the owner who has one. I'll give you her phone number on the Big Island. She doesn't usually take people there, but call her and see what she says."

"What time does your flight get in? We'll meet you at the airport. You can stay with us," said Leslie's soft voice at the other end of the phone. I was awed that I had "stumbled" upon this keeper of the gate and that she, a complete stranger with only a vague introduction, was offering to take me to the Pele cave. I was extremely touched that she was also offering me transportation and housing. The first gate had opened.

Leslie and her friend, Franco, met me at the airport. We drove out into the countryside in a pickup, eventually pulling over by a nondescript field. We scrambled through high, tough grass, and finally down a small slope. There, barely visible in the overgrowth, was the opening to the cave.

This entrance itself was a marvelous sight. The lush greenness of Hawaiian plant life grew around the dark lips of the cavern. My memory is one of large ferns reaching in, almost tickling, the deep interior. Here, already, was the entrance to the Mother's womb.

We stepped around the crystals, dried leis, and other offerings recent travelers had brought. In the beautiful simplicity of the Earth's wonder, these imported gifts seemed inappropriate and intrusive. We walked a little further in, turned a corner, and confronted the metal fence. It too looked out of place, but I could regretfully appreciate its necessity.

Leslie led us. She seemed like a being from another dimension. She was dressed in red and black, the colors of both molten and cooled lava. She wore a miner's lamp on her forehead, and *tabi*, heavy rubber booties with an individuated big toe. She tackled the padlock, but the key would not work. Oh, no! I thought, I've come all this way for nothing. Undeterred, Leslie pulled out some WD-40, sprayed it into the lock, and turned the key. We were in!

As a matter of fact we were *really* in. After we passed through this gate, Leslie locked the padlock behind us. I nervously scrutinized the tops and bottoms of the bars. They were cemented into the cave floor and ceiling; there was no way to get through, over or under them. Which meant, in my claustrophobic state of mind, that if anything happened to the key once we were in, we were lost forever.

We walked a little further in the darkness and came to the sacred yoni of

Pele. It was exquisitely, perfectly shaped, truly the yoni of the Goddess—like a woman's, yet larger, much larger. I could see where a few of the delicate folds of lava forming the labia had cracked and broken off from the stress of too many feet. The damage seemed a microcosm of the planet's wounding: the Goddess unable to survive the weight of too many human beings, however well-intentioned. I sat a respectful distance from the yoni to meditate, feeling the presence of the living Goddess enter my body.

When we were finished meditating, we climbed down into the lava tube beneath the upper cave. It was about twenty feet across and ten feet high, its length disappearing into the darkness. Franco told me that at the end of the tube, twenty-two miles along, an ancient altar had been found. As we walked along the lava tube with our flashlights, I marveled at the devotion and skill of the ancient Hawaiians. I could not imagine that natural torches would give light for very long. How did they find their way all those miles? The technology we had with us could only take us a fraction of the distance.

When we switched off our lights, we stood in the most total darkness I could imagine. I loved it—the silence, the velvety feel of the blackness. I turned around to see if any light was filtering down from the entrance, but no. The darkness surrounded me, enveloping me to such a degree that I could not distinguish directions. I could barely tell what was up and what was down, much less forward and back. The disorientation was a little frightening. I tried walking in the dark. Even though I had learned to walk at night along a potholed country road I once lived on, I could not walk in this cave. The challenge was extremely difficult physically and psychically impossible. I imagined the stamina of the ancient ones and the empowerment that must have resulted from taking the journey through this underworld womb.

We turned the flashlights back on and walked about half an hour into the lava tube. In places, tiny white lichens grew on the walls. How could anything live here? I wondered, and yet, they did. So also the occasional root system of a tree lived in the ceiling of the lava tube, dangling its roots above our heads. We were truly in the Underworld. I could see the tree, but only the part that was usually hidden from me, not the "tree" that I usually see. I was seeing the underneath of things—the foundation, the base, the support.

After about a half hour, our spare batteries began to wear out. We did not want to test their limits, as stumbling in this dark void would be a stressful return. We turned back to retrace our tracks. I stopped to tell the tiny luminous lichens of the overwhelming love I felt for them. We climbed up to the yoni, paid our final respects, and unlocked the gate for the last time. A few more yards, and we glimpsed the astonishing land of sunlight, green trees, and open sky. We sat at the entrance for a while to help us make the transition between worlds. Slowly, reluctantly, but also with a sense of rightness, we returned to the above world. I took the knowledge of another dimension with me. I had been to the Under-world, and it was beautiful.

It is impossible for me to say what effect the Pele cave has had on me. All I know is that I feel I have been altered in every cell of my body. I think of my long—and still ongoing—process of remembering how to listen to Gaia as an initiation, beginning with my visit to the kahuna. Years later the pilgrimage to the Pele cave enabled me to "get" the Earth's message on a much deeper, cel-lular level. Shortly after this experience, I started teaching others how to lis-ten to Gaia, more than a decade after visiting the banyan tree in Honolulu. In this way the journey has also been a training, so that I could help others remember.

———

Part of this lesson is learning to listen as well as plan. With the Pele cave, I had given up my plans and, by staying open to the people and events around me, unexpectedly found the one person who had the key. Significantly, the next time I went to the Big Island, I called Leslie and eagerly asked if we could go back to the cave.

"Oh, I'm sorry. It's closed," said Leslie's sweet voice. "The land has been sold. I no longer have the key."

It seems I had slipped through a narrow window of opportunity that I had-n't even known existed; so it is with pilgrimages and a life lived in harmony. We can plan to a certain extent, but the most important thing is that we just show up and listen. After balancing intuition with reason, we put our feet on the path and begin to walk. In this way, we can begin to find our way back to living in right relationship with our Mother, that she may continue to nurture us and we nurture her.

We need to listen to Gaia, not only to hear her cries but also to hear her love. Our inability to hear her and feel her love for us is precisely why we are so lost and why she is crying out to us now. We have forgotten that the Earth is a living being, we have forgotten that she speaks to us—we have forgotten that we are a part of her. For we are not just her children, we *are* her. Our tears and our sweat are made of the same substance as the salt and water of her oceans. All of our ancestors held this awareness on a cellular level, for their very survival depended upon being able to listen to Gaia—reading the clouds, the wind, the flights of birds, atmospheric changes. As a Balinese priestess once said to me, "Nature to me is like a book that I read."

Although we no longer live in a gathering-hunting, or even in an agricultural society, our survival depends on our ability to listen to Gaia, just as much as our ancestors' did. We need to be able to recognize when we have overharvested the oceans of fish. We need to know that cutting down the rainforest creates a hole in the ozone layer, that the Sonoran desert of Arizona cannot sustain the millions of people who now live there. If we begin to listen to Gaia and re-member the truth of her message of personal and collective healing, perhaps we shall survive—and thrive—after all. We shall see.

JOURNEY TO MU

REALITY CHECK. These are required once a day here on Pohnpei. First you must determine which reality you're operating from, and then if it is the reality you want to be operating from, based on whatever it is you are trying to be or not be.

It's difficult to sort out how much of the intensity and illusion of Pohnpei is due to its being home to one of the major sacred sites of the planet or to its being an isolated, fuzzy green speck floating near the equator on an expanse of blue infinity. In any case, without the assistance of reality checks, adjusting to Pohnpei's energy can prove too much for many outsiders, especially those who don't get off the island often enough. You think that Pohnpei is reality, but that's when you're really in trouble—when you think you have a handle on what's going on here. For the Pohnpeians it is an entirely different matter. This is their home, and the intensity and illusion feel normal. They feel disintegrated if they leave, so that there is always a tugging on their hearts that inevitably brings them back, sooner or later.

The issue here is not *just* the power of Nan Madol, Pohnpei's sacred site that is never more than an hour or so from any location, but the power of feminine energy. Raw and untamed on this sultry, sensual volcanic mass, this energy is something most Westerners have never experienced. Many emotional casualties may be counted among visitors or expatriates, stuck in the intellectual mode, whose programming can't adjust quickly enough to Pohnpei.

For several years now we've been told by our personal growth experts and spiritual teachers that what is missing, in our inner being and outer doing, is the feminine component; that Western culture with its left brain, aggressive, male-dominated, material existence is way out of balance; that each of us must begin with ourselves and restore our atrophied feminine side. Yes. But who ever thought of a place or culture where the *feminine* is so powerful as to be almost out of balance?

We foreigners must do our checks; we're unequipped to deal with a female reality. We don't know the rules. The *givens* have been pulled out from under us. Hallelujah—a crash course in experiencing the feminine or perhaps grad school is a better description.

And what are the characteristics of the feminine gone berserk? What does this over-indulged feminine look like? For starters there is this thick, musky, husky, sweaty sensuality that permeates everything alive or dead in, on, under, and around Pohnpei. Synapses dysfunction and will only process stimuli that pertain to having sex, having more sex, having different sex, having better sex, who's having sex with whom, who's not having sex at all (heaven forbid)! One cannot have dinner with an individual of the opposite sex without everyone assuming you're sleeping together. Why else would a man and a woman have dinner together anyway? In fact, a woman alone is suspect in itself—another woman would be with her if she wasn't trying to *koieng ohi* (get laid) and so the sexual dynamo keeps Pohnpei throbbing. This pulse is a bit too much for the typically repressed Westerner.

Thank God for the missionaries, at least they're trying to keep this uncivilized behavior under control. A hundred years of fear, guilt, and righteousness should do the trick. Put clothes on those natives, and no more dancing for those sinners. Why, they actually think sex is entertainment or recreation! Can you imagine no hangups—no psychological tentacles to strangle the simplicity and beauty of sexual expression?

Time for a reality check. Let's try it again with our next feminine trait.

Pohnpeians win the "being in the moment" award. They are absolute masters of this art; it is the prevailing state of mind. Is being fully present a function of the feminine? In the sense that you receive what life is bringing at that moment, and accept it, yes it is.

There is definitely no future here on Pohnpei. The feminine wins hands down. Plan ahead? No way. Save for a rainy day? Or even to get to the next payday? Be *on time?* Never. What happened to the time/space continuum on this island? They have calendars. The total disregard of time must be in their genes—or it's just plain laziness.

They are so irresponsible, how can they be so happy? so content? Do they actually think that everything will be *given* to them, with no hard work or planning? What about when the money runs out—who will take the responsibility? Don't they know that's *not how the world works?*

Reality check.

Caught you. The point is the world no longer works—as witnessed by its poverty, war, drugs, overpopulation, environment, and violence—and hasn't for a while. We must come up with a new way for it to work. In fact, that's why you're reading this book, isn't it? Looking for some alternative solutions?

We've lost sight of the fact that everything, both spiritual and material, was meant to come to us, effortlessly. We have lost our childlike quality of being totally in the present that allows us to receive automatically all that we truly require or, taking it a step further, all that we choose to create as a part of our reality.

Receiving. The ultimate feminine imperative. Also refined to an art form on Pohnpei.

The ability to allow and to accept without question of worthiness, exists at a cellular level here—totally unconscious, but effective. The innocence of expecting to receive that which you need—could it really be that simple? This ability to receive has been institutionalized, as Dr. David Hanlon points out in *Upon a Stone Altar,* his history of Pohnpei. The Spanish, Russians, Japanese, Americans, and the Australians have all come with their palms open—if Pohnpei doesn't *perform* according to the present powers that be, another country will come in, pick up the pieces, and give the Pohnpeians what they want.

This ingrained childlike innocence—the ability to receive and accept what the moment has to offer in its full abundance—drives Westerners crazy. If you're immersed totally in the present, you aren't thinking about cooking for tomorrow's party or a meeting that started fifteen minutes ago. And speaking of that meeting, do you know that five million dollars in foreign aid is at stake, depending on the outcome of that meeting, and that eight people are waiting for it to begin? Four of them are leaving on the evening flight, never to return if the meeting doesn't reconcile certain issues. Not to mention the insult of not respecting other very important people's time. Why are they always late? Can't they ever get organized, set priorities, and see what is at stake economically? Don't they want to get ahead?

Check.

No, for the most part Pohnpeians are content with what they have. Content enough, that is, not to disrupt their peace of mind to get *things*. What's meant to be will come to them in good time. What's the rush?

If you're in the moment, rushing cannot be justified. If you're helping a friend cook food for a funeral, you cook until you're finished. You complete the process and do not interrupt it because you had told someone you would meet them at a certain time for lunch. Now if the person who was to be met for lunch was a Westerner, s/he will be upset; if a Pohnpeian, s/he, being attuned to being in the moment will a) wait for a while and enjoy someone else's company; b) probably sense something isn't right and decide to continue with her/his current occupation; or c) just plain forget about it. The trick is to be tuned into the moment, so that your intuition can guide your activities on to synchronistic behavior.

By being in the moment and just dealing with what is in front of them, they assume life will create what is really necessary. Pohnpeians assume that if that lunch was really important, it would have happened; or maybe the lunch will be better tomorrow because they will have fresh sashimi instead of canned tuna.

We Westerners intellectually recognize this as being in the moment, but the Pohnpeians don't have to do the mental processing to reconcile life's surprises, they adjust automatically. Their contentment and acceptance looks much like emotional maturity most of the time.

I don't mean to imply that Pohnpeians and their culture have no faults. They are human, with everything that entails, and both men, and especially women, counteract their lack of outward power in a rapidly changing culture by an insidious use of the feminine in the form of secrecy, intrigue, manipulation, and sexual control—the worst of feminine traits. And as in every corner of the world, abuse of power and greed are no strangers to Pohnpeians, either. What is important is that theirs is a more feminine-oriented response to their environment, and it comes closer to achieving the ideal of balance.

Regretfully, as Western culture permeates Pohnpei, these positive values of being in the moment, receiving, and childlike innocence are being sacrificed to pursue the addiction of material consumption, with greed taking its usual toll. Although foreigners have been coming to Pohnpei for hundreds of years, with the exception of the missionaries, their influence lacked the enticements to motivate significant change. It is only now, with the seductiveness of materialism intensified by TV and its hypnotic commercials, that these positive traditional values may lose their priority.

Intensity.

Is this a quality of the feminine? It is, rather, a condition of being in the present all the time, which does not necessarily create intensity for local Pohnpeians, but does indeed for those not used to confronting every issue as it comes up.

Being in the moment is a form of receptivity, of not always wanting to change the present, past, or future reality by diversions, but of coping with it at the time. Most Westerners, because of our need to be in control, are unprepared to deal with this spontaneity; therefore we experience intensity as stress in what could be paradise.

Add up these positive feminine qualities and you have the makings of a mandatory crash course in functioning in the present, like it or not. In this sense, Pohnpei may be similar to other sacred sites around the world; only that it has its own brand of specialization—living in a feminine consciousness.

So what does all of this reality check business have to do with Nan Madol? To understand Nan Madol you must acknowledge that it is situated in the midst of a feminine island culture where perceptions may vary from ours. But more importantly, acknowledging Nan Madol's importance as a sacred site, not just an archaeological one, honors the feminine by accepting its mystery and power as real.

Do you suppose that the archaeologists who have worked on the site over the years did their reality checks? Was it clear to them that they were operating under a very skewed mentality in their examination process? Did they even consider that coming from the Western academic tradition of giving validity only to that which can be seen, heard, tested, proven, repeated, etc., does not make for a very open-minded examination of a sacred site? Dr. James Swan, in his book *Sacred Places*, lists a number of phenomena which contribute to a site being sacred, many of which are very real but are considered transpersonal and are therefore dismissed by many researchers.

Unfortunately, archaeologists and universities, by their very nature, are not overly concerned by the kinds of reality checks required on Pohnpei. For the most part, their activities at Nan Madol and elsewhere have been based on the single reality orientation dictated by the "scientific method." The scientific method is all well and good, and a necessary *component* for any kind of investigation or understanding; however, it is only one way to assess a situation and is most thoroughly permeated by Western cultural bias.

One wouldn't expect the "experts" to enter the Pohnpeian world of magic and spirits to understand Nan Madol—and they didn't.

It comes back to this issue of incorporating the feminine and keeping the right brain engaged while trying to understand what makes a place like Nan Madol tick. Equal time should be granted to information received from the intuition or from legends when experiencing Nan Madol. Researchers pay lip service to the oral histories, but do not take them seriously in pursuing their investigations.

Legend states *clearly* that Nan Madol was built by two twin brothers named Olshipa and Olsopha, possibly giants, who came from the outside. By using a special kind of magic, they were able to *fly* the heavy basalt rock logs into position. Their Pohnpeian helpers also learned these *mwanamwan* techniques and were able to use them during the construction process to make things lighter and easier to move them. There are Pohnpeians today who possess this ability, although it is said that they have forgotten the more difficult aspect of the actual levitation.

Nan Madol is many miles from the quarries of columnar basalt thought to be the source of its stone. How could a bamboo raft (the only explanation given by outsiders for how the rock logs could have been transported) float ten-to fifty-ton stones over a shallow reef that is less than four feet deep most of the time? The extraordinary high tides (approximately five feet) that occur only a few times a year would still not accommodate the displacement by the huge stones.

It is an insult to Pohnpeians that their history is not taken more seriously. Why have researchers ignored the magic factor and not done serious research how it might have worked, especially when there are still sources that are alive? This could be much more than an anthropological study, providing an invaluable source of information on the human mind and its capabilities in relation to the laws of physics, as well as a better understanding of past civilizations.

Another very important legend connected with the history of Nan Madol that is overlooked or ignored by "professionals" is that of Isokelekel. It is said that Isokelekel was the son of a Pohnpeian god Nahnsapwe born on the neighboring island of Kosrae by a Kosraean woman. He was raised to be a warrior and revenge his father's banishment from Nan Madol by the reigning Saudeleur (king), a degenerate descendant of Olsipha and Olsopha.

Three hundred thirty-three warriors were gathered by Isokelekel to return to Pohnpei, overtake Nan Madol, and put and end to the cruelty of the Saudeleurs. After a series of rather complicated maneuvers Isokelekel, with help from Pohnpeians, defeated the Saudeleur dynasty.

Three high chiefs of Pohnpei were not sure whom to make the next king. After some time had passed, they noticed a wooden outrigger canoe hovering over nearby Temwen Island. When they went to investigate, the three were lifted up into the still-hovering canoe and met with the God Luhk inside the canoe. Luhk outlined a new system of political organization for Pohnpei and indicated that Isokelekel should be made ruler of Nan Madol, thereby establishing the first line of Nahnmwarkis, which has existed until the present.

How could a canoe *hover* in the air? Was it an airplane, helicopter, or extraterrestrials? None of these possibilities fit into the scenario our archaeologists and historians have created about past civilizations. Since they are so off-the-wall and do not fit into presently accepted definitions of reality, they are simply discarded.

The most amazing example of denial regarding research at Nan Madol revolves around the selection of the physical site of Nan Madol. Once again, Pohnpeian legend is very straightforward and consistent about this oral documentation.

Olsipha and Olsohpa searched the whole of Pohnpei for a perfect site to build their new royal facility. They began construction at a few sites on the north and eastern sides of the island, but in all cases the sites were unsatisfactory. They traveled to Takai Ieu, a small pyramid-shaped mountain in Madolenihmw Bay and climbed to the top for a better view of sites that might be available in the vicinity. From the top they could see a magnificent city under the water. They then selected the present site of Nan Madol on a nearby reef named Sounaleng, or "Reef of Heaven," because of its proximity to the "City of Heaven" under the water.

Many Pohnpeians today believe in the existence of Kahnihmweiso which means "City of the Ancients," but no serious amount of time has been devoted by credentialed researchers to pursue this legend or find this city. When casual examinations provide no instantaneous proof, a generalized pronouncement is made that there is nothing is down there. All kinds of evidence abounds, but because it exists outside of the left brain mindset its validity is ridiculed. The Catch-22 may be that some phenomena exist only for "those who have eyes to see."

For example. I was scuba diving with my Pohnpeian friend and colleague near Nan Madol. He is quite knowledgeable about Nan Madol and its oral history, but also educated in a U.S. university.

We were swimming where the reef drops off perpendicularly to the site. Approaching what looked like a room-sized opening to a cave, we swam closer with our light.

At first we thought our eyes were playing tricks on us, because inside of the cavelike opening we saw three tunnels into the reef made of the same columnar basalt logs found above, in Nan Madol. Impossible, but here they were— two running out laterally and a third straight up.

A little further down the reef, we discovered two more tunnels. When what we had seen finally registered, we rushed to the surface in a combination of fear and shock. We had been given the privilege of seeing one of Nan Madol's secrets.

Numerous subsequent trips to the locations of the tunnels with cameras and videos proved fruitless. Once a giant stingray was positioned to "protect" the site. Other times, problems with gear and equipment inhibited the dives. When I would mention my frustrating ordeal trying to document these disappearing underwater tunnels to Pohnpeians, they would just smile and shake their heads knowingly. It was certainly not the first time they'd heard of time and space playing tricks with reality at Nan Madol. After all, Nan Madol means literally "between the spaces."

My relationship with Nan Madol began in *this* lifetime when, responding to Kennedy's call, I joined the Peace Corps in 1969 and was assigned to Micronesia. A look at the atlas proved Micronesia to be thousands of specks near the equator on the vast western Pacific—the Caroline Islands, Marshall Islands, Marianas, and Palau. These unfamiliar names, in black type floating on blue inked background, were the only hints that there might be land under them.

Armed with an Iowa upbringing, naïveté, and altruism, I set out to experience what would prove to be instrumental in discovering my true Self and life's work. Meantime, while, the young woman from Iowa was about to have her eyes opened. The feelings that surfaced while living on Pohnpei Island were very perplexing to my already emotionally confused being. What was this draw, this connection to the ocean, this melancholy of the unfulfilled?

And then my first trip to Nan Madol—a tour was given to the new group of Peace Corps volunteers. We had to leave before sunrise in small outboards, as the approach to Nan Madol required a high tide. Arriving in the darkness, we had no idea what was in store. As the sun rose, the sultry evening air was transformed to its usual steambath quality. Rising from out of the mangroves and the thick overgrowth were spectacular walls, some forty feet high, made of gigantic rock logs. These black basalt stones were *huge*, some weighing up to fifty tons. All appeared to be gigantic crystalline rock logs cut with five or six sides ranging from three to nineteen feet long. But no, we were told by our guide that they were of natural formation and were flown into place from sources miles away in the interior of the island. As we made our way through the myriad canals and some ninety-six artificial islets, the mystery intensified. *Why* would this enormous crystalline city be built on the reef rather than on land? And *how* did they move all of these thousands of stones?

I was intrigued and amazed by the place. But oddly enough, my dominant emotion was one of outrage and indignation. Why had I never heard of this place before? Why had no one ever written about it? Of course the island was remote, but considering Nan Madol's significance, it was unbelievable that most of the world was not aware of it. That my rather dramatic reaction could be considered odd never occurred to me at the time. But why should I, this Midwesterner, have been so concerned about the reputation of Nan Madol?

Later, I would come to understand the source of my feelings about Nan Madol that day, and they didn't go away. What was it about Nan Madol that so moved me to take it upon myself to be one of the first, aside from some archaeological research, to tell its story in print? This urge to write and to do research was totally out of character for me. At the time I rationalized it as a practical and beneficial way to spend the summer between my teaching assignments.

I had the honor that summer of having the assistance of the two men most knowledgeable on Nan Madol's oral history and its physical character. Masao Hadley and Pensile Lawrence held high traditional titles and had the courage to share legends and information freely with me. I say courage because Pohnpeian custom is not to share knowledge, but to keep it to yourself. If you give away all your knowledge, you give away your power and can even die. Obviously these experts were secure enough in themselves to see the benefit of recording their traditions for future generations, rather than to keep it secret for personal power to be lost when they die!

So I set about the task of interviewing the Pohnpeians and reading whatever I could get my hands on about Nan Madol, which was not much. Through a series of intensive tours with Masao, I learned that each of the many islets had specific functions such as clam fishing, spiritual rituals, healing, divining, making coconut oil, drumming, burials, and residences. Many fascinating legends were connected to each of these specific places and activities.

Living in a remote, tiny village, with no electricity or running water or *anything* except lots of pigs and approximately forty people provided a slow enough pace to focus on my work. Not expecting to run across a typewriter, I chose to hand-letter the whole booklet myself, which was actually fun for me as it provided the first opportunity to utilize my four years of training in fine art. Little did I know this would also be the first project of my professional design career, which would follow my leaving Pohnpei. The government flew me to its headquarters in Saipan to supervise the booklet's printing. My design was a bit complex compared to their usual 8½ x 11 jobs, but a miracle was in the making. "Nan Madol" was complete and ready to go on sale for a whole dollar, which would be used for the maintenance of the site, another theme that would dominate my later life's relationship with Nan Madol.

After almost three years on Pohnpei, I was forced to leave an extension of the Peace Corps contract prematurely. *That* is another story. I was heartbroken to leave this luscious though frustrating paradise, thinking I would never return to her incredible blue waters, reefs, and steamy jungles—this beautiful, melancholy island of moonlit boat rides and people who live from their hearts and souls.

The twenty-some years between leaving Pohnpei and my midlife crisis were largely spent creating a successful career and my own business, making substantial progress on my spiritual growth, and surviving two divorces mixed between numerous other romantic disasters.

Ironically, the events leading to my return to Pohnpei began with the ending of another relationship. My soon-to-be ex-boyfriend, who unlike the others was interested in spiritual matters, noticed a book jumping off the shelf at him, Norm Paulsen's *Christ Consciousness*. While reading away on the history of the Pacific's lost continent of Mu, he jumped up and showed me several pages on Nan Madol documenting it as a city of Mu (the Motherland of the ancient Hawaiians, also called Lemuria by scientists who theorized a lost continent to explain the migrations of the Madagascar lemur).

I couldn't believe it. After all these years I had never made the connection. When the outrageous Venezuelan astrologer who lived next door pointed out that the Caroline Islands once were part of Mu, the connection between Pohnpei as one of the Carolines made perfect sense. But I never took that obvious step further and associated Nan Madol as one of Mu's only remaining cities. This revelation knocked my socks off and I have yet to recover from this new version of addiction to Nan Madol.

As luck would have it, we broke up December 30. I just couldn't handle another ending and I was furious at God/Goddess for being alone again. In my rage I demanded to know just what the hell I came here to do anyway. I was sick and tired of the pain and wanted off this planet. If I couldn't have a meaningful relationship, then God/Goddess damn well better let me know what *else* is supposed to give meaning to my life, NOW.

Another gut-wrenching New Year's Eve.

Fortunately, I had just received a copy of an out-of-print science fiction that took place at Nan Madol. I couldn't put it down and spent my New Year's Eve devouring it. By reading between the lines I got my first inkling of the spiritual nature of Nan Madol and its magical subterranean component where battles between the "dark" and the "light" occurred. I'd never thought seriously of a return trip to Pohnpei, but after reading that book, I had to go back.

I also had to eat my words. So God/Goddess indeed had given me my answer. And just to validate it, my ex-boyfriend called the next day to tell me that he had met a woman at a New Year's party the night before. Her brother-in-law was an underwater archaeologist who had done lots of work in Micronesia. Of course he didn't mention he was again already romantically involved! There are times when I do *not* appreciate Spirit's sense of humor, and this was one.

In any case, these encounters with Paulsen's book and the underwater archaeologist were the first of countless synchronicities that fueled my obsession and eventually drew me back to Nan Madol.

I thought it the beginning of a grand spiritual adventure. Little did I know the experience was also going to be the most powerful healing that I was ever to receive. And thank God/Goddess I had no idea of what I was getting into and of what I'd have to let go of physically and emotionally before completing and dissipating the obsession!

The outer circumstances manifested as my creation of a nonprofit corporation to fund preservation, protection, research, and education projects related to the site of Nan Madol. At that time, there was little protection or management of the physical site, nor has that changed substantially since. Anyone, tourists and locals alike, may enter with no supervision and do whatever damage they may choose. Fortunately, Nan Madol's power as a sacred site has been strong enough to protect it *so far*. However, developers and golf courses have powers of their own which can be irresistibly seductive to vulnerable people whose economic future is so uncertain.

For a white woman with no personal or seed money to move to Pohnpei, a no (wo)man's land in terms of equality, and to start a nonprofit foundation was certifiable lunacy. The only saving grace was that I had lived there long ago, was able to speak some Pohnpeian, and had a few friends from the old days. However, this act of lunacy did provide a big-time opportunity for testing my personal belief systems concerning abundance and manifestation. If Spirit wanted it to *be*, then it would—despite any mistakes I might make along the way. I just had to be willing to be *out there*, literally and figuratively, and *listening*, and *willing* to follow the continuing synchronicities that would clear the path for me. A word again about the synchronicities. The point is that I had to receive them first, to be receptive and recognize them for what they were (feminine) and then act on them (masculine). In other words, I had to incorporate much more of my feminine side with my masculine. Most women struggle with bringing forth the masculine in order to balance themselves. Not me. That was a piece of cake, as witnessed by my years of relative ease and success in the "man's world." I was a totally independent woman, a successful professional, and had never asked anyone for anything, except for a client to pay his bill; even my ex-husbands never supported me financially. But incorporating the feminine was new to me. Luckily, I had the sense to know that the old way would no longer work for me in this situation.

No longer could I employ my skills from the business world to make things happen through sheer will power and professional capabilities—this time I had to *allow* things to happen and to *receive*. This receiving wasn't just clearing my issues about self-esteem so that I felt deserving enough to receive. I also had to *ask for help,* not just for money and various forms of government support, but for a place to live because I couldn't afford the outrageous rents! Wasn't that a painful blow to my pride—to be out of control and so *vulnerable.*

However, that was the whole point of this Pohnpei episode, to create a reality with a *balance* of the masculine and feminine. Pohnpei herself demonstrated the feminine in spades, so now I had to achieve the fine line in the middle. Other balancing acts with my feminine side took the form of patience/progress; sexual freedom/self-esteem; control/allowing; in the moment/past/future; etc. Observed more closely, most of these issues boil down to fear, in one form or another.

Sure enough, when I reached an understanding about these balances, often through extremely painful experiences, I felt a progressive release from the obsession of Pohnpei and Nan Madol. Now I was in a healthier position to see what my life's work was really about. Though I would always be linked closely to Pohnpei and continue working with Nan Madol, it had become time to expand my horizons to include not only Pohnpei, but the whole Pacific and its sacred sites. That I must focus on my relationship to all of these sites and not limit myself to only one piece of the puzzle became obvious.

Coincidentally, at about the same time, local politics surrounding ownership and control by the powers that be, namely men, intensified to the point of putting all activities related to Nan Madol into gridlock. This was more validation that my work should switch gears and locations for the time being so that I could incorporate Nan Madol into a bigger vision of my life's work.

Perhaps you're wondering why I'm not telling you more about Nan Madol. After all, this is a book about sacred sites, isn't it, and not the spiritual trials and tribulations of Carole Nervig. Yes and no. Each of us are sacred sites unto ourselves. To interact with a sacred site triggers clearing and healing in the individual as well as the site. There is no separation in these matters. In turn, our state of individual clarity determines the effectiveness of our impact with a particular site.

What we are called to do at sacred sites is to become one with them. We are not doing anything *to* these places, but merely acting as acupuncture needles to allow the vital energies to flow through us. If we as needles are rusty, dirty, or weak, we must be sterilized and tempered before insertion. So be prepared if you commit to doing this work!

As each power point/interdimensional portal is revitalized by our love and focus, allowing Spirit to surge through us, it is able to complete its connection with the entire planetary and intergalactic light grids in full force, not unlike the same process at an individual level in our body's meridian system. This is exactly what the ancients knew and practiced to keep Gaia in perfect harmony and balance. The activation of the flow of masculine energy from above and the feminine energy from below was executed on a precise schedule dictated by the stars. These rituals formed the core of the ancient cosmologies, many of which exist today in forms disguised by our modern-day religions. The people were conscious of their roles at the megalithic sites as catalysts in the maintenance of Gaia's nervous system and her intergalactic communication.

Humanity must now understand and embrace once again the importance of this process consciously—not just a few fringe eccentrics, but as a whole. The "establishment," the government and the scientific communities, must participate in the unfolding of the secrets of these Earth sanctuaries. Through the *balance* of scientific/masculine and esoteric/feminine information, humanity's memory can be triggered by presenting a *complete* picture of what these sites were in the past and humanity, once again, can be motivated to work with these sacred places to ensure a harmonious relationship with Gaia and our future together.

We must return to this understanding and practice not just to heal our planet, but more important, to heal ourselves. As we individuals become healed and whole and balanced again in terms of body, mind, and spirit, we will automatically take the appropriate steps in relationship to Gaia and her sacred sites.

Why certain individuals are drawn to a particular site or location has also to do with spiritual healing. We, especially those committed consciously to spiritual growth, become attracted to those places because they are the original entry points of our souls into physical embodiment. Revisiting in the physical can trigger a remembrance of why we came and what we were supposed to do on this physical plane. It can also be a potent catalyst in clearing the psychological baggage that impedes our self-actualization, preventing us from becoming who we actually are.

Like going home to the high school reunion, a perspective is experienced that illuminates where you are in relationship to your original goal; and presents an opportunity to get things back on track. However, the realization that we might be a bit off course hits with more intensity when we revisit a power place rather than a class reunion—it can even be traumatic in a positive sense.

As we come full circle in our third dimensional experiences by returning to our personal entry points, we focus not on ascending as pure spirit into the higher realms, but on ascending by infusing the physical with the divine right here on earth, the same theme reflected in sacred site rituals. It follows that our desire to reunite with our planetary points of origin heralds our yearning for this completion/ascension.

To restate all of this simply in the context of sacred sites and the feminine, we must not become *too* feminine, as we have learned from millennia of being *too* masculine. Everywhere we look in nature or in the cosmos we see a healthy balance, an achievement that is now humanity's ultimate challenge.

The Cave of Yeshe Tsogyel, Shoto Terdrom, Tibet. Photo by Leila Castle.

LEILA CASTLE

≡

THE FLESH OF THE DAKINIS: JOURNEY TO SHOTO TERDROM, TIBET, AND THE CAVE OF YESHE TSOGYEL

VULTURES WHEELED OVERHEAD as we practiced, sitting in a circle around the altar of stones, heart of Vajra Yogini, where bodies are offered. Ancient bird of the Goddess in her death aspect, the vulture mother takes the dead back into her own body. The Tibetans call them dakinis, enlightened female beings, and consider them sacred. We gathered their long black feathers along the path after our Chod[1] practice. It was raining as we walked. I held an umbrella over Tsultrim as we stopped to drink and collect water from the sacred spring, miraculously created by the founder of the Drigung lineage, that flows beneath the sky burial site. An ethereal rainbow appeared, arching across the valley as we left. She seemed exhilarated—marveling at her strength and endurance, I collapsed near her on the bus, completely spent after coming down the steep cliff. A mercifully short ride then took us to our waiting camp in the Shoto valley, the next valley over from Drigung, near Terdrom, after traveling northeast from Lhasa.

Drigung means "Camp of the She-yak," and is the principal residence of the guardian Goddess Apchi,[2] mandala of Vajra Yogini,[3] and seat of the Drigung Kagyupas.[4] The *dundro*, or "sky burial site" is considered to be identical to Siwaitsel near Bodh Gaya, the most famous of the eight Indian charnel grounds. There is a legend that they are connected by a rainbow.[5]

Freezing rain whipped the makeshift canvas tent as we huddled beneath it. I was so tired that black Tibetan night, cupping my steaming little mug of herb tea in my hands as I looked for a dry, rickety folding chair to sit down in after our climb to the sky burial site that day.

"Leila, come quickly, Tsultrim is ill!" I heard suddenly. What has happened, I wondered, hurrying on board the bus to find Tsultrim's seventeen-year old daughter, Sherab, and friend, Carla, already at her side. Tsultrim was lying in the bus driver's sleeping place. My cup in hand, I tried to get her to drink, but she didn't respond, as if in a trance. Quickly assessing her condition, I realized she was suffering from altitude sickness, exhaustion, and mild dysentery. But something else was going on. I applied several essential oils—rosemary and peppermint for faintness, to a tissue held to her nose, and then lavender massaged gently on her forehead for headache. It seemed that she could hear us but couldn't respond. I began having visions, as if I could see what she was experiencing, and realized she was on a shamanic journey with the dakinis.

Carla, Sherab, and I tried to assist her, but we became very worried as she seemed farther away, then began to convulse. Carla and I fed our own bodies to what seemed like the thousands of gigantic vultures tearing at her flesh, offering ourselves in her place, spinning the most powerful protective mantras we knew. Frightened, we realized she could be dying, yet somehow I felt a deep, calm presence and knew she was protected. Suddenly I understood I must do the Mandarava Long Life[6] mantras for her and sat quietly singing them in my heart, while Carla, with all her love and devotion, blew life energy into Tsultrim's chakras. As I sang, I saw Tsultrim surrounded in rainbow lights with multitudes of Long Life dakinis shimmering around her, and I knew she would be all right. Slowly she began to return, finally able to speak. Sipping tea and broth, while we stood vigil until she fully returned, she told us of her experience:

Feeling too much pain to move, I went into a light coma from acute mountain sickness. I could hear everyone talking but I couldn't respond or move. As my body lay there becoming colder and colder, my consciousness traveled back to the charnal ground. I saw myself on the rocks being eaten by vultures. The stones were like a grill with hundreds of butter lamps underneath. My body was on top. I could see a huge tubelike channel going up into the sky, through which the vultures approached. The vultures carried me through the channel into the sky to the waiting dakinis. They were of many beautiful soft colors and were moving in a wavy dance motion, creating spirals of color. They took me to their land which was not solid, so full of light. I felt I was finally at the place I'd been looking for all my life. The dakinis asked me to stay there with them. They looked like the flying angel-like beings in the Chinese paintings I'd seen in the Tun Huang caves on my way to Mt. Kailas. I longed to stay but then I remembered my three children and pulled away. It was so sad to leave them.

She had streams of tears running down her face—"This world is so heavy, so dense—we walk in a cloud, wandering, loose." We stayed with her for hours, making sure she was okay and comfortable for the night, before staggering into the icy wet darkness to crawl into leaky tents and finally to sleep, the sound of the rain and river in our ears.

Nine months earlier, on the Samhain full moon, Halloween, Tsultrim and I sat across from each other at a restaurant in New York City having lunch. She asked if I'd like to go to Tibet with her. I answered yes, though it seemed like a dream at the time. It is said that one's pilgrimage begins from the moment one decides to go.

We spoke of stories of our teachers and of Machig Lapdron, the great eleventh-century dakini who founded the Chod lineage—the practice of feeding the demons, in Tibet and to whose power place we would go on our pilgrimage. I remembered the first time I did Chod, the night I arrived on retreat in California in 1987 and met our teacher, Tibetan Dzogchen[7] Master Namkhai Norbu Rinpoche.[8] Chod was the first practice I did with him. I couldn't sleep afterwards, my body was singing with mantras and dancing with dakinis all night.

After lunch, Tsultrim dropped me off at the New York Metropolitan museum, where I meandered to an Egyptian room. Standing in the center of four great statues of the lion-headed goddess Sekhmet, I felt magnetized by her power. I stepped close to one of the black lionesses, fascinated by the beautifully carved image of a flower forming her nipple which I touched, feeling an indescribable electric union with her nature. Waking from this trance, a museum guard shouted at me not to touch the statue. One of the Tantric practices Tsultrim teaches is Simhamukha, the wrathful lion-headed Queen of the Dakinis, so similar to Sekhmet. This was the beginning of my pilgrimage—every aspect of my life was moving me toward Tibet.

Waking full of dreams in the frigid morning, my sleeping bag was an island floating in a puddle. I dreamed Carla, hip-length dreadlocked dakini sister from New York, and I were flying high over the gorges of Shoto Terdrom joining hundreds of dakinis going to a gathering—we soared with our arms outstretched holding hands. Shaggy black yaks wandered through camp as we emerged from our soggy tents to have breakfast beside the rushing snowmelt river. Thankfully Tsultrim was well. The last day of our pilgrimage together, tomorrow five of us will remain for personal retreat here, while the rest of the group who have traveled with Tsultrim, practicing at dakini places this last month, will return to Nepal, then the U.S.

We had come to Shoto Terdrom, which means "Box of Treasures,"[9] in hopes of visiting the illusive dakini, Tenzin Chodron, who resides here. Illusive, because we had heard of others who had made pilgrimage here to see her and were told she wasn't there, only to discover later it was in fact she who had told them! She is said to be an emanation of Yeshe Tsogyel, the eighth-century Tibetan princess and teacher who was the primary consort of the Tantric Master Padmasambhava, or Guru Rinpoche, considered to be a second Buddha and founder of Tibetan Buddhism. Yeshe Tsogyel lived and practiced here for many years of her life, alone, as well as with Padmasambhava and her consort, or mystic partner, Atsara Sale. Before she realized the rainbow body,[10] she promised she would always project an emanation of herself here. After years of dark retreat, before the Chinese invasion, Tenzin Chodron, now in her late fifties, was seen flying over the gorges, her shawl held out like wings—Sky Dancer, dakini, one who moves in the sky, *Khandroma* in Tibetan.

After fording the river on board the bus, we hiked toward the village nestled deep in a gorge, surrounded by towering mountains. The silhouette of the distant peaks form a descending V shape against the sky. The landmass itself, the steep sloping mountainsides, descends finally to a hot spring at the tip of another great vulva shape created by two rivers that flow along each side, converging at the hot spring, the warm mouth of the womb—cosmic cervix, place of the Great Mother.

The symbols of the vulva and V shapes are the most ancient images of the Goddess that exist, going back to Upper Paleolithic times—emblems of the Bird Goddess and her life giving, regenerative womb.[11] The primordial feminine in Tibetan Tantric tradition is Yum-Chenmo, the Great Mother. Her symbol is the descending triangle, the gate of all birth, source of dharmas.[12] She is the essence of space from which all is born.

Wandering into the tiny village, we were greeted by friendly nuns who live near the hot spring at the tip of this massive triangular landscape. They guided us from a beautiful dakini stupa built next to the river on a base of interlaced triangles, a six-pointed star, past steaming hot spring pools, residences of the guardian goddess Apchi. We followed them along a muddy, narrow path, abundant with fresh green nettles, to a crevice in a stone archway under which the two rivers merge. Padmasambhava threw his *dorje*,[13] or "magical scepter" from his cave high above, they told us, forming the tunnel the river flows through. Before this, there had been a poisonous lake here. The crevice is carved with mantras near a place they showed us where there is an impression of his shoulders, elbow, and staff, or *khatvanga*[14] melted into the rock. Beyond this is a small cave where Yeshe Tsogyel practiced, her footprints, one barefoot and one with a boot on, are nearby in stone. Soft moss and wildflowers were everywhere; it was a dakini faeryland, enchanted. I sat beside the cave, filled with *tsatsa*—little clay offerings, to meditate and saw Yeshe Tsogyel and Padmasambhava in yab-yum[15] embrace. We practiced Simhamukha here together before several of us returned to bathe in the medicinal springs blessed by Guru Rinpoche, while others continued on with the nuns.

Later we were allowed to practice in the nunnery gompa. Made from thick earthen walls, inside it was dark and dank, lit by butter lamps saturating everything with the pungent scent of yak butter, flickering to illuminate big statues of Buddhas and thankas. As we practiced Chod in the gompa, I began to cry—tears flooded my eyes, streaming down my cheeks in hot salty drops. Yeshe Tsogyel appeared to me in vision; she was standing beside the cave near the spring where we had practiced earlier, naked except for a white cloth around her hips. She entered me, became me. I felt her essence, totally wild, free—and realized this was my true nature, primordial wisdom. It was her, Machig Lapdron, Tsultrim, me—*everyone*, the essence of our dakini nature, our primordial essence. Filled with this energy, it overflowed from my body in the form of tears, as if flowing from my heart. Experiencing the most powerful compassion and liberation in her presence and blessings, I wondered how to bring this wisdom into the world and my life.

> Either I will be one with your own nature, or appear as your mudra. Now, for awhile, until your split minds are whole, parting will seem like separation. Be happy! When your split minds are one, you and I will be reunited. May good fortune and happiness be everywhere![16]

These were some of Yeshe Tsogyel's final words before she vanished into streaming, shimmering, iridescent rainbow light. I read them months later, after my return from Tibet, amazed to see her words spoken over a thousand years ago, true today.

After this final practice together as a group, we lunched on the usual hard-boiled eggs, white flour pancakes, and tinned fruit provided by our Chinese cooks. We bathed leisurely at the springs, then walked back to our camp. Before dinner we had a completion circle in the nearby meadow strewn with wild-flowers and yak dung, seemingly symbolic of the dakinis' lotuslike nature, beauty growing from the muck. It began to rain again, so we moved to shelter beneath the meal tent. After dinner we made toasts, singing and dancing together under the tent in the pouring monsoon rains for the last time.

In the morning, the mountains were dusted with snow like powdered sugar. The day was cold and drizzling. I dreamed of there being danger from rocks falling, and felt very cautious about our climb ahead. Angel-like nuns came down to the camp to help carry our bags to the hermitage where the five of us who will stay hope to do a retreat. After singing "Song of the Vajra,"[17] hugs, and an emotional, teary goodbye—our sweet Tibetan guide and the nuns were all crying too—five of us, Tsultrim, Sherab, Robin, Karen, and myself, dressed in layers of chubas (the traditional long dresses worn by Tibetan women), hats, coats, mittens, and rain ponchos, slowly followed the nuns, laden with luggage, up the mountain. Inching our way along the trail, in awe of the nuns' unbelievable strength and playfulness, we wound through the village, then up to the dakini's hermitage beside the cave of Guru Rinpoche. Shown several dark, damp huts along the way, wondering where we would stay, we were eventually, most graciously allowed to camp in the hermitage shrine room perched high over the valley.

Exhausted from the climb and altitude, we were grateful, *ecstatic*, to be given this beautiful, dry, abode with a sweeping magnificent view overlooking the mountain gorges. We rested, drinking delicious hot tea brought by the nuns. Told Tenzin Chodron was away, working on a prayer wheel at the entrance to the valley, we wondered if she would return while we were here. Her consort, Dutse, which means "nectar" in Tibetan, cared for us, bringing fresh yak yogurt he had made. Sherab and Karen pitched their tents on the nearby slopes, but Dutse insisted they be moved to safer ground away from rock falls, telling us people have been killed, confirming my dream warning.

Steps from the shrine room, up a ladder made from wooden poles, is Padmasambhava's cave. Inside it drips spring water, which also rushes along one side—deliciously fresh and singing. Indentations colored red with lichen mark where he took his bell and dorje, the scepter he threw to open the tunnel at the hot spring. A tall shaft reaching high into the solid rock ceiling is where he placed his khatvanga. Lush emerald moss grows on the stone and a natural altar is covered with prayer scarves, offerings, and sacred carved stones. Two metal khatvangas lean against the cave wall. I sat and meditated, merging my mind with the mind of Guru Rinpoche.

Earlier on the pilgrimage, after visiting Samye, where Padmasambhava established the Tantric teachings in Tibet, we stopped briefly beside the mountain Wolsar Drak. He and Yeshe Tsogyel magically flew from there to Shoto Terdrom to practice mystic sexual yoga in the cave called the Assembly Hall of the Dakinis. I heard as I meditated, "I am your staff, I will always be your support."

In the following days I saw khatvangas in the landscape made from natural formations of mountains and valleys. The khatvanga is a three-pronged trident staff that signifies one's inner consort. For a dakini, it represents her integrated male energy or animus, skillful means and great bliss or compassion, symbolic of the presence of Guru Rinpoche in union with her wisdom nature. For a daka, or male counterpart of a dakini, it represents his integrated feminine energy or anima, symbolic of his union with the primordial wisdom nature. At Samye, Yeshe Tsogyel appeared as the khatvanga of Padmasambhava miraculously before the King of Tibet in the eighth century.

Then, at Sangri Kharmar where we traveled next, khatvanga teachings continued, as I sat at the convergence of two mighty rivers across from the Red Citadel of Machig Lapdron. The mountain facing me has a gigantic khatvanga etched into the cliff. Rainbows danced in the sky as I received understanding of my consort/mystic partner, in both inner and outer manifestations. Simultaneously experiencing all the pleasure and pain, joy and sorrow of our relationship, love and death mingled in me as I sobbed beside the roaring rivers, until some alchemical process completed, a deep compassion rose in my heart. Realizing that Padmasambhava is the inner consort, my union with him my inner male, bliss united with emptiness, I knew that I would always have this presence within for support. Tsultrim met me on the riverbank after this experience, going to the same spot to meditate. She showed me two smooth, small river stones marked with khatvangas she had just found, and had also seen the huge khatvanga image on the cliff. (Synchronistically, as this was written, I looked down at the photograph leaning on the computer in front of me and noticed for the first time that there was a perfect image of a khatvanga stained in black on the rock above me as I sat at the entrance to Yeshe Tsogyel's cave. Its shape and color were just like the one Robin gave me when we returned from Tibet—she and Tsultrim had found it in a shop in Kathmandu and bought it for me. At this same moment, the phone rang and it was my consort.) Inner and outer aspects of my life seemed to blend into the Dreamtime realm revealed by the dakinis as they chop away at my egoic illusions of duality with their blades of wisdom.

We took turns sitting in the cave beside the hermitage before dark that first night. Tsultrim, Robin, and I slept in the shrine room dimly lit by flickering butter lamps that cast an eerie, supernatural luminosity on a statue of Padmasambhava. His eyes bulge from his face, looking completely wild, crazy. The room had no heat, though we were warm nestled deep inside our zero-degree down sleeping bags and felt protected and peaceful lying on lumpy carpets spread over prayer benches against the thick earthen walls. A weird wailing sound, like a dakini singing, awakened me in the middle of the night. I felt the presence of a dakini, sort of hovering in the corner of the room. In the morning Robin told us of the dream she had:

> In sleep I had a very intense dream image of a fierce dakini spirit hovering over my bed in the corner closest to the Guru Rinpoche cave which was right outside. I could see she was beckoning me to follow her up some stairs that led up and out of the corner of the room, into the cave, and through it to the dark beyond. It was as if I could see everything perfectly, both inside and outside of the room I was sleeping in, and in some way it seemed perfectly logical that I should just walk through the wall with her and into the cave. I kept trying to do just that but each time I got almost to the cave I would awaken out of breath. During my waking moments I could not see the dakini spirit physically, nor could I see through the wall and into the cave like I could while dreaming, but I was still possessed by an awesome sense of presence in the room. The air was still and thick, my skin was filled with goosebumps, and everything appeared rather surreal. Had I not been a student of Buddhism and metaphysics over the years, I might have been

frightened, but instead I was drawn to continue to try and follow the dakini through the wall, the cave, and into the dakini realm beyond. I tried and tried all through the night but each time I awoke panting and out of breath. Towards morning, I finally acknowledged to the dakini during one of my waking moments that I was probably not going to be able to take my physical body into the realm she wanted to show me. It became clear to me that there was no other option at the time, other than stopping breathing and death, for going with her. The decision to die in order to go with her was one I could not bring myself to agree to and finally had to surrender to the fact that whatever supernatural state of being was needed to enter the dakini realm was not at my access or ability at that time. In a final slumber, the dakini seemed to acquiesce, merge into me with some screeching, high pitched noises which my roommates claim awakened them, and vanish.

Sharing our dreams became part of our morning ritual, like ancient priestesses dreaming at sacred sites together. The dreams of the site are another dimension of its teaching, like a secret doorway. We had tea and breakfast, then practiced, moving very slowly, adjusting to the higher altitude, around 17,000 feet. I bathed next to a tiny spring trickling from the mountainside, washed dishes and clothes, and then sat on the hillside writing, enjoying the deep blue sky and sunshine, overlooking the green valley covered with wildflowers high above the rivers rushing deep in the gorges far below. We were taking it very easy, resting that day. The altitude made it impossible for us to do anything else.

The next day, we woke and shared our dreams. I dreamed of my children and lover and that I should do Guru Yoga.[18] Tenzin Chodron still hadn't returned. Our Tibetan friends here were so kind. Dutse, wise, protective, and playful, cared for us bringing hot tea and water for washing, yak cheese, yogurt, and rice. I made an aromatic oil for healing his knee which was bothering him. By his actions I learned about how a consort supports the realization of the deep feminine, serving the wild nature. He tended the shrine in the room daily and loved to visit and talk with us. Tsultrim could speak a little Tibetan and translated. Nuns came by to visit and watch us practice—they were calling us the dakinis.

Cloudy and cold, with some brief sun that afternoon, we were led by Ani, the head nun, to the cave of Yeshe Tsogyel. A very strenuous climb from the hermitage up steep rocky cliffs, we inched our way skyward, stopping to rest and catch our breath every few steps, our hearts pounding. A great golden eagle soared by us, effortlessly gliding. Approaching the cave, the entrance is formed by a magnificent V-shaped stone archway, like a pubic bone—the descending triangle, sky womb. It was as if we first entered her vagina, damp and slick with spring water, adorned with the most precious wildflowers, and then her womb.

Deep inside the innermost cave, wet and dripping, we practiced Chod together with Ani Phuntsog Drolma. Visions began of dharmadayas[19] made of light, thousands of them emanating one within the other. The rock walls of the cave seemed alive, undulating, fluid, as if no longer solid. Tibetan script, just beneath the surface of the stone, covered the cave walls entirely. I felt Yeshe Tsogyel's incredible strength, discipline, will, and power. I am so soft and weak in comparison—for me just to get here has taken all my determination and strength. Living here one would have to be nearly superhuman. I later discovered she was called the White Cotton-Clad Dakini when she practiced Tummo (the inner heat) here, protected by nothing but a white cotton cloth. The nuns' cheeks and earlobes were reddish purple from frostbite. With snow on the peaks in August, how cold must it be in winter?

Tsultrim had brought a crystal to leave as an offering. We all prayed with it before Sherab climbed to place it in a high niche in the cave wall. As she did this, a chunk of rock was dislodged, tumbling down and grazing Ani below, who was luckily unhurt, aside from a bump on the forehead. A perfect image of Padmasambhava in his rainbow body form was then revealed where the rock had fallen away. "Practice in all those places where there is a naturally manifest image of Guru Rinpoche, particularly in Tidro[20] itself,"[21] so Padmasambhava instructed Yeshe Tsogyel.

Ani reached into the niche and handed us all a small portion of damp red clay, telling us it is called the Flesh of the Dakinis, and to eat it, which we did, tasting its earthy nectar. It is medicinal and imbued with blessings. Like placenta or blood, the essence of the dakinis from the cave womb of the Great Mother was nourishing to us, her newborn daughters.

Months before this journey, on a dakini day (the tenth day after a full moon in the Tibetan calendar), I dreamed I was standing in a pool of clear, warm water up to my belly, giving birth underwater. Reaching between my legs to gently hold my daughter as she slides from my womb, I gazed at her lovingly beneath the water. She was incredibly beautiful, smiling at me, and felt as if she was made of nectar—lush, blissful, and completely aware. I realized she was a dakini as she grew very rapidly and had a very fine eye in the center of her brow. She spoke to me as I held her to my heart.

That dream happened about two months after I'd had an abortion. Nine months previous I had conceived unexpectedly and unintentionally, at a time when circumstances made it impossible for me to go through with a pregnancy. It was a very difficult and painful decision to give up the potential of that pregnancy—all that might have been. I felt devastated, and that dream was especially healing as I grieved. Now the dakinis had brought me here, to Yeshe Tsogyel's cave, rather than actually giving birth.[22] I was giving birth to my true nature, from the womb of the Great Mother.

The following day I walked down to the hot spring after practice. Bathing in the warm bubbling pool strung with prayer flags, I soaked, and then washed clothes in the river. Snakes lived there, apparently not afraid of us, almost friendly. One slowly slithered over to me, then went its own leisurely way. Sitting beside the spring, Robin was surprised by a snake coiling from beneath her, as if coming from her yoni. Perhaps they were nagas, water spirit guardians of treasure. A woman, ghastly yellow green with hepatitis, came and sat by the pool. She looked weak and terribly ill. The springs, blessed by Guru Rinpoche, are said to cure any illness. Another old woman came and asked for healing. Karen laid hands on her where she felt pain, Sherab gave her clothes.

Walking back up the steep mountain path to the hermitage later that afternoon, two young nuns accompanied me. They stopped at a large boulder to show me the handprint of Yeshe Tsogyel. The tiny details of her hand in solid rock were astounding, as if her touch had melted it like soft butter. I placed my hand on hers, so much smaller than mine—like a girl's—touching her touch.

> And in numerous minor power places rocks were marked with my hand and footprints, and mantras, seed syllables, and images were placed there, left as articles of faith for the future with prayers that qualified devotees will discover them.[23]

In *The Language of the Goddess*, Marija Gimbutas discusses the symbols of hand- and footprints in the Paleolithic and Neolithic art of Old Europe. Hands and feet represent divine touch, imparting the energy of the goddess and symbolic of her presence—stimulating, healing, protective. Upper Paleolithic cave walls going back to 20,000–10,000 BC are decorated with the handprints of women. More recent are stones with miraculous footprints of the Virgin Mary, Jesus, and saints that are held in deep reverence in the Catholic countries of Europe. They have the power to heal, strengthen, and protect.

Reaching the hermitage, I climbed onto one of the flat rooftops of a nearby hut overlooking the valley to meditate. I did Guru Yoga and sat, feeling my mind open to the presence of pure mind. Form seemed to dissolve, the mountains suddenly no longer seem solid, but fluid-looking. At dusk, Robin and I did Chod for Tsultrim. Afterward by the pale candlelight, she helped us with details of the practice, explaining Tibetan pronunciations and the sound *phat*, which means "to cut, sever attachment." That night I dreamed my body was huge, laid out over the sky burial altar at Drigung. My arms and legs were stretched out in the four directions pointing to the four dakini stones.

During our pilgrimage we had gone to sites that are sacred to many forms of the primordial feminine in the Tibetan tradition—Tara, Machig Lapdron, Yeshe Tsogyel, and Vajra Yogini—who are all said to be emanations of each other. I experienced union with Machig Lapdron at her sacred site, with Tara at hers, with Yeshe Tsogyel at hers, and with Vajra Yogini at hers. And I was in the present company of Tsultrim, who is said to be an emanation of Machig Lapdron, who is said to be an emanation of Yeshe Tsogyel and Tara, and we had come here to visit Tenzin Chodron, who is said to be a present emanation of Yeshe Tsogyel, who is said to be an emanation of Vajra Yogini and Kuntuzangmo herself, the primordial female Buddha!

> In reply to your specific question about my emanations: I, this Supreme Being, Yeshe Tsogyelma, I will never withdraw my compassion from Tibet. Radiating the light of skillful means through emanation, I will guide all beings of the future to happiness. In particular, five emanations of Body and five of Speech, five emanations of Mind, five of Quality and five of Action—these twenty-five emanations will constantly sustain Tibet. Each of these twenty-five will project five secondary emanations, and each of these will project tertiary emanations, etc., until all sentient beings are apparitional beings, united with the blissful Great Mother, gathered into the matrix of delight, Kuntuzangmo's clear sky.[24]

I began to understand why all Buddhas are the same. In essence everyone's innate true nature, or enlightened being, is the same, though they express different qualities. When we realize this, when we experience this, we know its truth. That is why I see now how important, how compassionate is the vow of Tara—to assist continuously the realization of beings in female form. All women are dakinis, but we have forgotten this. In a world of patriarchal cultures, where male authority and values of domination have ruled, where enlightened beings, spiritual leaders, and religious figures are largely portrayed as male, women must be able to know their true nature's as women equal to men, not *as* men. It is very important for men and women to realize this, as well as understand the transformation that men can experience by integrating the feminine energy that the dakinis embody. This is why there are both Guru and Dakini, or dakas and dakinis, because as humans incarnate as either male or female, enlightened or realized being is present in both—it doesn't matter which. However for a woman surrounded primarily by examples and imagery of male divinity, the dakinis are a great help on her path of realization of her true nature; they are examples of an embodiment she may identify with, becoming herself. Daka and dakini, Guru and Dakini are models for us of partnership, of mutual devotion and love express-ing one's own inner sacred marriage, as well as a sacred relationship between women and men that supports the wild true nature of both. It is a coming home, finally knowing the essence of your true being and knowing this essence is shared with everyone. This essence is the mixing, the union of wisdom and compas-sion. I call it sky nectar, emptiness and bliss—open, spacious, sweet like honey in one's heart. This is the amrita, the water of compassion that flows from the Great Mother, the matrix of delight, Kuntuzangmo's clear sky.

How can I best assist in bringing this dakini wisdom into the world, how can I be a channel for the primordial feminine? I prayed, and listened, hearing:

> Practice yourself, become the practices, let this wisdom move through you in all ways, in your personal life, in all your relationships. Stay close to her within, always rely on your yidam. Become Samantabadri (Kuntuzangmo in Tibetan, the primordial female Buddha), allow her nature, which is your true nature, to flow through you like a river into the world through your heart to others. Being her awakens her as she is still obscured and sleeping in others, like a mirror she is seen.

Practices are methods or teachings one uses in order to have experiential knowledge of one's true nature, the enlightened being that one has always been, and to remain in the state of that knowledge. This is the dharma, which is embodied by the Buddha, the Buddha's teachings, and practitioners or *sangha*—the Three Jewels; and Roots—Guru, Deva, Dakini. To become the practices is to realize one's true nature and to live the dharma, to practice this in daily life—compassion arising in the present moment as pathway. The yidam is one's personal deity. Padmasambhava tells Yeshe Tsogyel, "Realize that you and the yidam deity are not two and that there is no yidam deity apart from yourself."[25] This is what I am to rely on. Through awareness of true nature and primordial feminine wisdom that Samantabadri represents, the heart emanates a riverlike flow, amrita, into one's life, in any circumstance that arises. When one embodies this, other people are affected because you reflect to them their own true nature.

Our last day at the hermitage, before we moved down to the village, gave us a final opportunity to climb to farther caves. After waking to telling dreams, tea, washing, and practicing, we hiked up to the top mountain peaks, looking for Machig's cave. Practically crawling straight up, beyond Yeshe Tsogyel's cave, I trailed behind Sherab and loosened a stone that thundered down the mountainside dangerously picking up speed. Luckily no one was directly behind me. We perched in a cave so high that we got vertigo looking down at the ridgetops far below, place of soaring eagles. The Hall of the Dakinis eluded us, beyond our reach, higher and farther still. We didn't have enough time for our bodies to adjust to the altitude, nor did we have the strength or endurance to get there, another week perhaps would do it. Ani gave us ringsel[26] from the Assembly Hall the day we left, in lieu of actually getting there. We gathered juniper, burned as offerings, growing from beside the caves as we descended, exhausted, mostly on our bottoms, returning to flop in the shrine room.

Dutse brought us tea and rice, and we rested, talking for hours about our consorts, sex, love, and relationships—maybe it was the energy of the place, or being away from our dakas so long. I love the passionately erotic and open, playful sexuality of the dakinis that is not separated from the spiritual. It is an unconditioned female sexuality, wild in this sense, also pure. The primordial lust of the dakini burns through all the layers of conditioning we experience as women in patriarchy and is powerfully healing. I went out on a nearby rooftop to enjoy the sun and wrote my lover a poem, missing him so far away. Everyone came out on the roof and our bawdy tales continued.

As we traveled from site to site, on an inner level I experienced an alternation of male and female energy within myself that related to the outer experience of the sites. Integrating with Padmasambhava at his sites, or with Yeshe Tsogyel at hers, creates a yab-yum effect within, where both one's wisdom nature and skillful means are activated and strengthened. I understood better now the importance of having a partner to practice with as these inner energies develop. Robin, Tsultrim, and I, although traveling together alone and experiencing our wholeness as women independent of partners, each have relationships with consorts, our dakas, with whom we practice and love very much. Our consorts, also practitioners, are deeply woven with us upon our spiritual pathways, yet we also have very ordinary relationships as lovers. This ordinariness is suffused with the luminosity of our true natures. This shines through and becomes a support on the path. We become each other's khatvangas, reminding each other, teaching each other, ultimately realizing our natures as the play of Guru/Dakini, Padmasambhava and Yeshe Tsogyel.

After awhile, our talk exhausted, Tsultrim and I did integration with the sky, so spacious, blue, with a white crescent-moon and thin clouds. I laid on my back, closed my eyes, and felt so full. Padmasambhava appeared in vision to me and placed a jewel in my heart. It was love and compassion and totally spacious at the same time, diamondlike, refracting rainbow lights. I felt deeply satisfied—strong, wild, pure, loving, open, spacious—like the sky with blessings raying out from this jewel. He told me this was his gift to me from this place, a treasure from his box. I vowed to bring this treasure home, and sent blessings to all from this state. At dusk we practiced, then organized our supplies for packing to leave in the morning. Ani and Dutse were there and it was getting very dark as I wrote by flashlight.

Box of Treasures III

Padmasambhava gave me a present
the day before I left.
I was lying on the roof
of a little adobe hermitage
below his cave
integrating with the sky.
He came and put a jewel
in my heart

It is like a diamond,
it filled my body/heart/mind
with light and rayed out
in blessings far beyond me.
He said it was a treasure
from his box, to share it
with everyone.
He said it had been
there all along,
the real gift is that
he showed me/
the real gift is that
it belongs to no one/
the real gift is that
it is yours too.

I woke to our last day in Shoto Terdrom, had tea and then went out to sit on the rooftop to meditate awhile with the diamond in my heart. It was magnificently clear, warm, and sunny, the most beautiful weather since we'd been here. Soon the nuns arrived to help us down the mountain to stay in a comfortable room above the hot spring beside the nunnery gompa. We spent the afternoon bathing in the springs. I laid in the water where on one side hot spring water flows, and on the other side cold, crystal snowmelt from the river hits me, luxuriating, splashing rainbow lights blissfully. We rested in our room before preparing the feast offering for the nunnery.

Nomads, toothless old nuns, and tiny children gathered at the gompa where we offered the feast in thanks for our stay. Dressed in my chuba, the dark golden color of Tibetan earth, I carried a large round bowl of food, transformed into nectar, offering it to all the people. The poorest seemed the most humble, hardly daring to take a morsel of meat or chocolate. Suddenly, it was as if I was in my painting, Dharma Lady, created after a vision in 1974, offering milk and blood to a gathering of people, blessing them. I was bleeding with my moontime and realized that somehow the vision had come to life. We gave away all of our food, and lots of clothing. Sherab fed jerky to the multitude of village dogs lingering outside.

Later, after dark, Karen, Sherab, and I bathed in the hot spring, soaking in the silky darkness, naked beneath the vast, deep black velvet sky studded with stars. We slept in a room above the kitchen—the primordial kitchen, with earthen walls blackened by cooking fires and huge cauldrons, saturated with the scent of yak butter and dung burning for fuel, the inescapable aroma by which we were awakened in the morning.

As the first rays of sun touched the highest peaks, we were on the frosty trail out of the village to meet our Chinese cooks (who had remained at the springs while we were in retreat at the hermitage) and their truck, which would take us back to Lhasa. Ani, Dutse, and nuns accompanied us to say goodbye. We were sad to go, but also glad to be going home. Dutse rode with us to the valley entrance, where Tenzin Chodron was working on a prayer wheel. Sherab had actually hiked all this way days before to see her with the river flooded from the storms, wading across water up to her waist. As we drove she showed us how the water had receded and we realized the road had been completely submerged.

We stopped briefly to visit Tenzin Chodron with her beautiful prayer wheel. Her long black hair was braided and wound at the back of her neck, dressed in layers of maroon chuba and clothing with a little felt hat; she was short and strong-looking. Her cheeks were red and rounded, her face kind and deeply knowing. She seems very powerful and gentle at the same time. Blessing the katas we gave her, and our beads, she was very concerned for our safety on the road to Lhasa. Saying that there had been landslides and floods with a bridge washed away, she insisted we leave quickly because of these dangers, protective of us. Dutse stood next to her and I could feel their love and devotion, the way their energy is blended. She asked us to walk around the building before we left, so we set out going clockwise. Suddenly I saw her tearing after Tsultrim ahead of me, with a huge knife, a cleaver in her hand raised over her head, an image of a wrathful dakini! Chasing after a yellow dog that was attacking Tsultrim, she attempted to protect her, but the dog bit Tsultrim's leg. She tended the wound, assuring Tsultrim she would be okay as we left, somewhat stunned.

Bumping along the rutted dirt road, we saw she was right as we reached the washed-out bridge. Our truck had to ford the wide flooded river, miraculously making it across, while we balanced our way on foot over logs lashed together. We arrived at our hotel in Lhasa safely, with just enough time to dash by rickshaw to the Barkhor market to buy some last-minute gifts for our children and loved ones. Robin and I circumambulated the Jokhang, along with throngs of Tibetans, several times, buying turquoise, prayer flags, and butter lamps, while

Tibetan women taught us how to tie our chubas properly, they said—so we will attract husbands. We all laughed. Robin and I could hardly breathe, they had tied the belts so tightly around our waists. After dinner and a few hours sleep we left Tibet in the early morning to return home, halfway around the world.

REFLECTIONS

I am lying in the warm sunshine after practicing in my garden, surrounded by fragrant wild rose hedges, blackberry brambles in bloom, and apple trees full of tiny baby apples—so far from Tibet. Why did I go to Shoto Terdrom? How could I have imagined what would happen to me by going there? As I write, I enter into the Dreamtime of the place, its sacred space that is within. Sometimes this has been so strong that after a paragraph I have had to go sit out in the garden for several hours and open up to the experience unfolding further in my awareness and understanding. The Dreamtime is not bound by time and space—its entrance is in the awareness of the present. The sites remain within us, part of us.

I see the face of Tenzin Chodron and hear Yeshe Tsogyel's voice, "Either I will be one with your own nature or appear as your mudra. When your split minds are one, you and I will be reunited."[27] My journey to Shoto Terdrom has been a journey to my true nature—*know thyself*, the principle of the Pythia at Delphi.

This trail has not been easy. I had to walk into all my worst fears and let go of everything most precious in my life. My fears were of never returning, of never seeing my children again, of losing my lover, of suffering some horrible illness or accident in a remote foreign land, of the atrocities of the Chinese. We all knew we could die there, and in a way, we did. On a somewhat more humorous note, I remember thinking as I climbed up the cliff to the sky burial site at Drigung Til, my heart pounding so hard it felt like it was about to burst, that if I were going to die, this seemed to be a pretty good place to do it. I was stripped naked, stripped of my hopes, dreams, and fears.

There is a price for teachings that has nothing to do with money, even though it cost a tremendous amount to go to Tibet. The price is our surrender. Not to someone else, but surrender to our innate wisdom. It is this innate wisdom the dakinis embody and reflect. It is this wisdom I am learning to trust, to dance with.

We hardly spent half an hour in the presence of Tenzin Chodron, yet my entire journey was a teaching from her, Yeshe Tsogyel, and Tsultrim, of the primordial wisdom nature of the enlightened feminine that they embody "until all sentient beings are united with the blissful Great Mother." I think of Tenzin Chodron often. I understand now how she protects the Terdrom valley; I see her at her prayer wheel calling everyone to remember. The valley, caves, and mountains are soaked in the blessings of Padmasambhava, Yeshe Tsogyel, and the power of the place, practices, and practitioners spanning over a thousand years. The dakinis are dancing at the sacred sites, and they invite us to join their wild dance.

NOTES

1. The practice of Chod, first transmitted by Machig Lapdron in the eleventh century in Tibet, is often done in charnel grounds or desolate places and involves the practitioner visualizing the offering of him/her body while singing and playing a damaru (drum) and bell, summoning all to feed from him/her, destroying dualism and egoic attachments. See Allione, *Women of Wisdom* (London and New York, Arkana, 1984).

2. Vajra Yogini (or Vajra Varahi, "Diamond Sow") is a Sambogakaya dakini form of the Great Mother, the primordial feminine wisdom.

3. Apchi, the guardian Goddess of Drigung, was originally a dakini who married an exorcist, ancestor of the Drigung lineage. She became a powerful protectress of the Drigunpas and the area. See Dowman, *The Power Places of Central Tibet* (Routledge & Kegan Paul, London, 1988).

4. The Drigung Kagupas are one of the Kagyu schools of Tibetan Buddhism in the lineage of Milarepa. See Dowman, *The Power Places of Central Tibet* (Routledge & Kegan Paul, London, 1984).

5. Keith Dowman, *The Power Places of Central Tibet* (Routledge & Kegan Paul, London, 1984).

6. Mandarava was an Indian princess and consort of Padmasambhava, who with him realized the yoga of immortality practice of the Buddha of Long Life Amitayus. The Mandarava Long Life practice is a terma from Namkhai Norbu Rinpoche, received while on retreat at the Maratika cave in Nepal in 1984, where Mandarava and Padmasambhava practiced together.

7. Dzogchen, the primordial yoga, or "Great Perfection," is an ancient form of contemplation and essence of all the Tibetan teachings. See Namkhai Norbu, *The Crystal and the Way of Light* (Routledge & Kegan Paul, London and New York, 1986).

8. Namkhai Norbu Rinpoche is a Tibetan Dzogchen Master who currently lives in Italy and teaches worldwide. He is the recognized incarnation of the great Dzogchen Master Adzom Drukpa.

9. Shoto Terdrom, meaning "Box of Treasures," refers to the terma tradition there. Terma are treasures, teachings hidden primarily by Yeshe Tsogyel and Padmasambhava and meant to be discovered by people destined in the future, tertons, in order to benefit their time so that the teachings remain fresh. Many terma were hidden and have been discovered in Shoto Terdrom.

10. The rainbow body ('ja'lus), or body of light, is realized through Dzogchen practice when the material, physical body dissolves into its essence, the five-colored rainbow light. See Namkhai Norbu, *The Crystal and the Way of Light* (Routledge & Kegan Paul, New York and London, 1986).

11. Marija Gimbutas, *The Language of the Goddess* (Harper & Row, 1989).

12. Tsultrim Allione, *Women of Wisdom* (Arkana, London and New York, 1984).

13. Dorje is Tibetan for the Sanskrit word *vajra*, a ritual object representing the indestructible true nature; it means " King of Stones, diamond scepter."

14. See page 117 for further explanation of the *khatvanga*.

15. Yab-yum, father-mother form of deities in sexual embrace with their consorts representing the integration of male and female energy, samsara and nirvana, relative and absolute, wisdom and compassion, emptiness and bliss.

16. Keith Dowman, *Sky Dancer* (Routledge & Kegan Paul, London, 1984).

17. The "Song of the Vajra" is a song in the language of the dakinis that helps the practitioner enter into the state of his/her true nature by integrating with the sound of it.

18. Guru Yoga is a practice to experience the unity of one's nature of mind with the Master's, or Guru's mind. A Guru can be female.

19. A Dharmadaya is a six-pointed star, the shape of interlaced triangles, representing primal duality and the union of masculine and feminine.

20. Tidro is Shoto Terdrom.

21. Keith Dowman, *Sky Dancer* (Routledge & Kegan Paul, London, 1984).

22. I have two precious children, Gaea and Raven (now teenagers) from my first marriage. They were born at home and I cherish and wanted them both very much. The early months of my pregnancies are extremely difficult, having miscarried and been hospitalized in the past.

23. Keith Dowman, *Sky Dancer* (Routledge & Kegan Paul, London, 1984).

24. Ibid.

25. Erik Hein Schmidt, *Dakini Teachings* (Shambhala, Boston and Shaftsbury, 1990).

26. Ringsel are tiny seedlike relics that appear spontaneously at sacred places or from the blessings of enlightened beings.

27. Keith Dowman, *Sky Dancer* (Routledge & Kegan Paul, London, 1984).

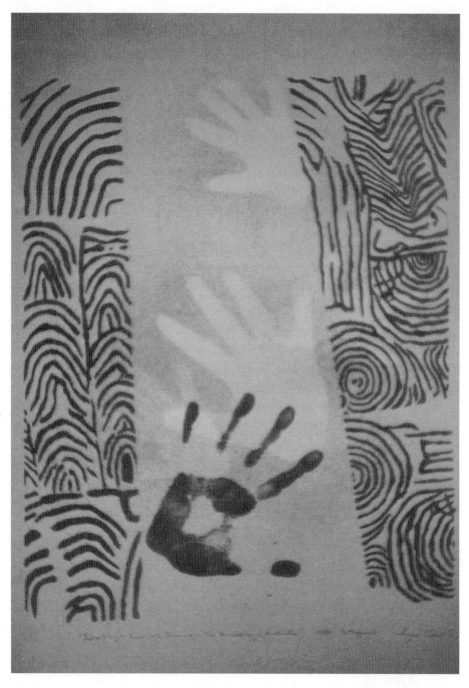

Lynne Wood, "Identity"

LYNNE WOOD

A CAILLEACH IN THE ANTIPODES

WRITING OF MY EXPERIENCES at sacred sites presents something of a dilemma for me. As a fourth generation Australian strongly aware of my Celtic origins, I have often felt a sense of isolation within the Australian landscape.

In the early 1980s, I spent five years in Britain where I met with many people who helped put me in touch with the culture and landscape of my ancestors. Five years of focusing on the ancient monuments in Britain, and gaining a personal understanding that my body and the land are one gave me a new perspective on the Australian landscape when I returned there in 1985.

Before traveling overseas I had worked in the outback regions of Australia, teaching art in remote schools where many of the students were Aboriginal. It felt paradoxical that I should be teaching a Western European art tradition to native Australian people, whose art holds a power and vision long since lost by much of contemporary Western art. Since the late 1970s, the international art world has had the opportunity to experience the unique beauty of Australian Aboriginal art, so closely bound with the people's relationship to the land.

I began teaching in Aboriginal communities in the late seventies. After returning to Australia in 1985, when I lived in the Central Desert for a year and for shorter periods in other areas, I was fortunate to experience teachings from women of the indigenous Australian culture, which had many parallels with the teachings from my own traditional culture in the remote areas of the Scottish Hebrides. The ancient sense of one's body and the land being one flows through both cultures; the difference in traditional European culture is the strong emphasis on the Great Mother Goddess embodying the life of the land.

In Australia, the land expresses the life force of the ancestors, both male and female. Giant animal/human ancestor characters lived and moved through the landscape, creating landforms, mountains, rivers, and rocky escarpments, while following lines of energy within the Earth and then entering the Earth themselves, becoming the landforms or being accessed at water sources. This same awareness appears in British ancient teachings as the Mountain Mothers who formed the landscape in the Celtic countries, after which they became parts of the landscape (for example the legends of the giantesses of North Wales, Ceridwen; the ancient Goddesses in Ireland such as Tea, Ethniu, etc; and the Cailleachs in Scotland).

In Australia, Aboriginal people believe that human inhabitants can become one with the ancient ancestors through ritual—acting out his or her story in song and dance, keeping the energy of the land alive. When humans follow the lines of energy within the Earth between the sacred sites, the land is kept fertile and energized and all plant, animal, and human life can live in harmony with the energies of the Earth. At birth (and sometimes earlier), each person indicates a relationship with some aspect of life, animal or plant (their Dreaming), which in turn has its special place within the landscape. That individual person is then responsible for the continuing life of that plant or animal, particularly in reference to its special place.

Within the social structure, each person holds a position in relationship with other people, depending on his/her responsibility to the land and their Dreaming. As well as individual responsibility, each family group or clan has collective responsibility for an area or region. Then there is "women's business" and "men's business." As a woman, I was only ever able to see something of women's business, focusing on women's sacred sites in areas where I was living.

From my own childhood I understood that storytelling was a way ancient traditions were passed from generation to generation. Before I ever visited Scotland and Wales I had inherited a sense of the landscape of these countries from family stories and songs, told to me from a very early age. The Celtic essence was still alive even after generations of isolation from the land of origin.

In the Hebrides I was fortunate to meet Annie Macloed, a guardian of the sacred site of Callanish and teacher of the ancient traditions of the land itself. With Jill Smith (who still lives on Lewis now), I was given powerful teachings on the relationship of the land and the moon, the ancient monuments and the importance of keeping alive human relationship with place, and holding the energy of the place within one's own body.

In Central Australia, I was to find women guardians of the land teaching similar awareness of relationship to Earth energies.

Earlier, in the 1970s, I had lived near one of the major river systems in western New South Wales. While there I met a very old Aboriginal woman, who lived in a cave hollowed out of the high cliffs along the river bank. Local people said she was the oldest person still living in tribal conditions. She remembered being chased by early white settlers, being shot at, and seeing members of her family killed by the bullet or by poisoned flour. But she had survived, living on what she could catch from the river and wild plants, as well as government assistance later in life. Mostly though, she kept to her cave and to the river itself. Children said that she kept the spirits of the dead and the yet to be born in her cave, and would show them matchboxes where she kept the spirits. Known by indigenous people in the area as a woman of wisdom, she told stories and it was said that she performed spiritual healing, even in advanced old age. I was never told her name.

A river guardian, she told stories of the female river serpent moving across the land from the mountains in the east, across the desert to the sea, forming a deep valley in the Earth. When she reached the sea, she took a long drink, the water passed through her body into the earth valley she had created, filling it with water and forming the river system. It was said that women lived at places along the river, singing the songs of the river woman, inviting fish, birds, and animals to share in her life along the river, keeping all in balance.

Unfortunately, with the coming of white people, most of the women river guardians had disappeared and my old friend was one of the last. But she believed that with the pollution of the river would come a return to the old ways, where people of the native tradition would teach the invaders to respect once again the waters and life of the river. She believed that the Europeans would not act until it was almost too late, which is now being seen in the panic over the blue-green algae in this part of Australia that is causing the water of the major river system to go stagnant, due mainly to chemical fertilizers washed off the land into the rivers.

In her cave by the river, this old woman was holding the old ways and teaching respect for them. This experience led me to understand that I had a choice to make between staying there, and living as her people live, to learn the ancient lore, or returning to the land of my own ancestors and meeting with my own tribal people. I now believe that if all white Australians could go back to visit their own country, hear the stories and the songs and relate to the land, they would understand how Aboriginal Australians feel about their country.

My sense of feeling out of place in Australia, along with a sudden inheritance a year or two later, helped me to decide to travel to Britain, my ancestral place, and to spend some time living in my tribal country. I immediately felt at home in Britain and at one with the ancient sacred sites, identifying with the Celtic culture in particular, and the ancient Goddess religion of Europe. From women such as Monica Sjöö I understood the ancient tradition of women and the land, so long hidden from women in Western mainstream culture. From Annie Macloed on Lewis I understood the long tradition of my ancestors from the time of the Goddess, through Celtic culture and the Viking invasions and the strict rule of the Church of Scotland. The old ways were still there in the person of Annie Macloed, who sent me out into the landscape and talked with me of the ancient ways, the Sleeping Beauty Mountain and the moon times.

Coming back to Australia in 1985, I felt a strong pull to go to the Central Desert around Ayers Rock. Initially, I planned a week's holiday but found myself staying there for almost a year. I worked as a cook in one of the old motels near the rock, and spent much of my spare time wandering in the desert landscape drawing. From Aboriginal women, Pitjantjajara people of the Mutjulu community, I learned the unique subtle beauty of the place, to observe exquisite delicate plant and the unique animal life that had adapted in remarkable ways to the desert life.

The conditions that Aboriginal people were living in shocked my middle-class complacency beyond belief. People live in third-world conditions at a major tourist site, while right next door motels provide comfortable beds, abundant food, and alcohol for tourists who come to take photographs of the "quaint natives" living in unbelievable poverty conditions. It stirred all my guilt about being a European Australian living off the fat of the land stolen from these people. Time spent with traditional Aboriginal people can alter one's perceptions considerably.

Among Aboriginal people in traditional situations, there are some who have escaped the ravages of alcohol or petrol sniffing or the general hopelessness of their situation. Some of the old men and quite a few of the women still hold fast to the old ways. Powerful women still work ceremonies around special sites in the area, performing initiations for young people, abundance, and ritual healings for people and the land. The special places for spirit children waiting to be born, caves where sexual magic was taught and performed, and sites where the oldest mysteries of life were taught still hold their power, regenerated through ritual. Both men and women still work at sacred sites to counteract the damage perpetrated by tourists, white Australians, and overseas visitors looking for the sense of spirit so sadly lacking in their own culture.

There were occasions when I was fortunate to talk with women who recognized that I had teachings from another sacred place. Once when there was a need for rain, women spoke of how they knew that my country had lots of rain. They spoke of how they now needed some of that rain at Uluru, although not as much as in my country. It seemed that my presence there at that particular time, with my personal links to Hebridean weather and singing, was to help with ceremony at Uluru to invoke the spirits of water, resulting in spectacular thunderstorms with a couple of days rain, enough to fill waterholes and underground springs.

Rain at Ayers Rock is something marvelous to behold. Waterfalls tumble over the surface, disappearing into one cave and emerging out of another. Myriad rainbows come and go, so quickly. Water on the surface turns the Rock a deep chocolate brown, or silver when the sun is reflected off the surface. Without the rain, the Rock is a rich red ochre color, in vibrant contrast with the intensely blue sky, which sets up optical effects in the shimmering heat that occasionally allow one to see it as a great pulsating organ—like a heart beating. Other times the surface appears to be alive, to be moving like thousands of writhing serpents.

Old women with "secret bags," drawstring bags which they always carry containing stones, feathers, and crystals, perform healing ceremonies. They will sing and touch the body of the patient or smear the skin of the affected area with goanna fat charged by the power of healing crystals. Patterns painted onto stones or wooden sticks and onto the body itself can produce powerful responses in a patient that defy the rational explanations of Western medicine.

When I left the Central Desert to return to Britain for a year, I was given a long wooden digging stick by the women of Ayers Rock. There was a sense that places in Britain needed to be linked with Australia through the knowledge of women. The digging stick traveled with me to London and then up to

Oxford, where I stayed with a friend who was taking care of a house for visiting Tibetan lamas, helping them acclimate to Western culture. After I left Oxford, I realized that I had left the digging stick at my friend's house. A week or two later when I returned for the stick, my friend told me it had been in the shrine room, where it had been blessed by a number of visiting lamas. From Oxford it went to Callanish in the Hebrides where Annie Macloed and Jill Smith kept it when I returned to Australia. It continues to reside there, bridging the cultures.

One of the major focuses for ritual at Callanish on Lewis is the lunar standstill which occurs every 18.6 years (see Jill Smith's piece "A Woman and a Mountain"). At the lunar standstill the moon appears to sit on a mountain that is viewed from the stone circle at Callanish, giving the mountain a silver glow, which explains its name Sithean Airghid, "Silver Maiden." Local stories say that when this occurs the land and all life is regenerated.

The last lunar standstill was in September, 1987. I was living in Adelaide, South Australia at the time. I had booked a ticket to return to Scotland for the standstill to be part of the event at Callanish. In late July, I received a strong intuitive message that I should not return to Scotland, but that instead I should go to Broome in Western Australia. For a while I ignored this and continued plans to go back to the U.K., but the message became so strong that I decided to make the journey to Broome.

In August that year an event known as the Harmonic Convergence occurred heavily sponsored by the New Age movement from the U.S.A., getting lots of publicity here in Australia. The lining up of planets was said to create a harmony of energies that would give the Earth a strong energy charge, altering mass consciousness. Organizers were urging those of spiritual inclination to gather at sacred sites and to perform simultaneous meditation rituals at that time.

Here in Australia, a big gathering was being promoted at Ayers Rock. From my contacts there, I had heard that the Aboriginal people were strongly opposed to strangers moving into their sacred place, ignorant of the forces which govern the site at all times and imposing rituals and ideas from other places and cultures. Unfortunately, "enlightened" New Agers were ignoring Aboriginal protests and some actually desecrated the site against the wishes of the guardians, the traditional people. I found it interesting that the sponsors of the Harmonic Convergence would be so ignorant of the lunar standstill, happening a month later in September. I read this as yet another example of dominant patriarchal insensitivity to this area of the mysteries (that is Women's Mysteries), ignoring it as unimportant.

My instincts at this time led me across the Nullabor Plain from Adelaide to Perth, then north up the western coast, with a stop at Monkey Mia to play with the dolphins. It was a day before the full moon and, although I had another day of travel before me to reach Broome, I felt I should stay another day with the dolphins. When finally I arrived in Broome, on the day of the full moon, I discovered that it was festival time. Japanese pearl fishermen living in Broome were celebrating a full moon festival dedicated to a Shinto Pearl Moon Goddess. Also at this time in Broome was a phenomena known as the Stairway to the Moon. Everyone was excited about it but it took a while to find someone who could explain it to me. I discovered it was important that I be on the shores of Roebuck Bay that night.

I looked for a camping site to pitch my tent and found a good spot on the edge of Roebuck Bay; I then realized I was camped on the spot for viewing Stairway to the Moon. On the full moon in September (that is closest to the equinox it also happens at March equinox) the low tide is so low that the whole bay empties of water. As the moon rises, it shines across the wet sand of Roebuck Bay, creating a silver reflection which, as viewed from my campsite, looked like a shining path or stairway leading across the bay to the edge of the moon itself.

With all these coincidences falling together I began to realize why I was in Broome rather than Callanish. As the moon rose that evening I set up a ritual meditation at the entrance of my tent, a shrine with a photo and stone from Callanish, a stone from Ayers Rock, and another photo given to me before I left Adelaide by a friend who had just returned from a trip to Easter Island. While this friend had no real conscious interest in sacred sites or rituals, he felt he should give me this photo of one of the stone carvings of the Bird Man of Easter Island next to a Christian image of a saint. On the back of the photo, he had drawn a map of the island, marking all the major sacred sites. I'd taken the photo on the trip with me, not really knowing why.

As I sat watching the moonrise, I was conscious of Jill Smith and Annie Macloed and other friends at Callanish preparing for the lunar standstill. My meditation was focused on the moon and its energy entering the Earth at Callanish and also there in Broome touching the land to produce the Stairway. Suddenly, I was aware of being high above the Earth, looking down to see the silver light of the moon touching the Earth in the northern hemisphere, like a fire igniting a fuse. A spark of silver light moved along pathways south into Britain and across the planet entering Australia at north west where I was sitting. I saw my physical body glow silver and felt a powerful energy hit me and then move into the Earth along the energy lines southeast through Ayers Rock, leaving the land in south eastern Australia, and then cross the Pacific Ocean to Easter Island. It happened all in a matter of seconds, sometimes I was viewing it from above and then I was on the Earth feeling the force in my physical body. Perhaps I had been drawn to Broome as a bridge between the ancient teachings of my own ancestors at Callanish and the need to link with the land of my birth and its ancient teachings in Australia. The whole planet needed the energy of that lunar standstill and I was in the right place at the right time to make the link between the cultures, both of which have a living contemporary awareness of the energy forces of the Earth and their cosmic connections. By following my instincts, I had been part of an amazing experience of connection.

An interesting footnote to this experience occurred when I returned to Adelaide a few weeks later and spoke on the phone to my mother, who lives in New South Wales. She thought that something had happened to me, as she'd had a vision on the night of the full moon. My relationship with my mother had not been very close and we have never discussed my spiritual life, but it seemed that on the full moon she had just gone to bed when she saw me appear at the foot of the bed, dressed in a white robe, glowing as if from an inner light. Mother said that I appeared to be very much at peace, showing a serene smile, and she thought it meant that I was dead. She had no idea of my work at Callanish or any of my ritual work, but what she saw gave me a powerful verification of what had happened to me at Broome, at the same time giving me a sense of connection with the line of my mothers—the women of the moon, my ancestral line through my mother's Welsh Celtic ancestors.

Over the years since these experiences at Australian sites, I haven't traveled much, but have settled in Adelaide, South Australia, working as an artist and curating exhibitions of Aboriginal Art as well as that of contemporary women artists, working from a spiritual perspective. There is a growing interest in Australia in Celtic culture, mythology, and related arts and I have been teaching courses and workshops, particularly about the women in Celtic myth—Brighid, Scathach, Macha, Rhiannon, and Ceridwen, among others. What I hope to do with my teaching and my art work is to study the traditional cultures of British Australians so that we can try to build awareness, within our own ancestral memory, of our relationship with the land, with other life forms, and with each other. Between the different cultures we can develop a shared awareness of the spiritual harmony of all life, expressed in symbols and stories. Although the form may be different between cultures, we are all touching the same essence of awareness, the same human needs, the same mythological themes and symbols.

My own unease at writing this piece comes from feeling Celtic and living in a land with which I have no ancestral bonds. Australian Aboriginal people have taught me much about their relationship with this country, and I feel an understanding of their bond in terms of my own connection with the lands of my ancestral culture in Britain. My experience of sacred sites in Australia is as a Celt with ancestral memories of my own traditional country. What I speak of in experiencing the land in Australia is as an outsider with a parallel experience, which can never adequately express the personal experience that an Aboriginal woman has in this land. However, I was born here, as were my parents and their parents. (How long does it take to be of the land of one's birth?) When I am in Britain, I still feel connected to Australia, while in Australia I have a powerful sense of not belonging, a yearning for my ancestral place, that sense of longing embodied in the Welsh word *Hiraeth,* a chronic Celtic condition.

So here I am, a woman of the land belonging to two places and torn between them. Perhaps the lesson is that when one is bonded to the land, it doesn't matter whether it is one's own place or not, so much as the awareness of being part of the whole Earth, registering one's place as being wherever one is at the time. All places are sacred places. In the times ahead perhaps we will all join together with a sense of wholeness, and cultural boundaries will dissolve. The shared experience of special places will flow together, creating a bond across the Earth, a network of love and healing, nurturing the whole planet into new life.

GOREE ISLAND: THE BEGINNING OF MY AFRICAN ODYSSEY

MANY SACRIFICES WERE MADE so that I could pursue my dream of being initiated in Africa. This story is written in memory of Ella Barnes and the ancestors of the people who passed through Goree Island. Egun re o! Egun re o! Egun re o!

Eshu, Crossroad's Guardian, Messenger between Humans and Spirit, open the road to more knowledge about the ancestors and their lives, for each person who reads this work. Aché.

I stood on the Air Afrique plane looking out a window at the approaching sun of a new day. "Dreams can come true," I thought, as we flew toward our first African destination—Dakar, Senegal. I traveled with Luisah Teish and her husband, David Wilson, my spiritual elders, mentors, and friends, and two other people. David and I were going to Africa seeking initiation into the mysteries of the Ifa religion of the Yoruba people of Nigeria.

Oshun, the deity of love, art, creativity, sensuality, sexuality and fertility is my personal deity. When I first realized, through divination, that initiation was on my path of destiny, I began to dream about going through that process in Oshogbo, Nigeria. That is Oshun's place in the world. That is where the original source of her power, the Oshun river, flows. And although initiations are carried out here in this hemisphere regularly, I wanted to be initiated in her forest by the Oshun river.

I got a photograph of Oshun's altar in her forest in Oshogbo and placed it on my bedroom wall next to a map of Africa. Every morning when I woke up and every night before I went to sleep I focused my attention on that wall. I visualized myself there in Oshogbo, in the altar area, going through my initiation, and the river running freely nearby.

As an African American female this trip was also important to me because I was going to the motherland, the place where the African part of my heritage began. I have no family stories passed down through generations of ancestors about what tribe my people come from, nor any idea who my people were in Africa. So all of Africa was important to me. I couldn't wait to see the land, gaze upon the people, or taste the food. National Geographic wouldn't have anything up on me anymore.

Standing at the window, the plane coming out of the dark of night as the morning sun waits for us, I feel my heart fill with joy. I look at the distant clouds laid about the sky full of promise. I wait for my first sight of land. Slowly we begin to descend and there it is, Africa—the motherland!

We are home—Dakar, Senegal. It is the first soil of this continent we will touch. We will rest and begin to acclimate ourselves to Africa here. As we stand on the top step of the plane looking out at the airport building and surrounding terrain, I observe that the military is everywhere. Looking. Checking each passenger as they walk from the plane to the building. Within our party there will be no touching or kissing of the ground by any of us of African ancestry. Our African heritage is still strong within us but the unexpected military presence makes us restrained.

Inside the airport, we each confront our culture shock, as things are stark in color, giving off little energy. We proceed through customs quickly and easily. Then it's out into the hustle and bustle of Dakar. We step out of the airport with our luggage and immediately twenty to thirty men surround us, offering their services, their cabs, their information, or begging for money. Jabber. Jabber. Shout. Attitude. We are like lambs led to the slaughter, backed into the outer wall of the airport.

"Non," I respond when asked for money.

A little albino girl approaches Teish and I, saying, "One dollar lady. One dollar lady." I watch as Teish looks at the child and stops her physical recoil in mid-response. Together we search for some change and finally gift the child with some money. It is not enough for her and she demands more. Her face covered with the sores of leprosy, her eyes walling back in her head, the child reminds me of the ads on American television about the suffering people in Africa. We find more money. As this vignette is happening, chaos continues around us. I move from the wall in an attempt to get some air and escape the enclosed, suffocating environment.

"What's your name?" a soft, smooth voice asks. I turn and catch a glimpse of a dark, handsome, smiling man. Home training causes me to answer quickly but so that my name is not heard. French and broken English are hurled at us, as bartering for our transportation becomes relentless.

Finally we secure the services of two taxi drivers for eleven American dollars each. Luggage is placed in the trunk and then in the back seat of the taxi I'll share with one of my companions. I get in our taxi, watching as the cab carrying Teish and company leaves. Our taxi jumps out on the road moving eighty miles an hour! We are a mile down the road when I realize we passed the other cab back at the airport.

Our taxi continues to move fast. Our driver looks in his rearview mirror and makes a quick right turn onto a dirt road. Immediately all my sensors go up. Where are we going? I scream inside. As if hearing my inner dialogue, my companion says, "It's alright." But I'm not so sure we're safe yet. My inner fear is complemented by the threats of extreme speed, semi-reckless driving, and no lanes marked on the road in either direction.

Through a maze of twists and turns we move on quickly. I look in amazement as we travel in the streets of a housing area in the desert, followed by rural land, filled with what I assume are growing vegetables, and into the city proper. As we travel I look at how colorfully the women are dressed, the long robes of the men, and the wide eyed children. And then the Novotel Hotel looms ahead, up on a hill overlooking the city.

Our driver stops in front of the door. A cart is brought for our luggage. I get out of the taxi and gaze downhill looking for the other cab. We pay our driver the agreed-upon eleven American dollars and he balks. It is not enough for him. Inside the hotel lobby all calm is broken as a shouting match ensues between my companion and the taxi driver. A crowd of people gather from the commotion, as my inner restraint snaps and I begin to pace back and forth across the lobby.

Where is everyone else? Are they safe? Will they get here soon? Back and forth I walk, worried and wondering. The argument in the lobby subsides as the hotel staff talk with our driver and help to settle the dispute. Encouraged to fill out my registration card by my companion, I say, "No, I'm not doing nuthin', 'til everybody else arrives." I look up at the sound of a motor and suddenly everyone else arrives with a wild story to tell.

After leaving the airport, their driver had driven them past the airport twice. From there he traveled through people's backyards and got stuck on a thirty-foot-high cement embankment. As half the taxi teetered over the embankment, everyone left the vehicle, except Teish, who remained sitting in the rear. The driver, along with the local citizenry, watched in astonished disbelief as David and our other male companion pulled the taxi back from the possibly fatal drop, got back in the taxi, and were ready to go. But now we were all together in Novotel Hotel. We check in, get our rooms, and head for a soothing bath and sleep.

Upon awakening hunger pushes all of us to the hotel restaurant. Succulent food awaits us—lamb, chicken, and fish. After our meal Teish and David go off together and I am left with our other traveling companions.

Sitting and talking we become aware of another group of Black Americans in the restaurant. As they prepare to go I approach them, exchange greetings, and invite them to talk with us. They are four women traveling together. Eagerly they share with us some of their experiences from the Pink Island to Goree Island to the Gambia. As they continue to talk, I go find Teish, knowing she needs to talk to these women. Senegal with its veiled and clitless women has been too much for her already.

Teish agrees to come and talk. When we return our group has grown with the addition of two Senegalese men—Jerra, who agrees to be our guide the next day, and Adu, a magazine publisher.

Jerra, who was at the airport when we left, tells us he is happy to see that Teish and company got to the hotel safely. "That man who was driving your taxi was crazy and stole the taxi to get the money for himself," he says. We all look at each other and laugh. This piece of information adds new drama to the entire story. We sigh and thank the Orishas for protecting us.

We continue talking long into the night and before retiring we decide to talk again before each American group departs Novotel Hotel.

The next day our traveling group eats breakfast while we plan out our day. The men have an outing of their own to complete, while Teish and I go shopping at one of the local grocery stores. We decide that we will all go to Goree Island together in the afternoon. The men leave and we dress to go shopping.

Teish looks very African, clothed in a long African print dress and head-wrap. I'm dressed in jeans and a T-shirt, very American. But we're both covered up as Senegal is an Islamic country. A couple of the women from the night before join us and we walk down the hill from the hotel past the local vendors, who call to us.

The women tell us the store we seek is another block and a turn to the left. We continue to walk together as more street vendors move in offering all kinds of trinkets, cassette tapes, and make-up. We get bunched together. Suddenly I feel a hand inching into my pocket. "Non! Stay away from me!" I declare loudly. The man backs away from me, muttering as we move quickly along, my sense of security and freedom shattered. In my mind everyone now has the potential to harm me.

We pass a man begging on the street. He has no hands. One of the women walking with us tells us to give him nothing, as he was probably a thief or pick-pocket. In Senegal they attempt to fit the punishment to the crime. The first time a thief is caught one of his hands is cut off. If it happens a second time they cut off the second hand. "Sometimes it's hard for some people to learn to not steal," I think.

Arriving at the store we tell the women good-bye and go in to shop. We gather the items we want and return to the hotel without incident. Once up in our room, we pull out Teish's tarot cards for guidance. Jealous women, delayed journey, gifts that are bribes, and change are constant themes. Information follows information, until we can't stand anymore. We decide to go down to the pool until we leave for the island.

Goree Island is located twenty minutes away off the coast of Dakar. To reach the island, one has to ride on a ferryboat. Originally discovered in 1444 by the Portuguese commander Denis Diaz, Goree Island became important during the years of the slave trade.

The Portuguese used Goree Island after 1492, as part of a network between Lisbon and New World ports in Brazil and the West Indies. In 1617, the Netherlands bought the island after using it for 29 years, and built two forts. The French took the island in the latter part of 1677. Although the English would acquire La Goree twice, once in 1693 and again between 1758–1763, French culture dominated the island.

Once the slave trade began, slave ships stopped at Goree Island to take on provisions for the Middle Passage. Many times while ships anchored at the island, the Africans who would become slaves in other parts of the world were kept in cells on the grounds. And then they were taken through the Last Door back to the ship.

The Last Door was the portal through which each person walked as they were taken to the ship that would carry them to other places in the world to be slaves. For many it was their last sight of their motherland.

Standing on the ferry, the island stood before us. Jerra, our guide, talked about the geography of the area, Senegalese culture, and puberty rites for females to help pass the time during the journey.

As we disembark the ferry, I am struck by the quiet and empty feeling of the island. There are people here, yet they are a mute background to the silent buildings all around. Jerra leads us up stone steps, towards what is called Maison des Enclaves (House of Slaves) courtyard.

From the courtyard, we walk into a small room, the slave office, we are told. On one wall hang iron balls and chains, and on another iron neck collars. I reach out to touch these shackles of bondage and I am inwardly moved by the coldness of the metal and the weight of them. They are bigger and heavier than I had ever imagined. I am carried upon a wave of compassion as I feel the energy of the former fettered slaves surging through the chains. And they were used on humans!

I turn and look at the posters across the room. Jerra tells us about the posters as he recites the history of the island and of the millions of people who passed through Goree to lives as slaves in the "New World."

The tour guide rises from his desk and begins to deliver a talk about the island in French. Many things he says are repeats of things Jerra has told us. As the guide speaks I find my sense of right is stretched beyond my concepts of right and wrong. I look around the room at all of these implements used to enslave generations of my people. And I begin to weep over the lives lost, the senseless cruel acts perpetuated against them. I cry, lost in a deep inescapable sadness.

I go to David seeking comfort. I hear another sob and look up into the eyes of an African man across the room. We look at each other and move into each others arms, crying together over this heartbreaking rape of our motherland—each person taken away from Africa robbed her of some source of knowledge, change, and kindred.

It is time to continue the tour. We break apart, each returning to our companions, looking at each other, feeling the pain of the separation of our people. We move to the men's room, where men were punished for trying to escape. Next is the women's raping room, followed by the babies' room. And in each room I hear something—the moaning of the men, the screams of the women, the crying of the babies.

The silence room sits to the right, before turning the corner left towards the Last Door. The silence room is small, built under stairs leading up to another floor of rooms. It is built so one can only squat or sit on the cold ground or lie in a fetal position, but not stand up. This was a place built to punish and break the spirit of its inhabitants. And I cry. More and more I cry.

We turn the corner and walk to the Last Door. We peer out of the door, before stepping out onto the rocks below. We look out to the Atlantic as our ancestors did. I imagine the scene with ships waiting in the distance to take all of them away. The Last Door, the first nail in a nightmare-filled coffin.

It is here that all of us of African descent gather to light a cigar and pour libation to begin the ceremony honoring our ancestors. I stand beside Teish as she begins the Moyuba, a prayer to honor the spirits of Goree Island. I am given a chance to speak and pray for those ancestors whose lives were forever changed by coming to the island and were lost in the Middle Passage. I pray and ask for their strength, courage, and ability to survive, as I begin this new phase of my life. We finish, and do what our ancestors never could do as we walk back through the Last Door.

We cross the courtyard and leave the area to go to one of the sitting areas outside the small restaurants on the island. Once again I see the African man from the slave office. We smile at each other and he comes over to join us. Speaking French, with Jerra interpreting, he talks to me. He speaks of his frustration of not being able to talk directly to one another. "Because our people were separated so long ago, today we share no common language," he says.

I hold up one hand and haltingly say, "Je m'appele Uzuri Amini." He smiles and introduces himself, telling me he is Senegalese and on vacation. We talk a little more and then return to our friends. We can't leave the island yet as the ferryboat is behind schedule.

As we wait I pull into myself, thinking about my visit to the island, the ways in which the energy and spirits here touched me. I am ready to return to the hotel.

The ferryboat arrives and we all line up to find a seat. Once on board and underway, I look at the island until it is a speck upon the horizon. I know that one trip to the island has changed me and given me renewed respect for my ancestors. And now I will have an ancestral story to tell to my grandchildren about Africa.

That night as I fall asleep, the day washes over me and I find myself again on the island. I am there, standing in the whipping room. A room with only one window . . .

. . . A one window cell is continuously buffeted by forceful winds. Pleading voices carry through the air. The wind blows against the sun-covered stone walls, an invisible fist fighting to liberate the people. Just a breeze.

It was just a memory—the wind, driven through the window. Air to cool hot, cramped bodies. A breeze that does not relieve.

It is night now. Time has slipped away into a deep nothingness. The wind can be heard moving through the night, relentless in its continual scouring of the land. Can the land ever be free of the memory of betrayal?

"Oh ancient wind, born before the first mother, the first father, the first child, weave with the dark places of the sky, as your melodic song dances between the trees."

Listen. Are you sure it's the wind? I hear thousands of human voices blended into one, singing and moaning through the night. Spirits, grieving the ancestors sold away from everything they held sacred. Ancestors, on Goree Island, who walked through the "Last Door."

Iba se gbogbo Egun Goree Island.

What is remembered lives!

Eshu, thank you for opening the road to the sharing of this part of my spiritual journey with others. Aché.

In writing this piece I got information from *Black Genesis: African Roots* by John Devere & Jurgen Vollmer (St. Martin's Press, New York, 1980).

This is an excerpt from a work-in-progress about my journey to Africa to be initiated. Also, as all things begin and end with Eshu, in my spiritual tradition, so it is with this work.

NORTH, CENTRAL, AND SOUTH AMERICA

$$\overset{\displaystyle =}{\frown}$$

WUTI AXIS

Wupatki is an Anasazi ruins complex built around a very unusual feature—a blowhole that breathes like the entrance to a cave system. The ruins of Wupatki recall a living tradition in which our own bodies reflect that of the earth, sending our breath into the storms and drawing it back again, just as the caverns inhale after the storm to begin the breathing cycle again. Since the process is one of creation of fluid waters, this image series is titled *Wuti Axis* from the Hopi Indian word "Wuti" meaning female.

The Hopi Indians are the living descendents of the Anasazi and in their cosmology the clouds are born inside the earth. The innermost realms of lightning are also inside the earth. From the deep dark cavern solitude, the sounds of vibration echo and resound, setting the breath in motion. The moon draws the mists out into the atmosphere.

The Hopi view corn, the staff of life, as their children—needing to be tended and sung to. As the corn grows with its long leaves spiraling out from the center of the earth, the indigenous mind gives the process of emergence the symbol of the spiral.

Wuti Axis was created from S-VHS video images and still photographs. These were edited and composed using a prerelease version of Altamira Composer Software Program on a DOS-based IBM computer. I use concepts of the ancient world on the electronic systems of today to send a message from the future to the present. Electricity appears to be our slave but we have forgotten our source: The Great Matrix of lightning and fertility cycles.

Joan Price, "Gate of Transformation"

Joan Price, "Flower in the Cave"

Joan Price, "The Corn Plants Are the Children"

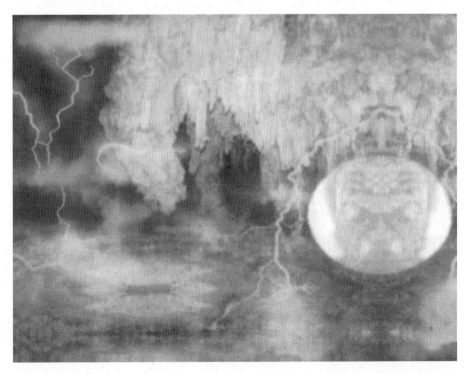

Joan Price, "Source of Clouds"

CINDY A. PAVLINAC

DEATH VALLEY JOURNEY: A DAUGHTER'S SEARCH FOR RECONCILIATION

MY FATHER DIED when I was nineteen, nine months after I ran away from home to attend college. Seven years later I wished to observe the anniversary of his death and shocked myself to realize I did not remember the exact date he died. Searching for my copy of his death certificate, my casual inquiry became a compelling demand for action to consciously mourn and to deliberately end mourning. My personal remembrance blossomed into a self-reflective journey to honor my father's memory, reconnect with my ancestors, transform the distress of abandonment, define my role as a woman artist/healer, and proclaim myself as a daughter of this American continent.

The remembrance impulse began as an image to spend a night alone in Death Valley, fasting, praying, waiting, conjuring my father's ghost from within me to say the good-byes I never had a chance to say in life. I felt a physical need to understand profoundly my role on Earth, and sought to ground myself with the teachings I had learned from American Indian medicine people. They showed me respect for the land with their sense of sacred limits, consequences, nature, and community. They taught me to focus intention and how to behave, pray, sing, thank, and giveaway. Through ceremony I touched the matrix of cosmic order and glimpsed the ancient integrated world of ancestors and relationship to place. In the macrocosm of ancient American archetypal landscapes, the Desert is the Determiner. I wanted the toughest desert landscape I could drive to from my house in northern California to help push me through this opening threshold. Death Valley leapt to mind. If I could touch bottom in the lowest point in the western hemisphere, perhaps I could rise renewed, soaring to new heights. I also chose Death Valley because of its reputation for swallowing pilgrims.

Some of my earliest memories are pictures from family vacations: a great white expanse of sand, seagulls as big as me, people swimming out into green water and not returning. My lifelong hunger to travel was fueled by books of secret and forbidden cultures, and ultimately formed a quest—to claim as my birthright the ancestral knowledge held encoded in the sacred landscapes of ancient civilizations. A personal relationship to land seems fundamental to our psyches. Acting out ritual remembrance evokes deep participation and immersion in the landscape. The physical location is my primary concern when I create a ritual. Once I recognized my need to go to Death Valley, I trusted that a ceremony would emerge from the land itself. Transformation could come when I emptied myself and opened to being held in the land. The austerity of the desert landscape dissolves pain of separation, incarnation, living, and loving. By immersing myself wholly in a specific landscape, I evoke the potential for transmutation into a timeless landscape. I left for Death Valley on a May Sunday morning.

I park the car at 2 AM, seven years to the hour of his death. The moon had passed its first quarter, like my life. With a woolen cape I had made from a rummage sale coat, a pine box of feathers, and a wooden flute, I walk out into the black cold silence to meet my father. Crossing a dry riverbed, I huddle by a talking bush, half expecting it to burst into flames. There is no shelter in this harsh landscape from the wind, from the cold, from the night, from myself. Listening intently with every fiber of my longing I realize my father is not here. He is not anywhere. He is dead. All that I would meet in the desert is that which I have brought.

So I sit through the night watching stars arc overhead and think of him. Burning some sage, I remember how his five brothers hurt to see the youngest of them die first. The wind accompanied me as I played his double-flute from Yugoslavia. I imagine conversation with them, the brothers, sons of immigrants, wishing them well. None of them have spoken to me since the funeral and I am unprepared to suddenly know another brother has died. My grief includes their grief and all that we will never share, all that I will never know about who they were, all they will never tell me, all the thick silences and unspoken stories of their vanished world. Overhead, Mars crosses the dark sky as I ask for strength in my life, guidance, wisdom, grace. The Pleiades sparkle and I think of my mother's side of the family, aunts and grandmothers. They arrive to greet me one by one and depart into thin forgetfulness. The women's threads and stories of remembrance remain strong, whirling back into the mists of time much farther than the men's, perhaps all the way back. Two long bright strands of hundreds of people who never met each other meet in me. Wanting to give an intimate offering of myself, I pull out a few strands of my long hair and let the wind take them one at a time. Staring at the stars, I am an empty watcher in the night.

The sky began to lighten hours before I expected. Dawn swallowed the eastern stars as Mars and Saturn set in the west; the young warrior and the wise old man who ate his children. As the sun broke the horizon I stiffly stood to thank the Directions and the land host. Sometime in the night while dialoguing with the memory of my father we spoke of hair. I had always worn mine long and untrimmed. Any thought of cutting it brought to mind the story of Samson and his lost strength when his hair was cut, so I had refrained. The image of long blonde hair was an ideal of feminine beauty for my father and I now saw that I had kept my hair to please him, long after he could appreciate it. To truly claim my entire self I would have to eat my hair, to internalize my beauty and step out from behind my self-created veil.

Returning to the car I drank some water and drove on into the mountains. To help focus my intention before coming to the desert I had made a prayer arrow out of a stick and shells, feathers, pebbles with holes, and trinkets all wrapped with brightly colored yarn. Climbing 5,100 feet by late afternoon, I looked for the place to plant it. The Mountaintop is the place of giveaway. Walking up a dry wash I found a quiet rock with a commanding view. Setting down the prayer arrow laden with gifts and wishes, I gathered a fistful of bangs and severed my hair with my Boy Scout knife. Holding up the thirty two-inch shank of long hair in the wind I shuddered with the irrevocability of the act. Air chilled the top of my head. Shaking, I tied the hair onto the stick with bright thread and felt a resounding shock at what I had done. I had scalped myself. I had declared myself individuated, unique, visible. I cut another fistful of hair from the other side and added it to the stick. Planting the arrow in the rocky ground with sage and prayers, I became the offering. Wind lifted my hair softly and it danced around the medicine stick. It was alive and it was me, yet it was no longer mine. For a moment I thought I was the prayer arrow with my hair billowing in the wind on a mountain in the sunset. Yet I could stand and walk away. The last rays of the sun ignited the hovering hair and I said goodbye.

Returning to the car in twilight, I drove down the mountain like a hyper-charged demon. I was singing and shaking and crying and laughing and absolutely solid in my intent to cut off all the rest of my hair to claim the strength I found here. By embodying my story and cutting my hair to within a quarter inch all over my head I would make myself into a medicine offering and visual reminder of this event. Relieved of extra weight, my spine stretched taller, straighter and the euphoric energy release continued for several weeks as I lingered in an altered, timeless state of consciousness. Whenever I looked in a mirror or chanced to see my reflection I was forced to alter and update my inner picture of myself. My face no longer hid and my peripheral vistas opened up for the first time in my life. People approached me, intrigued, attracted, asking what had happened to me. They told me their most intimate stories of transformation and private wishes for healing. I found myself in a new role, not only surprisingly visible but a potent witness to friends and strangers. I had wanted to remember. I had wanted to change. It worked.

Through a particular honoring of a particular death I had sought to inte-grate the unique braid of my existence with those of my ancestors. What I found was a new relationship between inner and outer landscapes. By beginning to dialogue with the land, I touched the rich tapestry of creation and renewal. By physically enacting a rite of passage with self-sacrifice and celebration, I con-secrated myself as an individual woman, as an artist, as a survivor to the heal-ing continuity of the sacred.

Ritual, art, and sanctuaries were our ancestors' external memory reservoirs of encoded symbolic storage. The land reflects and remembers all alterations to its natural forms. We modern people no longer know who we are because we've forgotten where we've come from. Myth-making is soul-making. Through remem-brance, alignment, opening to the songlines we can use the power and gifts of our heritage. There is a place within me obsessed with travel to holy locations, a place with such intense need to linger within fields of sacredness that I become ill if I am too long away. Perhaps the the root of all sickness is homesickness, disconnection. During a recent nomadic Christmas, my profound alienation miraculously shifted to a warm glow of belonging and responsibility when I realized the entire world was my true home. I continue to travel as a pilgrim, seeking sacred places, and returning with offerings of photographs, stories, and songs, but I now carry within me a deep, ancient peace and essence of home. My inner soul landscape is fed, refined, caressed by visiting external sacred landscapes. My photography of prehistoric sanctuaries invites seeing with mythic levels of intelligence to glimpse a symbolic spiritual landscape created by our distant cousins. Even the pictures speak to our inner landscapes.

Our age holds before us the possibility, challenge, and demand of global citizenship and planetary stewardship. Each of us must find our own application of our life's gifts. Through creating our art, telling our stories, singing our prayers, and serving our communities from within fields of sacredness, we renew the ancient promise of our native sacred hearth. By honoring, but not imitating, the teachings of tribal shamanism we can consciously participate in the phenomenon of nontribal shamanic experience to regain the mythic and allow the sacred to emerge, enrich, and permeate our lives. Ancient tribal shamanism can instruct modern urban shamanism. All the beings who have fed us, dreamed us, sung us now wait in hope, wait to see what we have learned, and what we will do. By walking through Death Valley I transformed my memories, my separateness, my purpose. Listening to the inner landscape draws me to journey through external landscapes, and in my enchantment I discover internal sacredness, balance, harmony, and peace.

ANI WILLIAMS

HER SONG CHANGES EVERYTHING

The earth has come, the earth has come,
It is rising, it is rising,
It is humming, it is humming.
—*Porcupine's song, Northern Cheyenne medicine man*[1]

THE EARTH IS SINGING

EVERY CANYON, MOUNTAIN, and plain, every stream, wood, and meadow has its own unique sound signature, a symphony of sounds sung by the wind and the waters, trees, insects, birds, and animals. The Earth is also singing in inaudible sounds, those beyond our normal human range of hearing, yet these frequencies are still having their effect on all of life. Each element, every species is sounding, and together they form a chorus of tones, a symphony of life energy.

When we remove any part of this chorus—if we as humans alter the natural beauty and form of the Earth, or participate in the destruction of flora or fauna—the natural song of the Earth is altered, and all life forms are affected. Thus, we have changed the natural resonance of our beautiful home planet in a very short span of time, the greatest changes having occurred during this century and the industrial era.

In addition to changing the frequency of our world by altering its form, the opposite is also true: sound has the power to affect and change matter. It is this very theme that we find retold in numerous creation myths of indigenous peoples, and in all the world's great religions we hear of the creative word or sound issuing forth to create the Earth and the heavens, the moment of creation.

The creation myth of the Yavapai Apache tribe of Arizona so poetically describes this sound-creation connection that I include an entire story here. It covers several primary points of this work. First, that the creatress and chantress, first woman of the Yavapai-Apache, Komwidapokuwia, is *listening* to the song of heaven, and then sings for all of life—receiving and then giving the gift of song. Second, her body is made of the heavens; the *celestial and terrestrial integration* empowers her song; she shakes her rattle and everything changes. Because she embraces heaven and earth, there are no limits to her creative potential. Third, she has the courage to stand and sing her songs; she trusts what she hears and speaks for all spiritual life; *her songs are life itself.*

The Song of Kowidapokuwia

Pukmukwana, black stone powder grinding around,
Wove and talked into existence the girl Komwidapokuwia.
She came into existence and sang like this:
In the white morning
In the white morning
The small star in heaven wove.
In the morning, the small morning
It wove and made heaven.
After she had sung a little while, it became
White all over the world.
The girl came forth and stood and sang.
Heaven was used for her body.
She shook her rattle
And from its power it became white
All over the world.
That was White Morning Road.
Pukmukwana had woven and talked
Into existence the girl Komwidapokuwia.
Star powder heaven was used for her body
She came forth and stood and sang:
My talking and singing are life.
I speak for spiritual life
All over the world.
I speak and all the world
Lightens up to heaven.

This is the way I sing
When I listen to the songs of heaven
Small heaven with white circles her chest was woven of,
She sang to make different all the world.
This she sang for the sake of the shamans.
She sang and flowers bloomed in the sky.
This is her way of singing:
My songs were made for the beautiful sky.
My word went out into the sky.
The world stood still.
Everything was still.
My song changed everything.[2]

If we apply this beautiful creation story to our lives, to become more conscious of our role in co-creation, we must first awaken our faculty of listening deeply, to receive. Only then are we capable of giving something of quality to benefit life. And to be able to give, we must also be able to trust what we receive and have the courage to stand and speak for all life. We all have tremendous creative potential in our voices: what we say, the tones we use, and most important, the intention, the thoughts and feelings behind the sounds we project.

In ancient Greece, the Pythagorean schools of sound healing required novices to spend a substantial amount of time purifying the mind and developing compassion before even one tone could be sounded. Thus, the motivation and intention that directed the tones, chants, or music was clear, benevolent, and potent. Sound healer Jonathon Goldman has a wonderful formula that exemplifies this: frequency + intention = healing.[3] The sounds we express have the potential to benefit life greatly or to bring harm or destruction. Just this awareness alone can bring great changes to the quality of life we are creating. All life is resonance — variations of frequency manifesting as all the myriad forms and qualities of creation, colored by our thoughts, feelings, and beliefs.

The late Marija Gimbutas refers to the connection of sound as the creative force:

> In the tale of Er, the concentric spheres of the heavens turn around a spindle, like a vast spindle whorl. Each sphere is associated with a siren (Bird Goddess), who sings its particular note, creating the Music of the Spheres.[4]

Woman as weaver, creatress, and chantress sings the world into existence at the moment of creation, which is now. If we are to survive and continue living on this planet, we need to return to ways of being that support life. We are in a time of great remembering—we are learning from the ancient cultures how to live in harmony with the natural world, to make our lives as a mirror of nature. We are reclaiming our responsibility as co-creators of our current reality, and sound, how we use our voices is an essential key in our role as Keepers of the Earth.

When we surround ourselves with sounds of nature—the wind blowing through the trees, birdsong, waterfalls, ocean waves, or crickets singing at night—we are soothed and healed, comforted by the songs of our mother, the Earth. And who is there to sing back to the Earth—how are we using our voices, one of our greatest tools for creation? The Australian Aboriginal people say that the voice was made for singing. They say that the trees and plants are singing a silent song and all they ask is that we sing back to them.

To listen deeply to the song of the earth, to surround ourselves with natural sounds as much as possible, spending time in nature is to receive a gift of healing. And we can give back with song, in thanksgiving for the bounty and beauty of nature. Sound can become the language of communion, a way of reweaving our connections with wilderness, the natural world, and the sacred and harmonious in ourselves which have become so fragmented and separate from the Earth.

The following refers to the Yaqui tribe of northern Mexico and southern Arizona:

> Yaquis have always believed that a close connection exists among all the inhabitants of the Sonoran desert world in which they live: plants, animals, birds, fishes, even rocks and springs. All of these come together as a part of one living community which Yaquis call the huya ania, the wilderness world. Yaquis regard song as a special language of this community, a kind of lingua franca of the intelligent universe. It is through song that experience with other living things in the wilderness world is made intelligible and accessible to the human community.[5]

And on the other side of the planet, the Australian indigenous people are the oldest living tradition in the world, with over 50,000 years of continuous existence. These highly intuitive and intelligent (in the true sense of intelligence) people must have an incredible connectedness and knowledge of life to have survived for so long! One of their basic understandings is the existence of song in both the manifest and unmanifest realms, or the Dreamtime. Songlines are both the trackways of the ancestors, the people, and the lines of energy that move across the Earth, which must be continuously sung to keep the whole living community alive and well. The Australian Aboriginals consider song knowledge to be as essential to the life of the earth and all living beings as are food, water, air, and sunlight—in fact, without the intelligent use of sound, they say we do not have access to the proper use of the elements that make life possible.

> The definition of a knowledgeable person is the person knowing many songs, for without song knowledge, information about places, laws, correct behavior, healing, food sources, is unavailable.[6]

If, as the Yaqui people say, song is the intelligent language of the universe, and according to our Australian neighbors, the way to access knowledge of life, then song as a way of communing, speaking with other life forms, is a way of healing our separation from nature and each other. It is a way of reweaving the torn fabric of life, the lack of communication between humans and the wilderness world.

RETURN TO THE CIRCLE

The circle as a symbol becomes very important to us all now, representing the feminine consciousness, a return to wholeness. The Earth herself is round, and gives life and a home to all living things. And we, male and female alike, are birthed from the womb of our mother, rounded and nourishing like the Earth. At some point, there comes a time in our lives when we feel the need for change, renewal, a time to return to the sacred circle, the womb, to be nourished, cleansed, and to emerge with a clearer sense of who we are and what we are doing here.

This might take the form of taking time to rest, meditate, or to practice yoga, a return to our own center. Or our quest might take us on a journey to a sacred mountain, a beautiful place in nature, or an ancient temple, a place where pilgrims have journeyed for centuries, a place that has been honored as sacred, a place of origins, of power. Ancient cultures know of this need for renewal and many still practice the varied forms it takes—ceremonies of thanksgiving, sweat lodges for purification, a vision quest or journey into nature for communion and a return to ones center. And of course, celebrations with dance, song, and rhythm to bring the people together with the rest of creation, to honor the turning points in the cycles of the year, always returning to the circle.

In my own times of renewal, I have experienced and used many of these forms: quiet, meditation, time to be with Mother Nature, ritual, ceremony, and journeying to the sacred places of the Earth, to places where there is a sense of a special energy, which is sometimes felt as a profound stillness, and sometimes felt as increased energy and heightened perception. It is on these pilgrimages to sacred places that I began to learn to listen more consciously. I began to hear songs, and chants, and I learned over time to trust these gifts of song as the true gifts they are. I observed how song can increase the life energy of people and places. Through the language of sound, both in listening and then singing or sounding, I was able to access the deep magic and messages of sacred places. Often a strong teaching has emerged from a stone circle, a pyramid, a sacred grove of old trees, or sometimes visiting magical realms in dreams.

Perhaps one of the best ways to illustrate some of the gifts and teachings I have received from the sacred places of the Earth is to share some stories and dreams. Storytelling, songs, and dreams are some of our oldest ways of communicating knowledge and truth. According to the Australian Aboriginal women, ancient songs and rituals that have been forgotten, or new ones that are appropriate to add to the repertoire, can come in dreams. An ancestor may come to give a dream teaching along with the associated dance, song, myth, and ceremonial design to use. And since the traditions of many of our bloodlines have been broken, and knowledge lost, dreams and intuition can reconnect us with missing pieces of our own ancestral stories. As long as we have our stories that can be told to our children—songs that we may sing together, poetry, art, and dance—we have magic, creativity, and inspiration; we are truly alive.

WEAVER WOMAN

The Navajo, or Diné (meaning The People) of the southwestern United States, honor Spider Woman as the creatress of life. Most of the Diné women are excellent weavers and learn their craft from a very early age. They see the loom and the working area surrounding it as sacred, and therefore keep it in a state of order and cleanliness. They invite Great Spirit into their weaving and are beautiful mirrors of Spider Grandmother, creating beauty with design and color, sometimes dreaming it first. In the creation story, Spider Woman is not only a master weaver, but holds the sacred knowledge of all life. She is also singer, (en)chantress, connected to the realm of true magic and power, the realm of creation.

The Beauty Way is at the core of Diné cosmology. In many ancient cultures, the comb and mirror are tools of the Goddess. One might assume these the tools of vanity; however, if we look a bit deeper, the comb is also used to straighten and bring order, a weaver's tool to make a world of beauty and harmony, a healing-way. The mirror is what we create outside of ourselves, how we see ourselves in others, and how the world is a reflection of our state of being, mirroring our belief systems, our thoughts and feelings, our "webwork."

As Spider Grandmother spoke to White Shell Woman, she listened fully:

The loom, my child, is life itself. The weaving-way holds beauty. The loom, my child, is breath itself. The weaving-way holds power. Through weaving one can come to know the meaning of life and breath.[7]

One night I dreamed of Weaver Woman, sometimes known as Spider Woman:

She as weaver woman was peacefully sitting at her loom. Her shining long black hair flowed over a colorfully woven shawl, which was draped gracefully over her shoulders. She wove for some time, seemingly oblivious to my observation. After weaving several wefts into the cloth, she got up and crouched down on the earth, put her ear to the ground and listened a few moments. When she had heard what she heard, she returned to her loom and resumed her weaving. She repeated this listening and weaving over and over.

For me, this dream came as a reminder to listen well before creating, to rest before moving. When we listen to the Earth or our intuition before rushing into what we want to do, what we then create or weave into existence is more sacred, in tune with the whole circle of life.

WHEELS WITHIN WHEELS

We are the stars which sing,
We sing with your light,
We are the birds of fire,
We fly across the heavens,
Our light is a star which sings.
—North American Algonkian song[8]

Dartmoor is one of southern England's rare wilderness areas and is always a favorite place for me—a place of deep roots for my Celtic blood, especially since some of my ancestors departed on a ship in Dartmouth, not far from Dartmoor in 1640, bound for North America. Merryvale is an ancient circle of stones on a windswept hill in a remote part of the moors, barren except for the sheepshorn grasses and old stone fences lining the hills. Approaching the circle, one is first greeted by a long double-row of stones, an old entry avenue. I felt it the proper way to arrive at the circle, and as I walked slowly between the rows of medium-sized stones, I noticed one to the left that had more quartz crystal composition. Through years of working with stones for healing, I knew quartz to be a memory keeper, with the ability to retain energy or hold what is called a piezo-electric charge. I knelt before the stone and asked if there was a memory of this place within it. I placed my forehead against the stone, closed my eyes, and saw what seemed like a full color, feature film unfolding. Walking along this same avenue were little people wearing animal skins—they were of all ages, a clan of old ones, children, men, and women—chanting together, carrying torches in a ceremonial procession.

I thought this quite an impressive sight, but I thought, well, what can I learn from this? An elder of the tribe responded to my thought a bit impatiently, "Well, of course you must know we're here to honor the turning point, a time of the intersection of great cycles. We come together to honor the turning of the great wheels of time—of the sun, moon, planets, and stars. Our message is, if your people come together in circles again to honor the turning points in life, then harmony will reign in all realms and you will be at one with all life. If you don't, chaos and confusion will reign." The vision then faded away and I was again alone in the avenue of stones at Merryvale, current era.

Turning points can be viewed as the basis for all our calendric systems: the turning of the earth in one day, the earth circling the sun in one earth year, thirteen moon cycles in one earth year, as well as the greater solar, venusian, and other planetary and stellar cycles. Mayan, Aztec, as well as other ancient calendar systems were based on these galactic movements and those of other galaxies, according to my Mayan friend, Hunbatz Men.

These cycles and calendars form the natural rhythms that greatly influence how we experience life. Unfortunately, many of the calendar systems used in modern times do not reflect the natural cycles. For instance, we have thirteen moons in a year, and women's menses normally return in a twenty eight or twenty nine day cycle, like the moon, but our year is divided into twelve months. This puts our human rhythms into conflict and out of phase with the natural flows of magnetic energy and the movement of fluids in our bodies. When we begin to honor the phases and cycles of the moon, our rhythms are more in harmony—our intuitive, listening faculties may awaken, and we remember the timeless wisdom of the Goddess, a return to the circle of wholeness and healing.

The cycles and orbits of the heavenly bodies relate not only to rhythm, but also to resonance and sound. Musical tones have long been associated with the planets, moon, sun, and Earth in many ancient cultures: Indian, Chinese, Egyptian, and Greek, to name a few. To have divine order on Earth (as well as Earth harmony in the heavens), knowledge of cosmic cycles, rhythms, tones and how to use them is essential. The Chinese used certain musical tones, and scales to maintain social order; in the eastern Indian musical tradition the fundamental tone of C# is used for tuning most stringed instruments, which is the frequency 136.1 hertz, corresponding to the cycle of one Earth year.

Basically, the system of frequencies assigned to planets relates to cycles of time and relationship of distance, which all have numerical values; these are then translated into cycles per second (hertz). I will not go into a lengthy explanation here, but for those who wish to study this further, please refer to the book *The Cosmic Octave* by Hans Cousto.[9]

The Pythagorean schools in Greece taught the relationship of the planets with the diatonic (seven tone) scale and used specific musical modes or scales to effect moods and health. In ancient Egypt, the construction of temples was done with conscious knowledge of cosmic alignments and sacred geometry to create particular resonant tones in each chamber. These tones could resonate with and align the persons who entered these sacred places.

The therapeutic and morally transforming character of music was stressed not only in Greek music, but in China, where the study of music was featured in the training of scholars and future rulers, as the same principles of organization were believed to control music, the sky (the motion of stars and planets), the biological functions of the body.[10]

Recent research into the effects of sound for healing has confirmed many of the principles that these ancient cultures knew and used: that the changes and movements of the planets effect life on Earth, and that the positions of the planets at the time of one's birth indicate areas of ease and potential stress in physical, mental, and emotional health. There is a whole field of medicine developing called medical astrology, and one of its applications for healing is sound, using the appropriate tones corresponding to the planetary configurations in one's astrological chart.

Another way to assess the state of one's health (discovered by Sharry Edwards of Signature Sound Works), is by listening to the voice and observing which tones appear more and which are missing. The tones of our normal speaking voice ideally produce a range of tones that correspond to the twelve-tone chromatic scale and which relate to specific functions of the body and mind. If we replace the tones that are missing or that are in stress, the body can heal. When we have the entire spectrum of sound our systems can maintain a state of wholeness and health. Unfortunately, most of us have been deeply affected by emotional experiences that have "short-circuited" our sound bodies, or energy fields. Other ways that our frequencies are altered are through genetic influences and from sound pollution, inaudible as well as audible. If sound works at the level of creation, then the use of sound for healing should be implemented in all areas of medicine!

One of the most profound discoveries for me in this area of sound healing is the connection between missing notes in the voice, our separation from nature, and the world's worst killing diseases. The dominant natural resonance of the Earth, termed a Schumann resonance, is 7.83 cycles per second, or a tone between B and C. In testing the vocal tones of hundreds of women in different locales, most are lacking in these two notes. It has also been found that in most cancer and AIDS patients, B and C are missing or in stress. What is this telling us? Again, the separation from the wilderness world, from the natural beauty, sounds, shapes, aromas, and tastes that heal, is taking its toll in more ways than we can imagine. Our frequencies have become distorted by pollution, stress, and unnatural lifestyles, which creates a potential for dis-ease.

We all need to use our singing voices again, on a daily basis. Just sounding and humming can be of great benefit. Occasional spontaneous letting out of whatever sounds want to express themselves, is a great way to release and clear ourselves. But first we need to get our judgments of what is beautiful and "proper" out of our own way, to allow our wilder selves that expression. If you are not sure which tones you need to sing or sound, just listen inside for a tone that feels good and natural. Normally our intuition will know what is more beneficial, if we but ask. A Navajo acquaintance and flute player, R.Carlos Nakai once told me that if a person wants to know what their personal tone is, just ask upon waking every morning. The first note that comes into the mind should be noted, and this repeated for seven days. Of course, one will need to have a musical instrument or pitch pipe handy to find the note, unless one has perfect pitch. The note that occurs most often will be the major tone for that individual. I used this method years ago and the tone I found corresponded with one that was missing from my speaking voice and also was in a stressful aspect astrologically.

We can increase our knowledge of the use of sound to heal ourselves and the Earth in several ways. We can observe how indigenous peoples have used sound, and incorporate these ways into our lives. We can study the knowledge of ancient cultures and also the modern sound research being done—there are countless books and workshops available to us. And we can simply ask for guidance and trust our intuition. This is the basic method I used for years before I entered into any formal study. This is a way to access our own information, and bring knowledge, songs, and healing ways that will be appropriate for this time.

THE CHANTRESS IN EGYPT

For many years I listened to my intuition or inner ear for songs, and yet I didn't totally trust the validity of this method within our current cultural context. Using one's intuition did not seem as acceptable a source or credential as did having a university degree or a tremendous file of well-documented research, until I had many experiences that confirmed that both ways of accessing information are valid.

My first journey to Egypt was in August of 1987 during the Harmonic Convergence, an important turning point and the beginning of a new cycle, according to the Mayan calendar. The morning of August 17th was said to be the first day of this new cycle and was celebrated worldwide. With prior permission from the Egyptian Department of Antiquities, our group entered the Great Pyramid of Cheops and visited the King's and Queen's Chambers. Somehow I managed to be in the King's Chamber practically alone, with just one woman quietly meditating in the corner. I took this rare opportunity to tone and experience the deep acoustical quality that I had heard so much about. Still, no one else had arrived at the chamber, so I entered the sarcophagus, a stone-walled "bed," where initiates were said to be placed to test their spiritual attainment. I received a powerful message as I lay there: that all the blessings and gifts that I have received, are not for myself alone, but to be given away; that any songs, revelations, or teachings given to me are given so that I may share them with others. As this message completed, I heard many people chanting a Sanskrit mantra, and the sound resonance expanded through the chamber, making me feel like a group of angels had arrived. They were Earth angels from an ashram in New York—no matter, the effect worked.

I stayed and joined their harmonies for awhile and then found my way to the Queen's Chamber, where a few members of our group had already arrived. After sitting quietly for some time to attune to the place, I asked for a chant to honor the sacredness of the place and the time. I found a tuning that seemed to fit the feeling and began to play; it developed into a chant everyone could join. As the song went on, more and more people quietly entered and joined the growing harmonies. No one, including myself, "knew" the song, but we all sang as if we had been singing that melody together for ages, a melody that seemed very familiar. It was an extraordinary experience for all of us. At one point, I remember feeling the rising harmonies going right up and out of the top of the pyramid and spreading out to cover the Earth. I found out about one year later that one of our group had a remission of his cancer after that day, and attributed it to our group chant and the rich acoustics of the pyramid.

On my second journey to Egypt in 1992, I joined a research project with my friend Antoine Seronde, who had already been gathering data and historical evidence of the role of acoustics in the construction and ritual use of the Egyptian temples. We worked side by side: I used my faculties of listening within to receive the dominant sounds in each temple chamber; Antoine's method consisted of measuring all the dimensions of each chamber and then using a computer program to translate these figures into basic sound frequencies. (The dimensions of each chamber create a series of tones based on how the sound waves move between the walls and between the floor and ceiling.) We were each impressed with the fact that both methods arrived at the same results approximately 75 percent of the time. The sounds that I heard inwardly in each temple chamber corresponded with those arrived at with a more scientific approach.

Many ancient cultures used both science and intuition in knowing how to construct their temples, where to place stone circles, what songs to sing for healing, and basically how to bring the sacred into their lives. We all have the ability to dream, listen, and develop our intuitive faculties, and therefore may access the knowledge we need. Many great scientific inventions came from intuition and dreams!

The role of music was primary in the development of Egyptian temples: the use of sacred geometry in the design and construction, and the subsequent highly refined and extraordinary acoustics and harmonics. Music and incantations were an integral part of temple rituals and chantresses played a key role as temple musicians. As my colleague, Antoine Seronde noted:

> Desroches-Noblecourt ('La femme au temps des Pharaons') mentions that women were involved in medicine in official capacities as far back as the Old Kingdom: as physicians or healers and midwives to the royal family. She mentions that the royal midwives had medical training and that they acted as chantresses and temple musicians when not engaged in midwifery.

It was on this same journey to Egypt, researching acoustics with Antoine, that I experienced a most extraordinary resonance. In all my travels I constantly search for spaces that create unusual echoes and harmonic response—canyons, caves, cathedrals, hallways, wells, temples, large empty rooms—but when I first experienced the quality of sound at the temple of Abydos, I felt as if the temple walls were answering in response, and ringing with an aliveness I had not heard before.

In the rear of the main temple of Abydos there is a complex of chambers dedicated to Osiris, and according to friend and co-researcher Carol Horn, it is laid out in a design that approximates the body of Osiris. The acoustics seemed to have very different qualities at the opposite ends of the complex, so Antoine and I decided to begin in the chambers at the base, or feet, and move slowly through until we arrived at the "crown," or resurrection chamber. I began with tuning the harp according to the sounds that appeared to be dominant and more resonant. Then as I played and sang, I moved slowly from the first chambers, where the harmonics seemed to be deeper, lower tones, and then into the main hall, where the harmonics became much larger and more in the mid-range (harmonics are overtones and undertones that enhance a single tone, and contain complex harmonies of the original). As I entered the resurrection chamber at the end of the complex, the harmonics became so high and refined that I could barely sing with the rare beauty and quality of the acoustics. The effect of the sound was very profound, and indeed it seemed that the crown of my head opened up to a higher dimension of experience. Antoine perceived the same changes in resonance as we had moved through the chambers. After that experience, I was left with a great desire that we once again begin to build with more acoustical awareness, creating sacred space, so that more people could benefit from such transformative sound harmonics.

SACRED TIME

Whenever an eclipse occurred, the women painted themselves with red earth and sang.—"Selk'nam (Ona) Chants of Tierra del Fuego"[11]

During the past few years, series' of new songs have come to me at times of lunar eclipses and other turning points. I use my harp and voice to commune with the power and energies of those times. During one of those eclipses, I positioned myself under a large skylight in our home, with a perfect view of the approaching eclipse. As the shadow of the Earth began to cover the edge of the moon, I asked for an appropriate tuning for the harp and music aligned with the time. Inwardly I heard the notes G# A# C D D# F, to create the tuning on the harp— a scale that I had never played before. It sounded quite mysterious and beautiful and I continued to watch the shadow moving across the moon, playing what I felt. I gave the song the name "Lunas Trece" (Thirteen Moons) in honor of the yearly moon cycles. This song has some unusual rhythm changes and when

I took the time to count them out, the section with a chant to the moon contains measures with thirteen beats each. Then in later reading, I discovered that the G# tuning corresponds to the tone of the moon, a frequency of 420.837 hertz, which is based on the length of time between two new or full moons. Since G#, or A flat is not a commonly played tone in modern music, it is my feeling that it is an important tone to re-incorporate, as it relates to the moon and the feminine energies that are reawakening within all of us now.

All these experiences, dreams, and visions showed me the importance of listening and of honoring the earthly and cosmic cycles. In applying these principles to sound, I began to incorporate them more and more in my work at sacred sites. I began to see the cycles of time and turning points as sacred time, and to integrate this with sacred places; thus sacred time and sacred space become unified in a balanced world.

On one of my personal cycles, a solar return, or birthday, I was walking with a friend through one of the dramatic red rock canyons of Sedona, Arizona. This area has long been considered sacred to Native Americans, and now modern pilgrims and those on a search for deeper spirituality are coming there from all over the world. As we walked along, I heard a distinct chant in my mind and began to sing softly; the chant had syllables I was not familiar with, but I didn't really think about it, I just sang. Several minutes after I had stopped singing, my friend and I both heard the chant subtly singing from the stones! The time span between my chanting and the response was much longer than an echo in that area would travel. The red earth singing was a rare and wonderful birthday gift indeed; song as the intelligent language of the wilderness world, a gift received and given.

Music and chant has long been used by many cultures and religious groups to bring unity, order, and to affect life. The Sufis are especially versed in the power of the human voice as inseparable from the breath of life. I had the opportunity to attend an evening of Sufi ceremonial chant in Mexico City, and experienced firsthand how they use song and breath together. This integrated use of tones, sacred words, and breathing had a very powerful effect, and I entered into an altered state of consciousness in a very short time. The Sufi wisdom teaches that sacred dance and song are a path to the divine. They say that the human voice is the barometer of the state of our mental, emotional, physical, and spiritual selves.

What kinds of music can heal? Singing is the most powerful, for singing is living. It is prana (the sacred breath of life). The voice is life itself ... the breath touching the heart of the listener.[12]

At one time, there were on the earth many perpetual choirs, a tradition of constant chanting to keep divine order on Earth, and as a form of life energy to feed all living things. The Druids used the sounds of these choirs to connect the lines of energy between their sacred centers. The Tibetans still employ these perpetual choirs in some more remote areas of Tibet and in at least one Buddhist center in the U.S., to feed and bring beneficial energy to the earth. Great stones and mountains are also said to be singing in order to keep the connections alive between certain rocks and hills. At Ringing Rock in California, and Pena Bernal (Singing Mountain) in Mexico, the neighboring indigenous people tell of hearing the songs of the earth there, and that these songs are communicating with all the other stones and hills in the area.

CHANTING BRINGS ORDER OUT OF CHAOS

Glastonbury, England, has been a sacred center throughout many cultural and legendary eras—the ancient "little people" of the elemental and faery realm; the Goddess worshipping traditions, Druidic, Arthurian, and early Christian. Some historical sources say that Joseph of Arimathea and perhaps Jesus and Mary all frequented the "Glas Isle."

Arriving in Glastonbury England after a long trans-Atlantic flight and a three-hour bus ride, my friend and well-known chantress Lisa Thiel and I were so exhausted we couldn't sleep. We were staying in a little cottage nestled at the base of the famous Tor, the central landmark of the ancient Isle of Avalon. This sculpted green hill forms an intricate labyrinth and is said to be an entrance to Annwn, the "Otherworlds," where the veils between dimensions are unusually permeable.

So there we were, our minds so tired that we were in an altered state of consciousness in addition to being in a very powerfully charged sacred site. Our room was very dark, but we both began to observe little sparks of light darting about every which way, seeming to playfully dive-bomb us. It became increasingly difficult to imagine ever getting to rest with these little elemental Earth

Energies or faeries zooming around the room. Lisa began to chant the Tibetan hundred-syllable Vajra Satva mantra, a chant used by many Tibetan Buddhists to bring harmony and divine order. As we chanted, we observed the little lights begin to dance in circles, gradually joining in one harmonious ring of movement together. With ourselves relaxed and the spirits of the place appeased, we both slipped into a deep sleep.

SONG INCREASES LIFE ENERGY

Marius Schneider has shown that the Sanskrit root *bra* can mean both grow and adore ... Brahma the God grew to the degree that his praises were sung. The universe expanded through song. —*The Third Ear* by Joachim-Ernst Berendt.[13]

A legend of the Stanton Drew stone circle in the Mendip Hills of Somerset says that the people came to this site to learn how to use sound to move the stones. It is said that this was done by projecting sound to disintegrate the stones into tiny particles, and then reconstruct them in a different place. It did seem peculiar that the composition of these great monoliths appeared to be thousands of small pieces of different colored stones "glued" together, or perhaps that is how the legend started! Either way, what occurred to me at the circle supports the belief that song can change and increase life energy.

I had with me a small bard's type of Celtic harp and a set of copper dowsing rods, and set out to test the effects of song on the stones (dowsing is a method of measuring Earth energies). I began with a dowsed control measurement of the one stone chosen for the experiment. Then I played an improvisational song for the stone; measurement afterwards showed an increase of about four feet in the stone's aura, or field of energy. I then made an offering of incense to the stone, thanking it for its presence. Aroma is another important medium used for energy and healing work, and this expanded the field about three feet more. After this, I dowsed the fields of the other stones in the circle and all of them had increased their fields of energy to the same degree. Just like a circle of friends, all being affected by beauty or healing energy—they were in perfect resonance with one another!

In the Aztec culture of Mexico, dances are still performed today which contain rhythms and dance movements that correspond to the natural movements of life: to the four directions and to the four types of movement in the universe (Nauhi-Ollin). The intricate foot movements relate to sacred geometry and are danced as a language, a way of speaking to the Earth. Central to their cosmology are song, flowers, dance, and poetry, and these themes continue to flavor contemporary ceremony, prayer, and artistic expression.

"Flower and song were the highest things on Earth that can penetrate the confines of truth."[14]

Nahuatl musical instruments such as clay flutes take the form of jaguars, birds, reptiles, shells, flowers, and deities. Drums (Huehuetl) and wooden percussion played with sticks (Teponaztli) are carved with figures part human, part bird or animal, showing the integration of terrestrial and celestial natures. The representations of the instruments honor their connection with the wilderness world, and are used to speak with all its realms.

The Goddess Xochiquetzal, meaning "precious flower" or "flowering bird," is honored in some modern day ceremonies. I attended a ceremony for a seven-year-old girl, an important time of change for every child. Every seven years we move into a different stage of our human development and these rites of passage are still honored in many indigenous cultures. This beautiful and gracious young girl was honored with prayers from her mother, father, and relatives that were so supportive and positive it made me reflect on the great and lasting effect this would have in her life. She was honored with showers of flower petals, songs, the Aztec sun dance, and prayers from the more than one hundred people there. Can you imagine the profound depth of acknowledgment for that child, and how different our lives might be if all children were thus honored by so many family and friends?

Hallie Iglehart Austen speaks of Xochiquetzal in her wonderful book, *Heart of the Goddess*: "... the Goddess of pleasure, sexuality, beauty and flowers."[15] If we embrace earthly sensuality as the divine flowering of beauty, and are surrounded with this acceptance from an early age, we have a sense of wholeness and integration with our bodies and the body of the Earth.

One of the Nahuatl fourteenth-century poems by Nezahualcoyotl reflects this integration of beauty and nature in their culture. It has become a song that I have played on the harp and sung for many groups because of its timeless message to us all. I include both the English translation and the original Nahuatl version, for the beauty and depth of the old language:[16]

In the house of paintings the singing begins	Amoxcalco
Song is intoned—flowers are spread	Pehua cuica
The song rejoices	Yeyecohua
Your heart is a book of paintings	On ahuia cuicatl.
You have come to sing,	Quicoyahua xochitl
To make your drums resound	Icahuaca cuicatl
	Oyohualli ehuatihuitz
	Zan quinanquiliy
You are the singer	Toxochayacach
Within the house of springtime	Quimoyahua xochitl
You make the people happy	On ahuia cuicatl.

We have all come to sing, to celebrate life, and within our hearts are all the colors, poems and songs needed to bring the flowers and the new life of a springtime on Earth.

On my first visit to Palenque, in Chiapas, Mexico, I was deeply moved by the beauty of the temples and lush rainforest vegetation, and also a feeling that I had come home. After exploring most of the temple areas, I found myself at the eastern edge of the complex, below the Temple of the Foliated Cross. The windows in the front of the temple look like keyholes, or goddesses with heads and wide skirts. Nowhere else have I seen this shape of window. As I ascended the meandering stone pathway, I noticed a proliferation of moist green grasses and moss, butterflies and flowers, all signs of the presence of the Goddess. When I arrived at the temple, I made an offering of cornmeal to the deity inside, which is said to be the Corn Goddess. Then I offered a song on my bamboo flute, and as I played, I saw children begin to climb up to where I was. There were about nine, apparently attracted to the flute song. I was astonished, as each one arrived at the top and quite naturally took his or her place in a circle with me. I didn't yet speak Spanish, but without needing to speak, each child came up in turn and asked, with hand gestures, for some of the cornmeal to offer there. I began to play again and they hummed and danced around the circle, until their parents began calling them to come down from the temple and that "stranger." But before they left, each one came and kissed me on the cheek, and I felt truly blessed: by the place, by the Goddess, and by the beautiful children who remembered how to honor the place and so trustingly celebrated with their spontaneity of ritual, movement, and song.

THE EARTH IS SINGING

She stretched my heart, made it a drum, keeping time with everyone
She stretched my heart, made it a drum, keeping time for dancing
With the moon and stars and sun, keeping time with everyone
Keeping time for dancing, with the wind, with the rain
In a circle of friends[17]

The Earth is singing, She is humming, and if we just put our ear to the ground a moment and listen, we might hear her song, we might feel her heart beating. She is happy to feel more of her children drumming her rhythms, circles of people gathering and chanting once again, reawakening to the sacredness of life. It is helping her to feel once again places in her body that were numbed from the abuse and lack of respect—our songs help her to heal the long sadness and loneliness she has felt because Her children had forgotten so much.

Through the centuries of time, some of her children did remember why they had come here, how to listen to the star song, and how to live in harmony with the creatures of the Earth. They were named Earth Keepers and have long loved and respected the beauty of the Earth: the mountains as sacred beings, the trees and stone people who are singing a silent song, the winding rivers as serpent beings, the dolphin and whale people, who sing to keep the waters alive and the great oceans as the boundless body of the Goddess.

These Earth Keepers grow tired of caring for the Earth Mother alone. Their ways need to be heard and respected, their ways of being that keep all connected in the sacred hoop of life. If we open our hearts to one another, take the time to listen and learn to understand all the diverse beings that inhabit our planet, we may all become true keepers and protectors of life. Each one of us is an Earth Keeper, an Earth Singer—we have come to make our drums resound, to be the singers in the House of Springtime.

NOTES

1. Quoted by Evelyn Eaton, *Snowy Earth Comes Gliding* (Draco Foundation, Independence, CA).

2. Many thanks to Nicholas Mann for permission to quote from his book *Sedona Sacred Earth* (Zivah Publishing, Albuquerque, NM, 1991). This Yavapai legend was originally recorded by E.W. Gifford, as told by the blind shaman Muukyat.

3. Jonothan Goldman, *Healing Sounds* (Element, Inc., Rockport, MA, 1992).

4. Marija Gimbutas, referring to a section from Plato's *Republic*, in her book *The Language of the Goddess* (Harper & Row, San Francisco, 1989).

5. Larry Evers and Felip S. Molina, *Yaqui Deer Songs* (Sun Tracks and University of Arizona Press, Tucson and London, 1987).

6. Catherine J. Ellis and Linda Barwick, "Antikirinja—Women's Song Knowledge," in Peggy Brock, ed., *Women—Rites and Sites* (Allen and Unwin, Sydney and Boston, 1989).

7. Noel Bennett, *Halo of the Sun* (Northland Press, Flagstaff, AZ, 1987).

8. Quoted by Evelyn Eaton, *Snowy Earth Comes Gliding*.

9. Hans Cousto, *The Cosmic Octave* (Life Rhythm, Mendocino, CA, 1988).

10. Dane Rudhyar, *The Magic of Tone and the Art of Music* (Shambhala Publishing Inc., Boulder, CO, 1982).

11. Anne Chapman, translations and notes, Selk'nam (Ona) Chants of Tierra del Fuego, Argentina (Folkways Records album No. FE 4176, New York, 1972).

12. Hazrat Inayat Khan, *Music* (Samuel Weiser, New York, 1977).

13. Joachim-Ernst Berendt, *The Third Ear* (Henry Holt and Co., New York, 1992).

14. Samuel Aun Weor, *Aztec Christic Magic*.

15. Hallie Iglehart Austen, *The Heart of the Goddess* (Wingbow Press, Berkeley, CA, 1990).

16. Quoted by Christine Pruneda from the fourteenth century Nahuatl poem by Nezhvalcoyotl.

17. Lyrics from the song "She," by Ani Williams, Children of the Sun recording. Words adapted from the poem "Keeping Time" by Will Ashe Bason.

A PERSONAL JOURNEY

I COME FROM TWO CULTURES—Native American and European American, that is, Inuit, as well as Irish, some German, and a smidgen of Scots. My paternal grandmother was a full-blooded Inuit woman. My father was born in the Arctic Circle; his native name is *Nanoona,* which means "Little Polar Bear."

In the past several years, I've been coming to terms with the Native American aspects of my identity. Although I was born and brought up in California, far away from the Far North, I have discovered that I was brought up in a very Native American way. In general I was treated as an autonomous person, and was given choices and learned to make decisions at a very young age. From my father and mother I learned a basic respect, acceptance, and tolerance of others, and a certain degree of humility. From my father I learned a very important non-Anglo lesson—the value of the fullness of silence.

I used to believe that even though my grandmother was a Inuit, and even though my father was born in the Arctic Circle and grew up in the Aleutian Islands, these aspects of my reality did not directly affect me. After all, I was born in Oakland. I grew up in the Bay Area. I went to Berkeley, where I received my B.A., my M.A., and my Ph.D. My life seemed far removed from the Far North, and so was I—or so I thought. Little did I know or understand how wrong I could be. As a result of my experiences of the past several years, I can say for a fact that there is power in the blood, and that blood will tell: it will call you home, change and rearrange your life, and transform your identity and reality.

This story begins seventeen years ago, when my mother, to whom I was very close, unexpectedly and prematurely died of cancer. In many ways my mother accorded me and represented to me unconditional love. Her death was a great loss, and was also the cause of my first significant visionary experience as an adult. A night or two after Mama died, she appeared to me: I saw her face, full face, in color. Mama was looking straight ahead, not at me, her sight focused on some other point, her expression a very serious one, as if she were weighing or pondering very significant matters. I believe that because of my close connection to my mother I was allowed to see her after death as she evaluated her progress during her lifetime, weighing her soul.

Two years after my mother's death, a series of events took place that I won't go into, but which alienated me from my own family, for an extended period of time. Quite simply, the world turned upside down for me. I was totally unprepared for what happened and I didn't understand why it was taking place; I didn't know how to cope with it. I continued to have contact with my family, but it seemed very nominal, and everything was very different from what it had been. Of course this was complicated by the fact that my mother had died.

So about fifteen years ago, as a result of my response—body, mind, heart, and spirit—to my experience of rejection and my deep-seated feeling that I didn't belong, my skin gradually began to lose its pigmentation, a condition called vitiligo. White spots appeared and spread all over my body in a seemingly random, haphazard way. The cause of this condition was unknown. One possible cure was to ingest a certain pill and then expose the affected area to ultraviolet radiation: I didn't consider this to be an option for me, due to the dangers of ultraviolet light. This loss of pigmentation happened very slowly, but progressively. (An inner voice has at times told me that I am "marked by the Goddess" in respect to this skin condition.) Among other things, it made me feel old while still young. It also challenged my idea of what it means to be a woman, as well as my idea of my own femininity. Of course I experienced myself as being very different from others. I now realize that I grew up feeling I did not belong, not only because I was physically and intellectually precocious, and not only because I was discouraged from expressing negative emotions, but also because I strongly identified with my father, who, being what society calls a half-breed, felt that he did not belong. He never verbally articulated this feeling, yet the contents of his unconscious were clearly communicated to mine.

The experience of the physical condition of my skin and its accompanying imprint on my psyche has given me the opportunity to question virtually every assumption or notion I had previously entertained about the nature of reality and of cause and effect; it has caused me to ask why these events had happened to me—feeling rejected by my family, experiencing this physical condition, los-ing my mother, and missing her so.

I've worked very hard to clean up my act, as it were, hoping to effect a cure, a reversal of the process of depigmentation. I have attempted to recover a sense of wholeness and balance in my life. Many times I've had to cope with feelings of loss and abandonment, victimization, and learned helplessness. I have been on a philosophical and metaphysical search, experimenting with various holis-tic and metaphysical therapies and ways of looking at the world. On the whole it's been a challenging spiritual adventure—a journey. At times it's even been fun—I've recovered my sense of joy and wonder; I've discovered a youthfulness I never remember experiencing while young.

For me becoming healed, becoming whole, has meant coming home. Com-ing home has meant coming to Indian country, teaching and writing on Native American Studies, working with and teaching Native Americans. Coming home has meant coming home to the Native American worldview: realizing how familiar it is to me, and how meaningful it seems; understanding something of Native American values and attitudes; and as I mentioned earlier, understand-ing that I was implicitly taught many of these values and attitudes while grow-ing up. Coming home has meant learning about balance and the interrelatedness of all that is, the importance of cultivating right relationship while here on the earth plane.

I'm happy to say that over the years there has been a gradual but steady rec-onciliation within my family. Three years ago I and others began to see a slight but slow and steady reversal of the pigmentation loss on my chest. I've come to believe that we choose our illnesses in order to learn certain lessons. On a very deep level of reality, I freely and willingly chose this illness before I came into this life: I am not a victim, not a sacrifice. This realization took me aback: although I knew it intellectually I had never understood it on an experiential level of reality. Then on February 11 of this year, for the first time that I can consciously remember, I experienced a deep and profound sense of belonging. These matters are deceptively easy to relate in a few sentences, while in fact they represent giant steps in awareness, self-acceptance, self-knowledge, self-understanding, and understanding of others. But this is getting ahead of things.

By 1981 I had become increasingly weary and disillusioned with the acad-emic world: its narrow focus, its competitiveness, its worldliness, its cynicism, its overriding rationality, and its worship of the mind. Although I had been rigorously trained academically—I earned a B.A. in French and German, an M.A. in French, and a doctorate in Comparative Literature, which entailed learning nine European languages—I still felt somewhat like a foreigner in a distant country, ignorant of its customs, and ill-at-ease. I now knew that I wanted to turn my attention to Native American Studies because in the academic world I inhabited there seemed to be no room for the sacred, no appreciation for life as a mystery that cannot be solved or rationally understood, but that can only be intuited and vaguely grasped in its entirety. I was very pleased when I began to see life this way; it thus always guards its secrets, and I can always feel a sense of wonder at its myriad possibilities.

In October, 1981 I attended a literary conference at UCLA on medieval German poetry; I served as respondent and moderator. As I orally evaluated a noted Austrian scholar's paper, I simultaneously perceived a non-oral sound. As I became aware of this sound, I mentally experimented to make sure I knew exactly what it was, what it sounded like; I tried this sound and that until I understood what sound I was apprehending. This sound consists of a consonant and a vowel: it is the sound *yeay* (like the English word *hay*, but with a longer stress on and pronunciation of the diphthong). It sounds just like the Navajo term *yei'ii*, which means "the gods" in that language; this sound occurs in other Native American languages as well. Now, when I focus on this sound, it activates my third eye. A few minutes after I "heard" the sound, there was a minor earthquake. It took me quite some time before I realized that the sound and the earthquake were connected, and what that might mean. I now feel that what I heard was the cry, the call, of the Earth Mother. I suppose you might call this my initiation into Gaia consciousness. It was also an initiation into a much more expanded idea and experience of the sacred than I had previously known.

Since that first time I've had many visionary experiences. I haven't taken drugs such as LSD, or American Indian medicine such as peyote, to induce altered states. Drumming is one of the traditional journeying techniques of my ancestors; I participated in a drumming session last winter. It was a successful journey in that I met again with two of my allies as well as a being who is very important to me, but this experience didn't have the qualities of completeness, fullness, or immediacy of the spontaneous visionary experiences I have had. I've also had many spontaneous past-life memories and experiences.

My next significant experience relating to the Earth Mother was a waking vision I had in June of 1984, around 11:30 PM I was in bed saying the rosary, when I had a vision of an older, serious-faced Inuit woman. I felt she was calling to me. I felt she was related to me. At first I saw her face and saw that she was wearing modern clothes. Then I saw her face and she was wearing traditional clothes—a beautiful brown skin parka. There were other family members in the background. I felt this figure was calling to me, trying to reach me, to contact me. Was she my grandmother? It seemed so, but she also simultaneously embodied the spirit of the Inuit people and the land.

I mourned the loss of my Inuit grandmother, the fact that I had never known her or met her, and that I didn't even know her name. I cried sad tears while telling my unknown grandmother repeatedly that I loved and respected her. I couldn't understand why my grandmother would be trying to reach and contact me at the very time when I was longing to contact her. This waking vision frightened me, yet I can see that it was calling me home, and telling me that I was related, that I did belong, that I wasn't alone.

One morning a few months later I left my house in the mountains to drive to the University of New Mexico at Belen, where I was teaching. As I opened the door to my car, I was awestruck by a large white cloud hovering above, similar in size and shape to a dirigible, somewhat ovoid in shape. It was dense, thick and cottony, with an unusual shape and texture. I realized immediately that it was a spirit cloud, like a UFO. It was not a "natural" shape. I felt powerfully attracted to, connected with, and identified with it. In fact, I experienced a great deal of awe and some fear. I felt as if the cloud could literally sweep me away with it, if it wanted to—I was mesmerized by it.

It was hard to drive away from this extraordinary landscape, but I did. As I turned from North 14 onto West 40, I saw the bottom of another cloud, somewhat similar to the first. At first I thought it was the same one, but as I drove through Albuquerque and out on I-25 I saw the first and second clouds simultaneously: the second cloud was at least ten times larger than the first. To me the second cloud looked like a female polar bear on all fours, engaged in a meaningful trek across the sky. I felt that this cloud and the other one as well were manifestations of the White Goddess. It came to me that the She-Polar Bear was gathering together her lost and scattered children and that I was one of them. I almost had an accident on West 40 through Albuquerque as I peered intently through the rear view mirror.

It gradually came to me that this being, the She-Polar Bear, was the Great White She-Bear of the North. Of course the tie with my father and the Far North did not escape me. This bear must be one of my relations. And yet, paradoxically, I still didn't feel as if I were directly related to Native America, the Far North, or to my relations there, in spite of my ideas, attitudes, feelings, and worldview. I didn't feel I deserved to be related to my people up there; I hadn't been born there, and I didn't know the life from personal experience.

Two days later, at 7 PM, I saw the She-Polar Bear cloud again. As I came home and parked in my driveway, I found myself under an arc formed by the She-Polar Bear cloud with the moon below. Once more she was on all fours engaged in a great trek across the sky, coming by again to remind me and perhaps her other scattered children that it was time for us to gather together. At a time when I felt so alone, I was being given powerful visionary evidence that I was part of a group of people who were here for a purpose, and who had a mother who superintended them.

At the same time, on four different nights, the figure of an Indian woman of indeterminate age silently and repeatedly appeared to me. To me this personage was Old Woman, the Nootka Mother Goddess, as depicted so powerfully by Anne Cameron in *Daughters of Copper Woman*—more visionary testimony that I did indeed belong.

I have seen the Great White She-Bear of the North time and again. Among other things, I view her as the Great Cosmic Initiator. In a certain sense she is my mother—perhaps my clan mother, after all, my father is Nanoona, Little Polar Bear—and she is my protector. I believe that the Father-Mother god, the Great He-She, sent me a strong mother, to guide, nurture, and protect me, and to show me that I do indeed belong here, that I do have a place, and that I am an integral part of all that is, just like all aspects of creation. She is also a powerful source and stimulus of creativity.

Next I experienced the Earth Mother at Four Corners, where the states of Arizona, New Mexico, Colorado, and Utah join together. I had just read Page Bryant's book, *The Earth Changes Survival Handbook,* in which she identifies this area as the heart center of the earth. I felt compelled to make a pilgrimage there to the Earth Mother.

We arrived at sunset. I spent a long time walking slowly and standing directly over the Four Corners area, communing with the Earth Mother. While there I repeatedly and silently told her that I would like to help her; that I knew that she needed help and a cure, and so did I. In a Native American way, I promised her that I would help her, if she would help me. I knew she agreed when I felt a surge of energy coursing up through the soles of my feet, rising up my calves, knees, and thighs. It was a powerful moment, an ecstatic, exhilarating experience, a moment of dedication to myself and to the Earth Mother. I took a few small reddish medicine stones with me from that area to help me, and I remembered to thank the Earth as I did so.

In January, 1986, over a period of three days when I was doing work at the Yoga Center in Albuquerque, I had waking—actually walking—visions. I was walking when this knowledge came to me: that I am here to help anchor a force field of energy; that I am here to acknowledge womankind, and individual women; that my task here is to strengthen the womanspirit, and to help the Earth; that I am here to help birth the Earth and its people, myself included, into a new mode of being/seeing/sensing/knowing. The next day it came to me that a new center of gravity is emerging; that I am here with a group of people, men and women, and that together we are creating a new center of gravity.

I am one of the many women and men who are here to help, love, nurture, and support the Earth, and, by extension, the people of the Earth—since we and the Earth are one—as we enter a new and a more spiritual, nonphysical, dimension of reality.

In spite of all my work with holistic therapies, there were gaps in my life, something vital missing—some essential connection. I attended a lecture on Reiki, an ancient Tibetan way of balancing mind, body, heart, and spirit, which was rediscovered in Japan in the last century. *Reiki* means "universal life force energy": *rei* refers to universal or cosmic energy; *ki* is the life force which flows through everything that is living. I determined to learn to do first-degree Reiki in April, 1986, shortly after my birthday.

During the Reiki initiation, the chakras in the palms of your hands are opened, as are other higher chakras. Back in the summer of 1982, while attending the University of New Mexico's German Summer School in Taos Ski Valley, I had wondered again and again at the feelings in the palms of my hands when I placed them directly over the beautiful wildflowers growing there in the valley. Over the years, my palms had become more and more sensitive as I turned to metaphysics and holistic therapies.

The night before the Reiki initiation I saw and felt the Great White She-Bear of the North touch my palms; this was my pre-initiation initiation; I really felt her paws touch my hands on simultaneous physical and nonphysical levels.

Following the first day of Reiki initiation, I had a vision of a circle of polar bears—adults and cubs—joined together on a circular ice floe; they had green eyes and they were dancing in place. I have green eyes, and so does Copper Woman; green is also a vital color associated with the Earth. These visions concerning Reiki confirmed my intuition that it was appropriate for me to learn it then. On the night of my second day of initiation, it came to me that this was indeed a Cosmic Initiation, and that we who do Reiki are involved in soul-making.

At the time of the nuclear accident at Chernobyl, I only knew first-degree Reiki. Technically speaking, you can only send healing energy at a distance following your initiation into second-degree Reiki. However, I felt a great deal of sadness and identification with the people and land at Chernobyl. I wanted to do something to help them. The night I learned of the terrible accident, I lit white and purple candles, lay down on the living room sofa, and silently announced to the universe my intention of having my body take the place of the people and land at Chernobyl, while my hands would send them the healing energy of Reiki. I don't know if it truly did the people and land any good for me to do this; I only know that it definitely made me feel very good to do it.

That summer my husband and I visited Flagstaff and Sedona. While at Flagstaff I became very concerned about the San Francisco Peaks. I felt that they were in a very sorry state, undernourished, undernurtured, and that they needed a great deal of love and healing energy. As we left Flagstaff, I sent the Reiki energy to the Peaks; the very moment I finished sending the energy, there was a clap of thunder directly over our Chevy Blazer; simultaneously I had a vision of an ancient Hopi man, his face juxtaposed with a large, old Hopi pot. For some weeks following this visit I would periodically send Reiki energy to the Peaks. I had some surprising visionary experiences as a result.

Later that summer my cousin Mary, from the Far North, visited me for the first time, with her two children. She had called me that April and we spoke together about our family. It was an indescribable feeling to meet with her and hear her wild, hearty laugh, just like mine, to experience the same crazy sense of humor, and to hear her tell of my family, our heritage, and our traditions. For me this was an integration. One evening during her visit, the Hopi Sun God, Dawa, appeared to me as I lay in bed, entered my heart, and spread his shining, golden rays throughout my body. He took me by the hand (that is the "me" he took by the hand was about six or seven years old), and I knew that he loved me and that he had always loved me; that he had always been there at my side to love and protect me, even when I had felt most alone, desolate, and abandoned. I cried many tears of joy and great happiness; how it hurt, yet it was a good hurt. This was an ecstatic moment, a high point of wonder and radiance in my life. On the days that followed I noticed that my personality had become much sunnier than before. I think of this experience as my Sun God Initiation. When I think of the name Dawa, the sound of it activates my sixth and seventh chakras. I know now that the Father aspect of God was always at my side, and that he appeared to me as Dawa because of my Native American heritage and identification, and because I had tried to help Dawa and his people by sending healing energy to the San Francisco Peaks.

I was in Flagstaff again in May, 1987. While there I visited Sedona, and having learned of the vortices, or places of power there, I visited most of them. During my visit to the Airport Mesa Vortex, I had a powerful experience. While sitting there silently meditating, the area from my chest to my neck was cleared and enlarged on both physical and nonphysical levels. At the end of my meditation, I felt myself very attracted to one of the reddish stones lying on the ground of the vortex. I decided that it was appropriate for me to take this stone, and thanked the Earth Mother.

I had unusual experiences with that stone at my side. It literally shook me up. That very night in the motel in Phoenix, my knees and hands involuntarily raised themselves and knocked together. This happened a few more times in the next few weeks. My friend, colonic and Traeger practitioner Mary Caroline, told me that this stone was literally shaking me up in order to heal me. This shaking/knocking process continued when I was at home in Cedar Crest: it was rather awesome, somewhat frightening, and totally unpredictable as to when it might happen. When I returned to Sedona a few weeks later to attend a Harmonic Convergence workshop with Brooke Medicine Eagle—an inspiring Native teacher who is a joy to be with—I was very careful to return the rock as near as I could to its original home. What a relief! I was beginning to feel that this stone was too powerful for me to handle.

These then are some of my experiences relating to the Earth Mother. Before I knew her, I was experiencing a kind of death on many levels of reality. As a result of my interaction with her, I have experienced transformation, rejuvenation, and rebirth. This initiation into other worlds or levels of reality has made me a much happier, more fulfilled person; I have come to accept rather than to reject the visionary and spiritual gifts that are a part of me, and which were calling for expression, yet meeting with suppression.

I view myself as a person who tries to clear her own life, and her own personal environment, of negativity, and when appropriate does other things, such as sending Reiki energy to the San Francisco Peaks. With Brooke Medicine Eagle and many others, I believe that the Earth is a living being who apprehends the quality of life lived on her surface; that she can tell whether a person who walks on her surface is attempting to live a good life, one appropriate for his or her well-being and that of others. I believe that the Earth Mother can sense the difference between one who does and one who does not wish to walk in balance with her, and that those of us who try to walk in balance help lighten her burden for her. For me, walking in balance doesn't mean that one must lead a Native American lifeway—it means being in harmony with all that is.

This work was originally a lecture for the Indigenous Peoples' Panel of the Gaia Consciousness Conference, sponsored by the California Institute of Integral Studies in San Francisco, 1988.

JOURNEY OF THE MOTHERS

Machu Picchu, Peru

THE FIRST TIME I WENT TO PERU was in 1989. I went with my friend from Ecuador, Maria, and a small group of people led by an American psychologist and a medicine man from the Amazon. My friend and I had spent years struggling to understand aspects of our lives that had not been satisfied by the prevailing model of reality. Maria and I had met at Pasadena City College; she was my student and I was pregnant with my only child, my son Pisti. She had three children and was now a Marriage and Family therapist; thus our relationship began as mothers and women committed to helping our children and ourselves live as creatively as possible in a world that was revealing on a daily basis that it was dangerously out of balance. By 1989 our children were almost adults and we decided that this would be the year of intensifying our explorations outside our families and professions. So when we read about a small group of people who were going to visit some of the sacred places in Peru where they would meditate and focus on the healing of themselves and the planet, we knew that nothing could prevent us from going.

In March of that year we met the group in Lima. The morning after our arrival, we left for the beautiful countryside of Peru where we would spend the following weeks. It became clear very quickly that we had not made a mistake: the people in the group had similar interests and we worked very well together. The leaders were skilled in helping us to weave a single fabric of experience which honored each person's unique contribution to the unified effort to step beyond our rational construction of reality. Except for the shaman from the Amazon, we had all grown up under the influence of Western rationalism. I had just finished my Ph.D. in Comparative Literature at the University of California at Irvine; I was feeling an urgency to break through that intellectual view of the world and to participate in a visionary, spiritual reality—if, in fact, such a reality existed. All my life I had been open to such a possibility. I had studied world religions, indigenous spiritual traditions, and psychology. I had taught

Huayna Picchu. Photo by Ester Jenkins.

symbolic/mythic language for years and during graduate study had spent several more years studying various theories of how the symbol functions in the human mind. I had worked most of my adult life with my own dream symbolism. I was definitely open to the possibility of actual experience in dimensions of consciousness not constructed by the rational brain. I was open to the experience, but, other than dreams, I had had no such experience myself.

The first days seemed like weeks as the vastness of the Andes gently, almost imperceptibly, peeled away the layers of focused perception. I began to take in the environment through my body, and my senses became more active. As my brain began to relax its attention to detail and analysis, I began to feel a more direct biological response to the landscape. This felt like a new form of perception, but it surely must have been familiar to me during childhood. It connected me with the landscape in ways that resist articulation. Time slowed down and no longer seemed to dominate our days and nights; time was structuring our activities just as it had from the beginning of the trip, but it had sunk into the background of the field of perception. I realized that its position in perception dramatically changed its effects on my life.

By the time we arrived at Machu Picchu, however, these effects were translated into a pervasive sadness. I tried to reflect on this powerful feeling. I needed to articulate it, to understand it. I knew that it concerned my desire to go beyond my rational understanding of the world, and I knew that my rational self was beginning to suggest that this trip was a failure. My rational self devalued the effects of the shifts in perception, shifts that had actually given me pleasure. It concluded that nothing extraordinary had happened. I recognized the saboteur, but recognition did not reduce its power over me. I felt trapped between what might have been a biological reweaving of the tapestry of perception and the surgical reductionism of my own rational mind.

Before we entered Machu Picchu, we participated in a death ritual, a death to all that inhibited our ability to be fully present on this ancient sacred mountain. It was a beautiful ritual, but I could only experience the outer edges of its form. The next morning we entered Machu Picchu. The vastness of these mountains, the sky, the river below, the greenness of the earth began to spread out my vision and once again awaken a sensuous response. That highly focused camera of the mind extended its lenses and both mind and body became porous. We approached the Intihuatana, called the Hitching Post of the Sun, where we were going to have our first ritual. We made a circle around this ancient structure, and the shaman began to chant in Quechua. This is a haunting language, and when it is chanted, it sinks into the bones. The shaman himself was deeply moved. Each of us in turn stepped up to the sacred structure and placed our foreheads on the stone. This was, in a symbolic way, to awaken in us the memory of our own wholeness and our connection to all life. When it was my turn, I moved forward, kneeled, and felt the hard coldness. Something in me collapsed and an ocean broke loose. I experienced the profound lack of wholeness and the painful disconnection to life itself. I cried, but it was more than that; I was being cried. I cried for myself, for the terrible rape of my own creative source. I was both the victim and the perpetrator. And I was not alone. I cried for us all. I cried for the history of the world, and history cried through me.

Of course, I had known for a long time that the very nature of Western consciousness lay in its separation from all that was being awakened on this trip. I had been trained very early to devalue my experience, my feelings, my sensuous relation to the environment so that my ability to reason would not be compromised; trained to sever the outcropping of reason from its roots in the senses, the symbol, the vision, and that nonspatial, nontemporal world of being. I was taught to distrust every aspect of the mind and body that did not originate in reason. Theoretically, I had rejected this distrust, and I had even made a profession of teaching about cultures and people who also rejected it. Yet I could not overcome my own personal history. Western consciousness, including my own, had been constructed on a primary act of mental racism: only the rational mind could be trusted; all other modes of the mind were inferior. With the shifts in perception which had taken place, I was now able to experience in my body the consequences of this continuing historical act.

As I lay in bed that evening still shaken from the experiences of the day, I thought of my son Pisti and my husband Pista and how much I missed them. Maria and I whispered into the night about all that had happened and about our climb that afternoon to the moon temple at the top of the great mountain, Huayna Picchu, "Old Woman Mountain." Legend tells of the power and magic of this mountain, and the people of the Andes still honor it as a symbol of the sacredness of all life. I knew that I was not yet able to fully experience the sacredness of life, but I also knew that my love for my friends and my love for Pisti and Pista were at the heart of it.

After we stopped speaking, I lay awake thinking of how Lavinia in Shakespeare's *Titus Andronicus* is a symbol of our intuitive, feeling, visionary self, of all those modes of the mind that we reject as insignificant or deceptive. As daughter and woman she is potential mother, the very source of life. Yet her tragic fate is a chilling reflection of the consequences of our culture's mental racism. She was gang-raped by the sons of a man her father had captured in war. So that she could not tell her story, they cut out her tongue. So that she could not write her story, they cut off her arms. But she was not defeated. She took a stick by her teeth and tried to scratch her story in the earth. Yet even those scratchings have been ridiculed, ignored, or denied. Could it be, I wondered, that Lavinia might eventually forget she had a story to tell?

Since the historical denial of her story shapes the foundation of our model of reality, to remember Lavinia's story as symbolic of excluded reality is to break through centuries of addictive, abusive behavior. If we do not ridicule, ignore, or deny her altogether, we may seek her out only to do her further harm by demanding her to be what she uniquely is not. In our addiction to the rational mind, we say she must prove herself with the same "rigor" we demand of reason. We do not recognize that reason's way must demand rigor of itself, but it must allow Lavinia to present herself to us in her own way. To demand of her how she should do this is to rape her, to dominate her, to insist she be her opposite rather than herself. We fail to realize that we have so devalued and mutilated her that she cannot reveal herself to us in her full power—and this we take as proof that she has nothing to reveal. Our finest university cackle is reserved for anyone who would throw her a sop. In our attempt to uphold reason, we betray the very open, exploratory nature of reason itself.

My own complicity in this addictive behavior made me shudder. Just like an addict who has gone beyond denial, I wanted to be healed, but just like the addict, I could not resist the compulsive reaction to devalue and betray Lavinia. I regretted that I could not accomplish more on this trip, but only days remained. Soon I would return to Los Angeles carrying not only in my mind but also in my body the sorrow of our mutilated selves.

It is one of the wonderful and horrifying aspects of life that it brings to us enormous surprises at times and places when and where we would least expect them. I was back in California lying on the bed listening to music. I began to laugh uncontrollably. Some long forgotten memory began to flow through my body. Before it reached rational consciousness, I already knew it, knew it in my body, and the cells were laughing with memory. I saw a rather unclear figure move swiftly toward me with definite purpose. I knew she was Paccha Mama, the Old Woman of the Mountain, the source of all being. In less than a second she was no longer to be seen, but I felt her presence and I was back at Machu Picchu. I was up above the mountain looking down at what I knew was my dead body wrapped in canvas and tied with rope. It was on a hospital gurney that was being pushed quietly and quickly by four spiritlike beings. I had no remorse about my death—I knew the body was a symbol of my mutilated self. Suddenly I saw that I was being pushed toward Huayna Picchu. I was elated. I was to be allowed to enter the holy of holies—the ancient ones would speak to me, mys-

Paccha Mama Stone. Photo by Ester Jenkins.

teries would be revealed to me. But just as suddenly the beings stopped at the entry into the sacred mountain. In a flash everything changed. What my body had known from the beginning had finally reached the rational mind. While my body laughed, the images had moved in linear fashion to communicate with the brain. Now all of me remembered. What a joke I had played on myself! I *was* the mountain, the ancient ones, the Old Woman, the mystery, the Source. I laughed uproariously. Never had I laughed like this before. It was a molecular laugh, a laugh that vibrated in the cells and shot straight through the toe nails, skin, and hair. This was gnosis, that knowing for which no proof is asked because the experience is the knowing—to question it would bring forth more uncontrollable laughter. There was no egotism in the experience, simply memory of who I am, who we all are. Then I saw myself sitting in a forest, and I was surrounded by deer. I heard myself say, "But I can't create a world!" And a voice answered, "You just did create a world in which you cannot create! We can do nothing but create." I knew this, remembered this fully and completely. And with this memory, I flew past Huayna Picchu and spoke my creation: "Then I will create better games, games where all our children will be healed, where all our children will live in a world of ecstasy, joy, love, and peace." As I spoke, I myself was in a state of ecstasy. I was in love with the universe. I knew our world did not have to be as it is. I knew it is what we have created. In the moment this did not make me sad. I was experiencing what we can do, not what we have done. There would be time for sadness later.

This experience changed me dramatically, but not thoroughly. Other experiences came, and events in the outer world began to coalesce with the inner ones. Outer reality was now co-creating with the inner symbolic world. Maria's world was also changing since Peru, and together we stood amazed at the strange and unexplainable games our inner and outer realities were playing. Our rational minds ran after these games in our attempts to understand them. We loved reason with the same deep passion we always had, but now we were allowing it to walk around Lavinia's scratching in the earth, to observe it, to honor it. We restrained the rational mind's trained reaction to surgically extract and discard phenomena that it could not explain. This restraint created an enormous stress.

When reason is uprooted from its creative source, it constructs for itself a fiction of its own superiority, and it becomes dominant and abusive to anything outside itself that does not support this fiction. Now we were asking it to allow information which did not support this fiction to coexist with the very fiction whose trained response was to destroy it. The tension was often almost unbearable.

In his usual witty manner my son Pisti was able to help me with this tension. Pisti was a reasonable young man, yet he had allowed the Lavinia of his soul, if not to flourish, at least to communicate with him in extraordinary ways from time to time. Since he had always been painfully independent in his thinking, I was delighted that we shared many of the same interests. But I also wanted to share these experiences with my husband. I obviously did not realize what I was asking of him. I wanted him to hold within his consciousness experiences which he himself had not had, to honor them, and to respond to me with great enthusiasm. One morning while I was talking, I realized that he was looking at me with strained patience—not interest. I asked, "Pista, aren't you interested in this?" He answered, "I know what you are telling me is exactly what you have experienced, but I have never experienced anything even similar to what you are talking about, and I just can't relate to it." His newspaper was waiting politely between us. I was disappointed, but the bond between us was deep enough to allow this difference. I knew that it had been his strength, optimism, and independence that had nurtured me for years, and I knew that without the relationship with him I would never have been able to experience what he now could not assimilate.

This was to change. On October 29, 1991 we were both home in the late afternoon when we received a telephone call from Huntington Memorial Hospital in Pasadena. Our son Pisti had been in an automobile accident on the 210 Freeway. I answered the phone. When Pista heard me asking about Pisti's condition, he came into the room. I told him what had happened. I was calm. Evidently I had not absorbed what I had just been told, but he had. I heard him say, "Oh, no! Oh, no!" with a voice I had never heard before. On the way to the hospital, he drove with one hand and held my hand with the other in a grip so hard that pain shot through my arm. We were silent, both trying in our own ways to prepare for what a dear friend later described so well: "You are enduring what every parent dreads—the unexpected call, the jarring end of what you considered 'normal life' and the plunge into eternity—whatever that may prove to be."

That, of course, was written after Pisti died. Nothing would ever be "normal" again—and we were plunged into an eternity far beyond anything we could ever have imagined. One week after Pisti's death Pista mentioned to me that since Pisti's accident the pain in his heart was so strong that he was having difficulty breathing. He had begun to wonder if such pain could cause a heart attack. In our despair and my fear of also losing Pista, we lay down together, held each other, and cried. I don't know how much time had passed when Pista said, "Pisti was here." Both of us had experienced his presence. Pista's pain was gone. I continued to ask for days if the pain had returned, but it never did.

Pista explained to me that he had felt as though he left his body and with Pisti had gone to several of the sacred places of the earth, including Machu Picchu. Pisti told him that with Pisti's energy as a bridge we would now be able to remember our lives in their larger context. We would begin to understand how

Death Stone. Photo by Ester Jenkins.

his stepping into the other dimension was the beginning of a new kind of work together. They talked of the illness of the Earth and of the Earth's longing to heal itself. Pista remembered that the Earth would drink to the dregs the possibilities of its own darkness, and that out of that horrible knowledge it would create a world of exquisite light. Pista looked at me and said, "I had no idea what you were talking about earlier. I will never look at the Earth in the same way again." Before Pisti's accident I would never have been able to believe that the man talking to me now was the same man who had gazed at me across the *Los Angeles Times,* but we both knew that world no longer existed.

That same afternoon I had heard what sounded like Native American chanting and I saw a large spiral of people coming into the Earth and covering the globe. They seemed like indigenous peoples, but I knew they had come from the entire universe out of their love for the Earth. They were a response of the universe to the agony of the Earth. In that moment I knew this was the most natural response a loving universe would make, and I mourned how we on the Earth with our belief in our own insignificance and the emptiness of the universe had robbed ourselves of this knowledge. Out of the spiral I heard them say, "Our brothers and sisters on the Earth are dreaming a terrible dream." Pisti was with me as a kind of light body. Like Pista, I too had a glimpse of the great co-creativity taking place in the universe.

The sorrow remained, but there was also a joy that shocked us. We could now see our lives within a context of creativity. The rational mind's tendency to think of events as disconnected accidents holds it prisoner in a fragmented, meaningless world of victimization. In the experiences of that day each of us separately began to see how every event was related to all others and how our creating of these events began even before we had stepped into the time-space dimension. A vast tapestry of multidimensional co-creativity began to unfold within the consciousness of each of us. We recorded the events of that afternoon and of the days, weeks, and months that followed. They were so strange and wonderful that we feared our inability to hold their totality in our consciousness.

Pista continued to amaze me. Indeed he never did see the world in the same way again. I, on the other hand, lived between the shock and joy of my experience with Pisti in nontemporal, nonspatial dimensions and the murderousness of my own rational mind.

There were times when I thought the pain and disbelief of Pisti's death would destroy me. I wondered how I could fall back into this kind of despair after all we had experienced, but I came to understand that this is exactly what happens when rationality has been severed from its own roots. Once the experience is over, rationality begins to devalue it, to deny it ever happened, and ultimately to destroy it. Again it was Pista's strength, optimism, and independence from academic models of reality that helped me. He knew what he had experienced and, as always with him, he didn't care what anyone thought. So he became an anchor for me in this new reality. He was a businessman who had not concerned himself with these matters and certainly had not read about them. So my rational mind was stunned now at the knowledge his visions gave him, knowledge that often could be verified in the outer world. It was also stunned that Jenny, the girl Pisti loved so much, had similar visions, and that all our visionary experiences wove themselves into an overall pattern in which each of us was unique but delicately interconnected within a large web of being that appeared to all of us in surprising similarities. And it was not just the three of us. Maria and her daughter Jill stepped into eternity with us. We all were shocked, stunned, amazed, sad, and overjoyed. Standing in the deepest sorrow, we were experiencing the magic of the universe.

Yet, while Lavinia's body was regenerating itself, my rational mind was chasing her down to hack off her limbs once more, to demand yet more proof and more rigor. I was exhausted. The energy fields of my mind had been stretched to their furthest poles of opposition. One morning when I felt I could no longer bear this tension, I went into Pisti's room. He had reorganized and repainted this room two weeks before his accident, and he had placed on the walls the beautiful shamanic paintings of Susan Boulet. It had become our place of silence and meditation. Since Pisti's death it seemed that I was no longer just Pisti's mother. He had opened my heart to all children. Every child I heard about or read about became my child. The heaviest pain to bear was the self-destruction of a child, whether expressed outward against society or inward against the self. Sometimes I had come into this room and begged to have that kind of knowledge lifted from me. It was simply too heavy for me to carry. So I realized that my own personal sorrow could never be as heavy as the sorrow of some mothers.

I lay across his bed and cried. I cried because I missed Pisti's physical presence, I cried for Jenny who was now without him for a lifetime, and I cried for the world we have created for all our children. I cried for the children who had been murdered or who had murdered, I cried for those who suffered addiction or abandonment or abuse, I cried for the children who were confused and could find no way to create happiness in their lives, and I cried for their mothers and fathers. Suddenly I felt a bolt of energy hit me. I jumped up and stumbled back on the bed with my body pressed hard against the wall. I knew I was not alone in the room.

My eyes were open, but I was not seeing with them. I saw with an inner vision that can bring multidimensional worlds together in a single unit of time and space. (I knew this in the moment to be true, and there was no time to challenge it.) The room was filled with mothers from the past, present, and future. In fact, they extended far out beyond the room. Those closer to me were highly conscious while those at the edges were hardly aware that they were present. Their pain had been so great that they had fallen into unconsciousness. Yet there was a deep soul-urgency in all of them. Their energy was so strong that I was still pressed against the wall. They must have become aware of my limitations because as I thought of it, they too seemed to think of it, and I felt a subsiding of the power of their presence. These women had drunk to the dregs the possibilities of the earth's darkness, and out of this horrible knowledge they longed for a different world. Everything was communicated at once without words.

Later I tried to think this experience through in linear fashion as I described it to Pista. I told him that I knew the mothers were symbolic of loving, nurturing, parenting energy, yet I also knew that mothers were there who had abused or even murdered their children. In their souls too there was a deep unconscious longing for a transformed world. These women were like a hieroglyph of all the longing that exists here on Earth for a truly creative world, for ourselves and all our children. Within the delineation of their symbolic form, they embraced all of the longing of every single one of us for a better world. And I realized that this longing had reached the critical mass necessary for radical transformation.

So much happened during the next months that I didn't focus on this experience very much. I did wonder from time to time what was really meant by their message that the energy necessary for transformation was now available. It reminded me of medieval alchemical symbolism in which the temperature of the heat in the alembic had to reach a certain level of intensity before the two contrary elements could change their forms into what the German poet and modern alchemist Goethe had described as, "a new, a third, a completely unanticipated other." I wondered what exactly was in this alembic.

Meanwhile, as these thoughts flowed in and out of my mind, Pista and I began to plan a trip to Machu Picchu. We talked with a friend of ours about getting together a very small group of people who wanted to work at some of the sacred sites in Peru. This friend was the same person Maria and I had gone with on our first trip to Peru. It looked as though Maria would go also, but as it turned out, neither Maria nor Pista went. Two weeks before the trip Pista began to feel that he was not to go, that I was to go without him. We were surprised at this because Pista wanted to go as much, if not more, than I, but we had come to a point in our lives that we would not go against our deepest intuitions.

So I traveled alone to Miami where I joined the group. We went directly to Cuzco to begin our work at the navel of the ancient Incan spiritual world. There we met two men who were trained in the Incan shamanic tradition, one an anthropologist and the other an archaeologist. Together from this center we traveled the energy lines from sacred site to sacred site and performed in detail the ancient Incan shamanic rituals, structured to awaken ourselves and the Earth to our creative possibilities.

I was especially waiting for our trip to Machu Picchu. I had made arrangements to be on this sacred mountain one night alone because I was bringing Pisti's ashes to the Great Mother. A few weeks before his accident he had said to Jenny that if one were to die, the truly wonderful thing would be to have one's ashes scattered at some of the sacred places on the earth. When it became clear that Pisti would not live, we vowed we would do exactly that. When I left Los Angeles, Pista said that when I arrived at Machu Picchu I would know where to scatter the ashes. I had thought I would like to scatter them at the Paccha Mama stone, an area dedicated to the Great Mother. However, once we were at Machu Picchu, the leaders of the group felt I should not stay all night alone by the Paccha Mama stone but that I should work in a cave in the sacred mountain of Huayna Picchu. This immediately felt right. The group would hike down to the cave, which touched the edge of the jungle. There we would all participate in an ancient Incan ritual in the afternoon and I would stay the night. The leaders also did not feel comfortable with me being there completely alone, so one of them asked to remain outside the cave to do his own work while I remained deep in the belly of the Great Mountain.

After the group left and before I entered the cave, the two of us walked over to the edge of Huayna Picchu, sat down, and soaked in the view of the huge mountains around us. In such a place the arrogance of Western consciousness becomes embarrassing. Here the ancient Incan spiritual tradition was still alive, perpetuated by both the landscape and the powerful shamanic tradition that had been discreetly transmitted from shaman to shaman for over five hundred years. I knew something about how the ancient Incans viewed this place and this holy cave, but I wanted to hear how a university-trained man would express it, so I asked my friend what the cave meant to native people here. He looked at me, somewhat amazed at the question, but he answered gently, "It is the womb of our Great Mother." This was the response of an intellectual who had not severed his rational mind from its roots in its own creative source. He could speak of the reality of the symbol because he had experienced its power. Of course, such a position remains "absurd" to the intellect without this gnosis. I felt saddened by my tradition which had established itself as the gatekeeper of knowledge on the planet and which had perpetuated its mental racism as cultural racism against peoples whose model of reality was different from our own.

I entered the cave that evening wondering if I would ever completely heal the wound within myself. In spite of the balancing effects of nature and the work done during this journey, the old illness was still present. That night I felt utterly alone, severed from myself, the ones I loved, and certainly from any dimension of reality other than the cold wetness of the cave. I prepared for the ritual. Deep in the cave there was a natural stone altar. I scattered on this altar the dried leaves from the many roses Pisti had given Jenny. Since she had not been able to come, she wanted these to be scattered with his ashes as a symbol of their love for each other. In the tradition of the people native to this land I asked that the great circle be formed, that the sacred power of the four corners be present. And I asked once again to be healed, to be able to feel again the sacredness of all life. There was a part of me sick to death of healing, yet I remembered Camus' symbolism of the virus of violence in *The Plague*. He understood so well how we all carry this virus that can flare up at any time if we do not tend to our own healing from moment to moment.

I scattered Pisti's ashes in the womb of the Great Mother. I held in my hands the transformed substance of the son, more like bone than ash. I wondered how reason could account for this—the living child and now the bony ash. Within the space of this inability must surely lie the Mystery. As I continued to spread the ashes, they became the ashes of all our children. I could no longer think, and I could no longer mourn. I sat on the cold, wet stone below the altar. I would not leave this stone until early morning, and I would not remember much about the events of that evening until long after I had returned to California.

Pista met me at the airport anxious to hear about the journey. We both had anticipated extraordinary experiences at Machu Picchu since so many of our visions had occurred there. Often we had joked about this place being like a huge transformer between dimensions, but we didn't know what it really was that drew us to it in our dreams, visions, and in my case, actual physical journeys. I wished I had more to tell Pista, but I didn't. What I now think is that each experience at Machu Picchu was so contrary to the model of reality that had been programmed into my rational brain that my consciousness simply could not contain either one of them all at once. As we talked on the way home from the airport, Pista intuited this and suggested I be patient. "Just as before," he said, "you will remember and understand with time."

And so it was. Over a period of nine months, from the equinox to the solstice, through visions and dreams, each piece of the fabric began to emerge into consciousness. As each fragment revealed itself, there was time to reflect and assimilate. The progressive order and clarity astounded me. Each segment of consciousness prepared me for what was to follow. The old experience of the mental tension between the opposing principles of my mind was gradually subsiding. No longer did I feel as though my symbolic, visionary self was in the alchemical alembic under constant siege by my rampaging thinking self. Gradually Lavinia was healing and my rational mind was no longer attempting to mutilate her. Reason's fear of deception and betrayal was waning. They now stood on equal ground, she, as always, giving her gifts of creative love and wisdom, and reason finally giving her respect and trust. Having arrived at this point in the healing process, reason could now embrace Lavinia. In that embrace the rational mind was surprised to discover its own uniqueness. Instead of being diminished, it was awakening to its own vastness. Never before had reason been so rational! Just as Goethe had said, "a new, a third, a completely unexpected other" form of consciousness was taking shape. It was as though a beautiful tapestry were emerging out of the mist of the alembic.

It had not occurred to me earlier that the visit of the mothers had anything to do with my journey to Peru or my vigil that night in the cave. I later realized, however, that the entire journey was part of my work with these women. One evening while I was meditating in Pisti's room, I saw an old woman standing before me. Her eyes were large, unblinking, and sharply focused on my eyes. I felt she was piercing me with energy, attempting to raise me to a level of consciousness that would allow her to communicate with me. I decided I needed to lie down, so I went to the couch on the other side of the room. She came with me, sat down by me, and let her mind flow into mine. I was back in the cave and I saw that it was filled with the mothers just as they had once filled this room. I saw an image of the Pietá float past me; then I saw that each of us was a living pietá. The women carried their dead children to the altar where I had scattered Pisti's ashes that night. Our suffering and our darkness were so great that I had fallen into unconsciousness.

Not only had the suffering and the longing of the mothers been too powerful to carry in consciousness, there was something in the darkness that I had not yet been able to face. I thought I knew I had raped and mutilated the Lavinia of my soul. I had identified with her as victim of myself as perpetrator, but perhaps I had identified with her as victim more than I had taken responsibility as the perpetrator. Now I had to drink the dregs of my own darkness, and this was also the work of the mothers.

I—we—the mothers—had forgotten who we are. Because we had forgotten, we had allowed the mutilation of life itself. Only the love of the child could awaken us, but not until child after child had been sacrificed on the altar of our own darkness. We, the very source of life, had forgotten who we are. And we are all mother energy. We are creators, and having forgotten that, we created worlds in which we could not create—nor could our children because we bequeathed to them our myth of death. We had allowed our children to be born into a world of dead matter. Could we be surprised if they had no reverence for it, if they did violence to it—and to themselves and others? We modeled a myth of our own insignificance and gave it to our children as a sacred text.

I could still feel the presence of the old woman. I opened my arms and felt her enter my heart and say, "The sorrow of the past, the present, and the future can only be healed by creating new worlds." She was the mother of the Earth, the mother of us all and in us all. She began to sing in me:

Tell all my children they are the creators,
Create your worlds to keep me well.
You are the creators,
Create your worlds to keep me well.

She was the Old Woman of the Sacred Mountain. I am that woman, and so are we all. We were in the cave that night. We carried the murdered child, ourselves, our children, our Earth. And we prayed for a new birth, a new remembering. We are all the sacred women, every woman, man, child—and we are the sacred Earth. And we are pregnant and the Earth is pregnant with this memory.

VIJALI, WITH COAUTHOR PATRICIA SANDERS

EARTH AS SACRED SPACE

I FLEW! The thirteen hours of driving from the Hopi Reservation seemed like three. The spirit of the Kachina dances, the rhythm of the drum, the Earth's heartbeat still surged through me. But as time passed on the road, I could see and feel the light buoyancy of the northern Arizona air thicken and congeal around me as I drove into the Los Angeles basin. Breathing became an effort. My shoulders tightened. Heavy, brown smog obscured the horizon. My car joined the growing swarm on the freeway pressing forward relentlessly as if herded toward our destiny by some unknown slaughterer. As I turned off the freeway, highrise buildings enveloped me, blocking out the sky that had been so close to me on the reservation. I looked out the car window; people appeared sandwiched between smog and pavement. "How absurd! What am I doing here?" wailed some indignant voice within me. "Where is our power place, our Hopi land filled with meaning, our mountain peaks to summon the Kachina spirits? Where is *our* spirit-based community in Los Angeles? Where is *our* sacred mountain?"

Days passed. Early one morning, before sunrise, I sat up in bed with a start. "Yes, we do have our sacred mountain," I thought out loud. I remembered the first time I laid my eyes on Boney Mountain, its backbone of twelve-story-high stone pillars rising like a row of deities. It was love at first sight.

I jumped out of bed, grabbed my sleeping bag, climbed into my car and drove toward the mountain, pulled by the spirit of this sacred place. Driving up the long, winding earth road, I thought back to the Chumash medicine man who had told me that this peak, the highest ridge in the Santa Monica Mountains, was the power place of this area. The range runs east and west, sacred directions for Native Americans. I found the cave I remembered from my last trip—

a cave filled with Chumash pictographs—and prepared to stay the night in quest of my own way to live in harmony with the earth.

The mountain gave me an answer. I stayed on Boney Mountain from 1982 to 1987, trading the comforts of my Santa Monica home and the companionship of my husband to live alone in an abandoned trailer. My life took on a new simplicity. I began to synchronize with the rhythms of nature. Each morning I rose early to greet the sun from a high plateau and at the end of each day I returned to wish the sun farewell. Every simple act became a ritual—hauling water and bathing outside using a bucket and ladle, gathering wild greens for salads and sage for tea. I made peace with the rattlesnakes that lived beneath my trailer, and the bobcats and mountain lion that roamed nearby.

By living close to nature in this way, Boney was transformed into sacred space for me. I believe that a sacred space may be any place, not just ones designated by our ancestors. We may create them as I did on the mountain by entering into the spirit of a place through simple actions performed in a reverent way. Every object of my daily life took on a special meaning. The trowel I used for the toilet was as sacred for me as a chalice used in communion.

Even as a child I knew the sacredness of personal space. I remember going behind my grandmother's house in Dallas to a place where I could hide behind tall weeds. I would sit for hours in my circle of stones. As a ritual I placed dandelions and honeysuckle blossoms on the ground. That space was so special, I never revealed it to anyone, not even my closest playmates. How comforting to be there by myself as I mourned the death of a girlfriend or wept for my mother and father who had abandoned me at the age of two.

Sacred spaces can be created even in cities. In the late 1970s I felt a need for a sacred simplicity within my Los Angeles home. On a sudden inspiration, I took everything out of a closet and painted it white. Within this purified space I placed a stone, a leaf, a bowl of water and a sitting cloth from the Amazon— things special to me at that moment. I had created my own sacred space, my power place right there in the city.

For me as a sculptor, the process of carving and painting is itself a ritual. When I became frustrated with the commercialism of the art scene, I closed my studio and started carving stone outcroppings in wilderness areas. The first one was *Winged Woman* carved in the Simi Hills outside of Los Angeles. I found a group of large sandstone boulders that suggested a woman's face and a wing.

Beneath her lay a stone shaped like a man. By the time I completed the sculpture, I realized the woman reflected the need for feminine spirit to emerge in
our society. One day I returned to *Winged Woman* and found people sitting in
front of her and meditating. I realized, then, that art can be used to create sacred
spaces.

Years later—after my five-year retreat on Boney Mountain—I began an art
project of creating sacred spaces through sculptures and performances at twelve
sites circling the globe. I hoped that these would help recall communities around
the world to the sacredness of the Earth itself. Boney had taught me that a sacred
space was not just a personal power spot, but that the whole Earth is sacred
ground. It no longer seemed enough to sit on a stone and feel the interconnectedness of all life. The need to transfer the experience of a private sacred
space to all of nature led me to begin the project called the World Wheel: Theater of the Earth.

My journey has taken me from Malibu to the Seneca Reservation in upstate
New York, the Alicante Mountains by the Mediterranean Sea in Spain, the
Umbrian forest in Italy, an island in Greece called Tinos, the desert of Egypt,
the Dead Sea in Palestine and Israel, a tiny village in West Gengal, India, Shoto
Terdrom in Tibet, Kunming in South West China, Lake Baikal in Siberia, and
the wheel culminated in Japan.

One particular World Wheel experience shows how art can contribute to
making a place sacred. In May, 1992, I created a painted relief in a cave at 16,000
feet on the Tibetan Plateau in the Terdrom Valley. My Rainbow Bodhisattva is
a female figure, filled with prisms of color and seated in the lotus posture. Her
legs were molded from the red clay of the cave floor. Neither a Buddha nor a
Quan Yin, this is an energy body. I wanted to do a work traditional enough that
the Buddhist nuns and hermits living in nearby caves could identify with it, but
I also wanted to embody a universal image that was not limited to any single
concept of wholeness. This light-filled figure symbolizes, instead, the underly-
ing energy connecting everything, merging our innerspace with the space around
us. I made my Bodhisattva feminine because I was saddened to find the image
of Yeshe Tsogyal, the most prominent female holy figure in Tibet, shoved into
an obscure corner of the shrine in Shoto Terdrom. It was in the feminine folds
of this valley that she lived in a cave for many years during the eighth century,
and received her final illumination. I longed to see Yeshe Tsogyal represented

in shrines as an equal beside her spiritual mate, Padmasambhava, reflecting that harmony and balance so necessary for the health and continuation of life on this planet.

I did not know whether my creation would be recognized as a sacred site by Tibetans in the area. The answer came on the day I completed my work. Two nuns who were walking in the canyon came up to the cave. When they saw the figure they burst into tears, flushed, and flung themselves face down on the ground in three, full-length prostrations. That moment was my reward; I knew that this image had touched something within them that needed to be addressed and that for them, this cave would be, from this moment on, a sacred space.

The reverence expressed by those nuns is something most Tibetans carry naturally in their lives. They may wear only patched clothes against the freezing cold, but they regard themselves as blessed to live on their sacred land. We have much to learn from them. If I can generate even a fraction of their respect for the sacredness of nature through the process of creating the World Wheel, I will feel that it has all been worthwhile.

Creating art works is not the only way to acknowledge the sacred. Truly, the objects of ritual are always at hand. Stones are altars. Sunlight shining through leaves is stained-glass. Trees are pillars holding up the vaulted sky. Rivers are baptismal waters. Flowers are incense of the Earth. I worship the sacred when I lie with my back against the soil, my eyes gazing into the blackness of night.

The World Wheel is my way of walking in the world. It is my way of saying let's expand the idea of sacred space. Let us walk together the sacredness of the Earth.

CONTRIBUTORS

Tsultrim Allione, M.A., is the author of *Women of Wisdom* and founder-director of *Tara Mandala Retreat Center* in the San Juan Mountains of Southern Colorado. She has practiced, taught, and studied Buddhism for over 25 years. Formerly a Tibetan Buddhist nun, she leads retreats and makes pilgrimages to sacred sites around the world, exploring the interface between psychology and Buddhism. Her principal teachers are H. H. Karmapa, Chogyam Trungpa Rinpoche, and Chogyal Namkhai Norbu Rinpoche.

Uzuri Amini is a priestess of Oshun, the Yoruba goddess of love, healing, and art. She was initiated by the Oshun Society in Oshogbo, Nigeria, at the directive of King Ataoja in the Spring of 1989. She is a writer, artist, ceremonialist, and spiritual counselor. Her work has been published in *The Goddess Celebrates*, *Woman of Power* magazine, and the *Children's Advocate*, and she is currently writing about her own spiritual voyages. Her dramatic performances of poetry, folklore, and dance reflect the many faces of women inherent in us all. She is nurtured and advised by Luisah Teish, author of *Jambalaya* and *Carnival of the Spirit*. Together they have taught workshops and conducted rituals across the United States and around the world.

Hallie Iglehart Austen is a counselor, workshop leader, and author of *Womanspirit: A Guide to Women's Wisdom* and *The Heart of the Goddess: Art, Myth and Meditations of the World's Sacred Feminine*. She gives thanks and blessings to all mentioned in this story for their guidance, to Kim Johnson for editorial advice and to Gwendolyn Jones for invaluable help in making this article possible.

Jo Carson is a filmmaker and motion picture camerawoman who has worked with George Lucas's *Industrial Light and Magic*, and Tim Burton on *The Nightmare Before Christmas*. She is making a documentary, *Dancing With Gaia* which includes many sacred sites around the world as well as interviews with women artists, writers, poets, and performers with an awareness of the sacred Earth.

Leila Castle has studied and taught Goddess traditions for over 25 years, and made journeys to sacred sites since 1975. As former co-director of *Spotted Fawn Geomantic Arts* she taught and produced many geomantic events and exhibitions. She lives near the Point Reyes National Seashore in California where she creates natural botanical fragrances. Castle is a contributor to *The World of Aromatherapy* (Frog, Ltd.).

Charla Devereux, a native of New York, moved to Britain in 1984 where she is a trustee of the *Dragon Project Trust*, which has studied sacred sites and Earth energies for many years. She is editor of *The Ley Hunter Journal*, the foremost magazine of Earth Mysteries and author of *Diet Logic*. Her aromatherapy company is *Empress Ltd*.

Betty Kovacs has taught symbolic language/mythology and literature for over 20 years. She is a Professor in the English and Foreign Languages Department at Pasadena City College and holds a Ph.D. in Comparative Literature from the University of California at Irvine.

Caroline Nervig is President of the Nan Madol Foundation in Pohnpei which is committed to the preservation of the archaeological site of Nan Madol. She served in the Peace Corps on Pohnpei from 1969–71, has a B.A. in Fine Art, and worked in graphic design for many years before becoming owner and operator of a successful marketing/design/communications business serving the mainland and Pacific region. She now lives in Hawaii.

Cindy A. Pavlinac is a multimedia artist specializing in photography and computer imaging of ancient places. She has an M.A. in Arts and Consciousness Studies and has studied archaeology in Greece, shamanism in North America, and Celtic legend and European shamanism in Britain and Brittany. Her photography has won several dozen awards and has been published in *Sanctuaries of the Goddess, The Once and Future Goddess*, and *Sacred Places*.

Chesca Potter is an English artist and freelance illustrator. Her work has appeared in numerous exhibitions, publications, and book covers including *Priestess: Biography of Dion Fortune, Dreaming the Dark*, and *The Grailseeker's Companion*. She lectures on the British Mystical Landscape Tradition, sacred sites, and shamanism and is the designer of the *Greenwood Tarot* deck.

Joan Price is a video producer living in Tularosa, New Mexico. She is an author and lecturer on cultural forms of knowledge and has an M.F.A. from the University of California at Santa Barbara. She has published and presented her material in magazines, universities and conferences throughout the U.S. and Europe.

Serena Roney-Dougal received her Ph.D. in Parapsychology at Surrey University, one of only about a dozen people in Britain who have this qualification. She has had over fifteen years of study and experience in scientific, magical, and spiritual explorations of the psyche; has lectured and taught courses, seminars, and workshops in America, Britain, and Europe; and is the author of *Where Science and Magic Meet* (Element).

Monica Sjöö is a feminist artist, writer, and visionary. She is the co-author of *The Great Cosmic Mother, Rediscovering the Religion of the Earth* (Harper & Row), and author of *New Age & Armageddon* (The Women's Press). Originally from Sweden, she has lived in Britain for many years. She travels internationally, speaking and exhibiting her work on ancient sacred places and Goddess traditions.

Jill Smith is a poet and artist who has lived on the Isle of Lewis in the Western Isles of Scotland since 1986. She worked as a performance artist in the 1970s before creating ceremonial and ritual art. In 1984, she made a year-long pilgrimage though the landscape of England and Wales, linking sites by the path of her walking. She currently does readings and performances of her poems and stories as well as exhibitions of her drawings.

Vijali, an Earth artist and performer, is the originator of a seven-year art project called World Wheel: Theater of the Earth, in which she created sculptures in live rock and ritual performances in twelve countries circling the globe. She spent ten years as a monastic member of the Vedanta convent and has an M.A. in Fine Arts from Goddard University. Her work has been represented in several books including *The Once and Future Goddess*, *The Reflowering of the Goddess*, and *The Feminine Face of God*. She lectures and travels extensively.

Ani Williams is a professional musician who plays Celtic harp and ancient flutes. She is a vocalist, composer, and ethnomusicologist and has traveled and performed in the U.S., Mexico, Peru, England, Scotland, and Egypt. Her music, featured on radio programs nationally and distributed internationally, comes directly from listening to the spirit of nature and playing what she hears.

Lynne Wood was born in Australia where she lives and works as an artist, teacher, and curator in ancient European, Celtic, Aboriginal, and contemporary Australian art. She has a B.A. in Fine Arts and has traveled, studied, and exhibited in Britain, Europe, and Greece and has studied Aboriginal culture in Central Australia since 1980. She is currently working on a book of Celtic Goddesses, and lectures on Celtic art and culture and women's spirituality.

Nancy Carpenter Zak, Ph.D., of Inuit and Euro-American heritage, is a writer, teacher, and lecturer on Native American and Inuit studies. She has taught at the Institute of American Indian Studies in Santa Fe, New Mexico, as professor of English and of Native American Literature and Folklore for ten years. Her many teachers include: Morna Simeona, Sandra Ingerman, Brooke Medicine Eagle, Dhyani Ywahoo, and Tu Moonwalker. She has been helped by the healing practices of Bearheart Marcellus Williams, Bobby Medicine Grizzlybear Lake, Joseph Rael, Arvol Lookinghorse, Thomas Yellowtail, and Hunbatz Men. She was present at the Dalai Lama's historic meeting with Pueblo and Navajo civil and religious leaders, and recently received the empowerment of White Tara. Nancy honors the Goddess in all her guises.

BIBLIOGRAPHY

Allione, Tsultrim. *Women of Wisdom*. London and New York: Arkana, 1984.

Austen, Hallie Iglehart. *The Heart of the Goddess*. Berkeley: Wingbow Press, 1990.

Begg, Ian. *The Cult of the Black Madonna*. Harmondsworth, U.K.: Arkana, 1985.

Bennett, Noel. *Halo of the Sun*. Flagstaff, Arizona: Northland Press, 1987.

Berendt, Joachim-Ernst. *The Third Ear*. New York: Henry Holt and Co. 1992.

Bord, Janet and Colin. *Sacred Waters: Holy Wells and Water Lore in Britain and Ireland*. London: Paladin/Grafton Books, 1985.

Brock, Peggy, ed. *Women—Rites and Sites*. Sydney and Boston: Allen and Unwin, 1989.

Bryant, Page. *The Earth Changes Survival Handbook*. Albuquerque: Sun Books, 1983.

Burl, Aubrey. *Prehistoric Avebury*. New Haven and London: Yale University Press, 1979.

Caine, Mary. *The Glastonbury Zodiac*. Kingston, Surrey, U.K.: Self-published, 1978.

Cameron, Anne. *Daughters of Copper Woman*. Vancouver, British Columbia: Press Gang Publishers, 1981.

Chapman, Anne. *Translations and notes. Selk'nam (Ona) Chants of Tierra del Fuego*. New York: Folkways record album No. FE 4176, 1972.

Christ, Carol. *Laughter of Aphrodite*. San Francisco: Harper & Row, 1987.

Cooper, Powys, J. *A Glastonbury Romance*. Britain: John Lane, 1933.

Cousto, Hans. *The Cosmic Octave*. Mendocino, California: Life Rhythm, 1988.

Devere, John, and Vollmer, Jurgen. *Black Genesis: African Roots*. New York: St. Martin's Press, 1980.

Devereux, Charla. *The Aromatherapy Kit*. London: Headline, 1993.

Devereux, Paul. *"An Apparently Nutmeg-Induced Experience of Magical Flight."* Berlin, Germany: Yearbook for Ethnomedicine and the Study of Consciousness, VWB, 1992.

Devereux, Paul. *Places of Power*. London: Cassell, 1990.

Devereux, Paul. *Symbolic Landscapes*. Glastonbury: Gothic Image, 1992.

Dowman, Keith. *The Power Places of Central Tibet*. London: Routledge & Kegan Paul, 1988.

Dowman, Keith. *Sky Dancer*. London: Routledge & Kegan Paul, 1984.

Ehrenreich, Barbara, and English, Deirdre. *For Her Own Good*. New York: Anchor Books, 1979.

Eaton, Evelyn. *Snowy Earth Comes Gliding*. Independence, California: Draco Foundation, 1974.

Evers, Larry, and Molina, Felipe S. *Yaqui Deer Songs*. Tucson and London: Sun Tracks and University of Arizona Press, 1987.

Fontenrose, Joseph. *The Delphic Oracle*. Berkeley, California: University of California Press, 1978.

Gimbutas, Marija. *The Civilization of the Goddess*. San Francisco: Harper Collins, 1991.

Gimbutas, Marija. *The Language of the Goddess*. San Francisco: Harper & Row, 1989.

Goldman, Jonathon. *Healing Sounds*. Rockport, Mass: Element, Inc., 1992.

Goodrich, Norma Lorre. *Priestesses*. New York: HarperPerennial, 1989.

Harding, M. Esther. *Women's Mysteries: Ancient and Modern*. New York: Pantheon, 1955.

Jaynes, Jolian. *The Origin of Consciousness in the Breakdown of the Bicameral Mind*. Boston: Houghton Mifflin, 1976.

Jones, Francis. *The Holy Wells of Wales*. Cardiff: University of Wales Press, 1992.

Jones, Kathy. *Spinning the Wheel of Ana: A Spiritual Quest to Find the British Primal Ancestors*. Glastonbury: Ariadne Productions, 1994.

Khan, Hazrat Inayat. *Music*. New York: Samuel Weiser, 1977.

Kramer, Samuel N. *History Begins At Sumer*. New York: Doubleday, 1958.

Maltwood, Katharine. *A Guide to Glastonbury's Temple of the Stars*. London: James Clark, 1929.

Mann, Nicholas R. *Sedona Sacred Earth*. Albuquerque, NM: Zivah Publishing, 1991.

Marti, Samuel. *Music Before Columbus*. Mexico: Ediciones Euroamericanas, 1971.

Matthews, Caitlin and John. *Ladies of the Lake*. Wellingborough, Northamptonshire, U.K.: Aquarian Press, 1992.

Matthews, Caitlin. *Sophia, Goddess of Wisdom*. London: Thossons, 1991.

Matthews, Caitlin. *Voices of the Goddess:* Wellingborough, Northamptonshire, U.K., The Aquarian Press, 1990.

Michell, John. *The Earth Spirit*. London: Thames and Hudson, 1975.

Michell, John. *The View Over Atlantis*. New York: Ballantine Books, 1969.

Mowat, Farley. *Never Cry Wolf*. New York: Bantam Books, 1963.

Norbu, Namkhai, and Shane, John. *The Crystal and the Way of Light*. New York and London: Routledge & Kegan Paul, 1986.

Paulson, Norman D. *Christ Consciouness*. Salt Lake City: Builders Publishing, 1985.

Puharich, A. *Beyond Telepathy*. London: Picador, 1975.

Ratsch, Christian. *"Der Rauche von Delphi. Eine ethno-pharmakologigiche Annaherung,"* in *Curare*, Vol. 10, No. 4, 1987.

Roberts, Anthony. *Atlantean Traditions in Ancient Britain*. London: Zodiac House, 1970–71.

Roberts, Jack. *The Sheela-na-gigs of Britain and Ireland—an Illustrated Guide*. Skibbereen, West Cork, Ireland: Key Books, 1995.

Roney-Dougal, S.M. *Where Science and Magic Meet*. Shaftesbury: Element Books, 1993.

Rudhyar, Dane. *The Magic of Tone and the Art of Music*. Boulder, CO: Shambhala Publishing Inc., 1982.

Schmidt, Erik. *Dakini Teachings*. Boston & Shaftesbury: Shambhala, 1990.

Sharkey, John. *Ogham Monuments in Wales*. Felinfach, Wales: Clanerch, 1992.

Sharkey, John. *Pilgrim Ways: The Grand Pilgrimage to St. David's*. Dyfed, Wales: Ancient Landscapes, 1994.

Sherratt, Andrew. *"Sacred and Profane Substances: The Ritual Use of Narcotics in Later Neolithic Europe,"* in University Committee for Archaeology, Monograph No. 32, 1991.

Sjöö, Monica, and Mor, Barbara. *The Great Cosmic Mother: Rediscovering the Religion of the Earth*. San Francisco: HarperSanFrancisco, 1987.

Spence, Lewis. *The Magic Arts in Celtic Britain*. London: Rider & Co., 1945.

Smythe, Colin. *The Fairy Faith in Celtic Countries*. Buckinghamshire: Gerrods Cross, 1988.

Stewart, R.J. *Awakening the Sleepers and Regenerating the Earth*. London: Element Books, 1992.

Stewart, R.J. *Earthlight: The Ancient Path to Transformation Rediscovering the Wisdom of Celtic & Faery Lore*. London: Element Books, 1992.

Stewart, R.J. *Robert Kirk: Walker Between the Realms (The Secret Commonwealth of Elves, Fauns & Fairies)*. London: Element Books, 1990.

Stewart, R.J. *The Waters of the Gap—The Mythology of Aqua Sulis*. Bath: Bath City Council, 1981.

Stone, Merlin. *When God Was A Woman*. New York: Dial Press, 1976.

Swan, James A. *Sacred Places: How the Earth Seeks Our Friendship*. Santa Fe: Bear & Co., 1990.

Von Cles-Reden, Sibylle. *The Realm of the Great Goddess: The Story of the Megalith Builders*. London: Thames & Hudson, 1961.

Ywahoo, Dhyani. *Voices of Our Ancestors*. Boston: Shambhala, 1981.

Zak, Nancy Carpenter. *The Portrayal of the Heroine in Chretien de Troyes's Erec et Enide, Gottfied von Strassburg's Tristan, and Flamenca*. Gorppingn, West Germany: Goppinger Arbeiten zur Germanistik, 1983, Volume 1983.